Richard Acklam Araminta Crace

UPPER INTERMEDIATE

Book 2

Total English

Students' Book and Workbook

PEARSON
Longman

Contents

LESSON 3	VOCABULARY	COMMUNICATION	FILM BANK
Grammar: making comparisons **Vocabulary:** verb phrases about moving/travelling **Can do:** make comparisons about places and people	Travel	Travelling companions	Bhutan
Grammar: *have/get something done* **Vocabulary:** animal expressions **Can do:** talk about services	Prefixes	Can I help you?	Vikings
Grammar: *hard* and *hardly* **Can do:** write a report of survey findings	Phrasal verbs with three parts	Radio phone-in	Secrets of success
Grammar: relative clauses **Can do:** write an article	Newspaper headlines	Mind benders	Bullion Robbery
Grammar: *if* structures (2) **Vocabulary:** speaking **Can do:** talk about your regrets and resolutions	Commonly misspelt words	How does your mind work?	Yes Prime Minister

Tapescripts page 156

▶ Workbook follows page 162

6 Explore

Lead-in

1 Discuss.

1 What can you see in the photos?
2 Which of the places would you most like to explore? Why?

2 6.1 Listen and answer these questions.

1 What gave the speaker the idea to travel?
2 Why did she go to Spain?
3 How did she feel when she first got to Guatemala? Why?
4 How did she feel later?

3 **a** 6.2 Listen again and complete the expressions.

1 I began *to have* _______ *feet* and wanted to leave work.
2 I was a bit worried about *going into uncharted* _______ !
3 I *went as an* _______ *traveller*, on my own.
4 I spent a month _______ *around* the town.
5 I *was bitten by the travel* _______ and wanted to explore lots of other places.
6 The first two months were difficult and I *experienced real* _______ *shock*.

b Check the meanings of the expressions using a dictionary.

4 Discuss.

1 Why do you think people are bitten by the travel bug?
2 Has it ever happened to you?
3 Do you ever have itchy feet?

6.1 The jungle bug

Grammar Present Perfect Simple and Continuous
Can do write an informal email

Bitten by the jungle bug!

Sand flies, sweat bees, eighty-metre high trees ... Hell for most of us, yes, but all in a day's work for Charlotte Uhlenbroek. She moves as elegantly through the lounge of London's Savoy Hotel as she does through the Amazon jungle. But while she loves the adventure, she is also glad to be back in 'civilisation', at least for the moment.

She's just finished filming a TV series called *Jungle* – a gruelling nineteen-week job that involved her exploring the dense jungles of the Congo, the Amazon and Borneo. She says that it was fascinating, but daunting as well. So what was her most challenging experience? 'Definitely climbing an eighty-metre high tree in Borneo, when I'm petrified of heights! I had to keep going up and up, when a voice inside me was saying, "Down! Down!" I kept thinking the ropes were going to break and send me plummeting down below.'

And 'down below' was where the bugs were – clinging, stinging, sucking beasts. Apart from the usual mosquitoes, in the Amazon rainforest, she was plagued by sand fly bites. 'I've had some horrible bites but these really are the itchiest bites I've ever had. At one stage, I counted seventy bites on one arm,' she says. 'Just as annoying were the sweat bees in the Congo. They try to drink the sweat on your face and even the tears from your eyes. The most disgusting thing, though, was trying to pull the slimy leeches off your skin. The more I pulled, the more they stretched and the tighter their jaws clung to my leg. I kept shouting, "Get them off!" and the film crew kept saying, "Just a minute ... this makes a really good shot!"'

Charlotte's journey into the heart of the world's most significant rainforests was an inspiring experience. 'The rainforest really is like a city. Each tree is like an urban tower block with hundreds of residents. If you knock it down, you cause just as much disruption and damage as if those residents were human. The jungle is extraordinary because although it only covers about six percent of the world, it contains over fifty percent of all known animal and plant species, plus lots more that are unknown, too.'

Back in London, what has she been enjoying since her return to 'civilisation'? 'I've been having lots of nice, long showers,' she says. 'In the Congo I was always worried about using up all our water supplies. And I find that when I've been in hot, uncomfortable conditions for a while, the things I look forward to more than anything else are being with my family and enjoying my favourite meal.'

Reading

1 Charlotte Uhlenbroek spent over four months in the jungle. Before you read about her, discuss these questions.

1. Which things do you think you would find difficult in the jungle?
2. Which things do you think you would most like to do when you returned to 'civilisation'?

2 Read the text and answer the questions in Ex. 1 about Charlotte.

3 Read the text again and decide if the statements are true (T), false (F) or we don't know (DK).

1 Charlotte looks and feels 'out of place' in the Savoy Hotel.
2 She had to climb tall trees without the use of ropes.
3 The mosquito bites she had were the worst bites she's ever had.
4 She cried because she couldn't stand the sweat bees on her face.
5 The film crew helped her to get the leeches off her leg.
6 She compares a tree with a tower block because there are so many living things in each tree.
7 The water she used in the Congo was usually dirty.
8 When she gets home, she loves doing the cooking for her family.

4 Discuss. Would you like to go on a jungle expedition? Why/Why not?

Grammar | Present Perfect Simple and Continuous

5 Match the examples 1–4 with the correct rules A–D in the Active grammar box.

Active grammar

1 *She's just finished filming a TV series called 'Jungle' (and is glad to be back in 'civilisation').*
2 *I've had some horrible bites but these are the itchiest bites I've ever had.*
3 *I've been in jungles for a total of nineteen weeks and I'm going home today.*
4 *What has she been enjoying since her return to 'civilisation'? 'I've been having lots of nice, long showers'.*

A Use the **Present Perfect Simple** to talk about an action or experience in the past when the time is not important or not known.

B Use the **Present Perfect Simple** to describe an action that started in the past and continues in the present, when you're focussing on the finished action (or on the number of times the action has been completed up to the time of speaking).

C Use the **Present Perfect Continuous** to describe an action that started in the past and continues in the present, when you're focussing on the activity itself. We often use *for* (length of time)/*since* (starting point) to talk about the duration of the activity.

D Use the **Present Perfect Simple** to describe an action that happened in the past but has the result in the present. We often use *just, yet* or *already* in this case.

- *Just* means a short time ago. It usually comes between *has/have* and the past participle.
- *Already* shows that something happened sooner than expected. It usually comes between *has/have* and the past participle or at the end of the sentence.
- *Yet* shows that the speaker expected something to happen before now. It is used at the end of negatives and questions.

see Reference page 87

6 Correct the mistake in each sentence.

1 I've been to the Brazilian rainforest in 2003.
2 She's bought already her plane tickets.
3 I've been visiting friends in Italy three times this year.
4 What you been doing since I last spoke to you?
5 Have you yet seen that film, *Sahara*?
6 He just has spoken to the tour guide about it.
7 I've been learning Spanish since two months.
8 Have you been knowing each other long?

7 Complete the sentences by using the prompts in brackets. Use the Present Perfect Simple, Present Perfect Continuous or Past Simple.

1 _______ (you/go/ever) to a jungle?
2 _______ (you/decide) where to go for your next holiday?
3 How long _______ (you/study) English?
4 What do you want to do today that _______ (you/not do/yet)?
5 Where _______ (you/go) for your last holiday?
6 How much coffee _______ (you/have/already) today?
7 _______ (you/have/ever) a bad insect bite?
8 Where _______ (you/live) for the last year?

Person to person

8 **a** In pairs, ask and answer the questions in Ex. 7.

b Choose one of the questions you asked and ask your partner more details about it.

Vocabulary | adjectives with *-ed/-ing*

9 **a** Find these adjectives in the text on page 76. In pairs, discuss what you think they mean. Use the sentences around the word to help you.

1 fascinating (para. 2)
2 daunting (para. 2)
3 challenging (para. 2)
4 petrified (para. 2)
5 annoying (para. 3)
6 disgusting (para. 3)
7 inspiring (para. 4)
8 worried (para. 5)

b Look at the words and their context in the text again and choose the correct alternatives for these rules.

1 Use adjectives ending in *-ed/-ing* to describe someone's feelings.
2 Use adjectives ending in *-ed/-ing* to describe a situation.

c Write sentences with adjectives from Ex. 9a.

Pronunciation

10 6.3 Listen and mark the main stress for each adjective.

1 fascinated, fascinating
2 daunted, daunting
3 challenged, challenging
4 petrified, petrifying
5 annoyed, annoying
6 disgusted, disgusting
7 inspired, inspiring
8 worried, worrying

11 **a** Complete the dialogues with the most appropriate adjective from Ex. 10.

A: Do you like camping?

B: I can honestly say I hate it! I spent a week camping once and every night I was (1) _______ because it was so dark and I kept hearing animals. I even found putting up my tent quite (2) _______ . It's quite old and one or two of the bits were missing.

A: Are you scared of heights?

B: Well, no actually. I like being high up. I went up in a small aeroplane a few years ago. I was a little (3) _______ at first because it was a bit bumpy. But in the end I found the whole experience really (4) _______ . It made me want to do other things – perhaps even go parachuting one day.

A: How do you feel about eating food you've never tried before?

B: I don't usually mind new vegetables and things but I'm not very keen on eating meat I've never tried before. Actually, the other day, a friend of mine persuaded me to try snails. I was (5) _______ with him because he didn't tell me what they were. He pretended they were bits of chicken. Well, when I found out, I was nearly sick! They were really (6) _______ !

A: How would you feel about a job that involved working with animals?

B: I've just spent the summer holidays working at a monkey sanctuary and I loved it. You might not think monkeys are very interesting but they're (7) _______ when you get to know them. Some things were difficult – like catching them to give them medicine was pretty (8) _______ , but it was all very rewarding.

b 6.4 Listen and check your answers.

12 **a** Ask and answer the questions in Ex. 11a with other students. Use the adjectives in Ex. 10.

b Who has the most similar feelings to you?

Writing

13 Read the email in the Writing bank on page 153 and do the exercises.

14 Choose one of the situations in Ex. 11a and write an email to a friend telling him/her about your experience. Use Maisie's email and the paragraph plan below to help you.

Paragraph 1: explain where you are and why, and how you feel

Paragraph 2: describe what you've been doing

Paragraph 3: say how you feel about finishing

6.2 A magical kingdom

Grammar questions
Can do ask and answer questions about unusual places

Reading

1 **a** Look at the photo of Bhutan and discuss.

1. What do you think life is like there?
2. Why do you think few tourists go to this country?

b Read the text quickly and check your ideas.

BHUTAN is a country of about 750,000 people in the eastern Himalayas. Visitors may be surprised how much culture, tradition and nature are all flourishing in this very private country. The Bhutanese people believe that all forms of life, human and non-human, are precious and sacred. Because of this attitude, they live in harmony with nature and their environment remains pristine, with an astonishing variety of animals, birds and plants. The people live in harmony with each other too, with no discrimination of any kind.

In order to safeguard this rich natural environment and peaceful culture, Bhutan has adopted a cautious and controlled approach to tourism. In 2003, there were fewer than 6000 tourists and this number is not expected to increase greatly. No independent travellers are permitted in Bhutan; all tourists must go on a pre-planned, prepaid, guided, package tour. However, if you make the effort and manage to get a visa and arrange a trip, you will certainly have a life-changing experience in this magical kingdom.

2 Read the text again. Then, with a partner, summarise the text's main points about a) important beliefs of Bhutanese people, b) nature in Bhutan and c) tourism in Bhutan.

3 Discuss. Would you like to visit Bhutan? Why/Why not? Do you think Bhutanese people would experience culture shock if they visited your country? In what ways?

Vocabulary | weather

4 6.5 Listen and decide which of these questions each of the three people are talking about:

A: What's the weather like in your country?
B: What's your favourite type of weather?

5 **a** Look at the tapescript on page 156 and write the underlined words in the correct place in the table below.

COLD	WARM/HOT	RAIN	WINDY	SKY	WEATHER IN GENERAL
cool		*pours*		*clear*	

b In pairs, explain the differences in meaning between the words in each column in the table. Use a dictionary if necessary.

c Look at the words again and decide:

1. if each one is a noun, adjective or verb, e.g. *breeze* = noun
2. what other forms there are, e.g. *breeze* (n), *breezy* (adj)

6 Match one of the words from Ex. 5 on page 79 to each of the sentences.

It was perfect weather for flying kites. breezy.

1 The weather in Ireland isn't usually very hot or very cold.
2 I got completely soaked even though it was only a five-minute walk.
3 We had to sit in the shade until quite late in the afternoon.
4 The sky was full of clouds and the sun didn't come out all day.
5 It only rained for about ten minutes and then it was fine.
6 It was warm in the day but I was glad I'd taken a jacket for the evenings.
7 I like heavy rain but I can't stand it when it rains gently for hours and hours.
8 We were freezing when we went camping despite having extra-thick sleeping bags.
9 You'll need sun cream and a raincoat. You never know what the weather will be like.
10 It was a lovely place – blue skies and the light was really good for taking photographs.

7 Discuss.

1 How would you describe the weather in your area/country?
2 How would you like the weather where you live to be different?
3 How do you think this would improve your life?
4 Does the weather affect your mood? In what ways?

Listening

8 **a** If you were going on holiday to Bhutan what sort of things would you like to know about in advance, e.g. the weather?

b 6.6 Listen to a question and answer session with an expert on Bhutan and some people who are considering a trip there. In what order do they talk about the things in the box?

special events/festivals ☐ the ideal time of year to visit ☐ food ☐ what to do there ☐ what to take ☐ organised trips ☐

9 Listen again and complete the notes below.

TRIP TO BHUTAN

WHEN TO GO:
Spring and autumn are the best seasons to go
Don't go in winter because (1) ___________
Don't go in summer because (2) ___________

ACTIVITIES:
Trekking is fantastic – amazing views and a lot of different (3) ___________

CLOTHES:
Don't forget to take: rain gear and good (4) ___________
Also, for the sun: a hat and (5) ___________
Don't bring (6) ___________ or (7) ___________ for trekking (it's all provided)

FOOD:
One of the main ingredients used is (8) ___________

FESTIVALS:
The main reason for festivals is for people to (9) ___________

FLAGS:
The reason for the flags is for people to (10) ___________

10 Discuss. Would you like to go on the organised trekking trips described in the listening? Why/Why not? Have you been to any festivals or celebrations in your country or abroad which you particularly enjoyed? Give details.

Grammar | questions

11 Complete the questions in the Active grammar box. Then, look at the tapescript on page 156 and check your answers.

Active grammar

Direct questions

There are two main types of direct questions:

A *Yes/No* questions (1) ______ *to carry all our equipment?*
(2) ______ *provide a guide?*

B *Wh-* questions *What activities (3) ______ ?*
When (4) ______ the best time to go?

Subject questions are used when the question word (e.g. *who*) refers to the subject of the sentence. When a *wh-* word replaces the subject in a question we do not use the auxiliary verb.

Who (5) ______ with the trekking group?

Indirect questions:

Use indirect questions when you want to be polite (e.g. when you don't know someone). There are different ways of starting indirect questions (e.g. *Do you know ..., Can you tell me ...*).

Use the word order of positive statements. Use *if* or *whether* for indirect *Yes/No* questions.

Can you tell me what (6) ______ ?
Could I ask you what (7) ______ like?
Do you know (8) ______ any interesting festivals at that time?
I'd like to know (9) ______ to take anything special.

see Reference page 87

12 a Correct the mistake in each question.

You go on holiday every year?
Do you go on holiday every year?

1 Where you are living at the moment?
2 He has ever been trekking before?
3 Who did give you those lovely flowers?
4 What time you be here tomorrow?
5 You having a holiday soon?
6 When this company was started?

b Change the questions above into indirect questions starting with the words given.

Can I ask you if you go on holiday every year?

1 Can you tell me ______ ?
2 Do you know ______ ?
3 Can I ask you ______ ?
4 Can you tell me ______ ?
5 Do you know ______ ?
6 I'd like to know ______ .

Speaking

13 a Find out about two other types of holiday. In A/B groups write questions using the notes below to help you.

Student As write questions about camel trips in Egypt.

Student Bs write questions about bird watching in Mexico.

Think about cost, location, what the area is like, accommodation, food, facilities, activities/ organised tours.

b Student As read the text about bird watching in Mexico on page 147. Prepare to answer your partner's questions.

Student Bs read the text about camel trips in Egypt on page 145. Prepare to answer your partner's questions.

c Work in A/B pairs. Take turns to ask and answer questions.

14 Discuss. Which holiday would you rather go on: bird watching in Mexico, camel riding in Egypt or trekking in Bhutan? Why?

6.3 On the move

Grammar | making comparisons
Can do | make comparisons about places and people

Vocabulary | verb phrases about moving/travelling

1 Work with a partner. Match the <u>underlined</u> verb phrases 1–8 with the correct definitions a–h. Use a dictionary if necessary.

1. My parents are Scottish but they <u>emigrated</u> to Australia.
2. My brother has <u>lived abroad</u> for ten years so I don't see him much.
3. I've just <u>moved house</u>. Here's my new address.
4. My sister <u>left home</u> when she was 18 and went to university in York.
5. I spent a lot of holidays just <u>roaming around</u> the countryside, exploring.
6. After weeks of planning, we finally <u>set off</u> on our round-the-world trip.
7. We all cried when we went to <u>see her off</u> at the airport.
8. I'<u>m off</u> to the shops. Is there anything you need?

a) to live in a foreign country
b) to leave your house and go to live in another one
c) to leave your country and go to live in another country
d) to walk or travel, with no definite purpose
e) when you are ready to go or you're going to go somewhere very soon
f) to leave at the start of a journey (especially an important, exciting or difficult journey)
g) when a young person leaves his/her parents' house and goes to live somewhere else
h) to go to an airport, train station, etc. to say goodbye to someone who is leaving

2 Complete the questions with the correct form of a phrase from Ex. 1.

1. At what age do young people in your country typically _______ ?
2. Do you like people to come and _______ (you) at the airport?
3. What time did you _______ when you last went on holiday?
4. Which country would you move to if you lived _______ ?
5. What would you miss if you _______ ?
6. How many times have you _______ in your life?
7. Where _______ (you) to after class today?
8. When was the last time you went to a new place and just _______ without any clear direction?

3 **a** You are going to ask your partner the questions from Ex. 2. First, predict what you think his/her answers will be.

b Ask the questions. How many did you get right?

Reading

4 **a** Discuss. Do you think the following statements are true (T) or false (F)?

A Over a million British people emigrate every year.
B Spain is a popular destination for British people to emigrate to.
C Most people who emigrate go back home after a year.

b Read the text quickly and check your answers.

5 Read the text again and match each paragraph with the most appropriate summary A–G. Three of the summary sentences cannot be used.

A The appeal of many places is the price of property, better wages and the good weather.
B For most people who emigrate, it's the best thing they've ever done.
C Many people find that the grass is not always as green as they had hoped.
D There is a trend in recent times for increasing numbers of British people to emigrate.
E It's very difficult to get a work permit for popular countries like Australia and Spain.
F Some people go abroad for about three years in order to earn well and save money to go back with.
G Although emigrating can be hard, it can also provide people with greater job satisfaction.

ON THE MOVE!

1 **Every day, thousands of people are on the move and, either temporarily or permanently, setting up home abroad. Their move may be job-orientated or perhaps they think the grass is greener somewhere else. Whatever their reasons, it's clear that more and more people are stepping into the unknown and leaving their own country. In Britain alone, over 400,000 people make the move each year. But where do they go and why? And do they 'live happily ever after'?**

2 Typically a lot of people move abroad because of their jobs. They may find that their company is moving them overseas but many people make their own decision, believing they will have more successful careers abroad. Paul Derwin is a scientist who used to be based at a prestigious London university. He was dissatisfied, however, with the level of funding and recognition he was getting and decided to explore the possibilities California had to offer. 'Emigration is incredibly difficult, emotionally as well as practically,' he says. 'But after ten years here, I've got a far nicer life than before. I have a fantastic job and the recognition I wanted. People take my work much more seriously here. It would be difficult to give that up now.'

3 The most popular reason for emigrating, however, is the desire for a better quality of life. Destinations that place a greater value on leisure and have a more laid-back lifestyle were the most popular. People also look for places that will give them a sunnier climate and generally hotter weather. Britain is famous for its bad weather especially during the dark and cold winter months. Southern Spain becomes very appealing when you think of the 320 days of sunshine a year. Cheaper property is another reason given for moving abroad. The cost of living in America, for example, is twenty percent lower than in Britain and often salaries are slightly higher. For all these reasons, it's not surprising that the top five most regularly chosen destinations for Britons to emigrate to are: the USA, Australia, New Zealand, Canada and Spain. The fact that most of these are English-speaking countries is obviously also a major factor for British people. Sue Riddell, a thirty-year-old nurse from Birmingham, wants to emigrate to Australia with a group of friends. 'We're fed up of the conditions we work and live in,' she says. 'I went travelling to Australia after I left school and I loved it – the beaches, the fresh air, the sense of space. If I can, I'm going. And I don't know if I'll come back.'

4 Despite the fact that so many Britons move abroad, however, most of them go back home after only about three years. Often living overseas is not as attractive as it first seems. Generally people emigrate because they think life is going to be better. They sometimes want to do this because they get certain feelings on holiday and they romanticise about what it would be like to live there. They tend to focus on the best aspects and think it will be like this all the time when often that is not the case. Making enough money and getting work can be more difficult abroad than at home and people tend to find they miss family, friends and things they took for granted back home.

6 Discuss.

1 What type of person do you think you need to be to emigrate or study abroad?
I think you need to be an independent person.

2 Have you ever lived abroad?
 a If so, where did you go and what was it like? What did you miss?
 b If not, would you ever consider doing so? Why/Why not? Where would you like to go?

3 Is it common for people to emigrate from your country? If so, where do they go and what are their reasons? Do you think they find what they are looking for?

Grammar | making comparisons

7 Complete the rules in the Active grammar box.

Active grammar

1 A The comparative and superlative of one-syllable adjectives (e.g. *cheap*) and adverbs (e.g. *fast*) are generally made by _______ .

Exceptions:

B Adjectives which end in a vowel plus a consonant (e.g. *hot*). These comparatives and superlatives are made by _______ .

C Adjectives which end in *-e* (e.g. *nice*). These comparatives and superlatives are made by _______ .

2 A The comparative and superlative of two and three-syllable adjectives (e.g. *popular*) and adverbs (e.g. *carefully*) are generally made by _______ .

Exception:

B Two-syllable adjectives ending in *-y* (e.g. *sunny*). These comparatives and superlatives are made by _______ .

You can also use (*not*) *as* ... *as* to make comparisons.

3 A We use (*not*) *as* ... *as* to compare things which are _______ (e.g. *Often living overseas is not as attractive as it first seems*).

B We use *as* ... *as* to compare things which are _______ (e.g. *The lifestyle in New Zealand is as laid-back as in Australia*).

Some adjectives and adverbs have irregular forms:

4 A good/well → better →_______ ;

B bad/badly → _______ → the worst;

C much → more → most;

D little → less → least;

E far → further → furthest

We can't use *very* to modify comparatives, but:

5 A We can use *a bit*, *a little* and *slightly* to show __________ differences.

B We can use *far*, *much* and *a lot* to show __________ differences.

see Reference page 87

8 Complete the second sentence so that it means the same as the first. Use between two and four words (including the word in **bold**).

Spain is sunnier than Britain.

isn't: *Britain isn't as sunny as Spain.*

1 I find learning foreign languages far more difficult than my sister.
much: My sister learns foreign languages _______ than me.

2 I'd prefer to live somewhere drier than this.
wet: I'd prefer to live somewhere that _______ this.

3 I'm a bit more adventurous now than I was ten years ago.
slightly: Ten years ago I was _______ I am now.

4 At home my life was a lot more complicated than it is abroad.
much: My life abroad is _______ than it was at home.

5 I don't think I planned my time on holiday carefully enough.
carefully: I think I should've planned my time on holiday _______ .

6 My lifestyle in Canada now is not better or worse than it was in England.
as: My lifestyle here in Canada is _______ it was in England.

Person to person

9 **a** Write six sentences about yourself using comparatives and superlatives. You can use the ideas in Ex. 8 to help you. Four of the sentences should be true and two should be false.

I'm more adventurous than I used to be.

b Say your sentences to another student. Can he/she guess which two are false?

6 Vocabulary

Expressions with *go*

1 Match the expressions with *go* in **bold** with the correct definitions a–j.

1. We're **going away** for two weeks to stay with my cousin.
2. There's a lot of shouting next door. I wonder what's **going on**?
3. Which course have you decided to **go for**?
4. I totally trust Danielle. She would never **go back on** her word.
5. He **went down with** terrible flu the day before his interview.
6. I've never been skiing before but I'd like to **have a go**.
7. He's decided to **make a go** of the new business for at least a year.
8. I've been **on the go** all day and I'm exhausted.
9. It **goes without saying** that we'll all support you.
10. They **went to great lengths** to make the party a success.

a) to happen
b) to catch an illness
c) to take a lot of time and effort
d) to choose a particular thing
e) to attempt to do something
f) to be clear without being said
g) to be very busy or working all the time
h) to not do what you've promised or agreed to do
i) to make something (e.g. a business or a marriage) successful
j) to leave your home and go to another place for a few days or weeks

2 Work in pairs. Say one of the definitions in Ex. 1. Your partner should say the correct expression.

A: *to be clear without being said*
B: *it goes without saying*

3 Choose the correct alternatives.

1. When I'm abroad I always *make/have* a go at speaking the language.
2. We're going *away/out* for the weekend. Could you look after our cat?
3. Don't worry. It goes without *saying/talking* that I'll meet you at the airport.
4. There's something going *down/on* in the city centre. It's full of people.
5. Although they argue a lot, they want to *make/have* a go of their marriage.
6. I promise I won't go back *with/on* what I've said.
7. Can you help with dinner please? I've been *on/off* the go all day.
8. Your teacher can't be here today. She's gone *off/down* with a bad cold.
9. I couldn't decide which kitten to go *away/for*. They were all gorgeous.
10. He went to *great/long* lengths to make sure he was totally prepared for the interview.

4 **a** 6.7 Listen and check your answers.

b Listen again and underline the part of the expression with *go* which has the main stress. Then repeat the sentences.

When I'm abroad I always have a <u>go</u> at speaking the language.

5 **a** In pairs, prepare to tell a story using five of the expressions in Ex. 1. Your story should include one of the sentences below.

One day I decided that I wanted a bit more adventure in my life.

I'd always been fascinated by the idea of exploring caves.

I'd never considered myself much of an explorer before.

b Listen to other students' stories. Which did you think was the most exciting? How far were the stories based on true feelings/events?

6 Communication

Travelling companions

1 Discuss in pairs.

1 Which of the holidays in the photos appeals to you most? Why?

2 What is the best holiday you've ever been on? Why?

2 Do the quiz with as many different students as possible. When you're asking the questions, make notes about the other students' answers. When you're answering the questions, use the ideas in the quiz and your own ideas.

3 **a** Look at the notes you made about other students and read the descriptions on page 146.

- Which one do you think you are most like?
- Which one do you think each person you questioned is most like?

b Which students do you think would be the best travelling companion for you? Why? Which would be the worst? Why?

Lifelong learning

Travelling is learning

Travelling time is good learning time. Brainstorm all the ways to continue learning while travelling.

- watch English films on a plane
- listen to your coursebook CDs on a bus
- talk to English-speaking people you meet on a train

Who's your ideal travelling companion?

Are you an intrepid adventurer who loves sleeping under the stars or someone who prefers a home from home and all life's luxuries? Who is your ideal travelling companion? And who is your travelling companion from hell?

Do the quiz and find out.

1 What would your ideal summer holiday be?
package holiday/beach/pool independent travel alone/with friends camping exploring jungle/desert, etc. sports/activities (e.g. skiing, scuba diving, etc.)

2 What would you definitely pack in your suitcase?
romantic 'easy-reading' novels serious novels magazines guidebooks study/work books first aid kit sun cream sleeping bag penknife

3 How would you spend your ideal evening on holiday?
in the hotel restaurant in your tent
in local restaurants trying different food
in various bars and nightclubs

4 How long do you like your holidays to be?
not more than a week two weeks
at least three or four weeks open-ended

5 What do you dread most about your holiday?
missing favourite TV programmes missing friends/family
being bored spiders, mosquitoes, etc.
toilets that don't work properly
being on a beach with only people of my nationality
not being able to speak the language
getting robbed

6 What are you most likely to bring home?
cheap cigarettes and perfume lots of photos
souvenirs from the airport a tropical disease
a fantastic suntan arts and crafts made by the locals

Present Perfect Simple and Continuous

Use the Present Perfect Simple to talk about an action or experience in the past when the time is not important or not known.

I've visited several countries in South America.

Use the Present Perfect Simple to describe an action that started in the past and continues in the present, when you're focussing on the finished action or on the number of times the action has been completed up to the time of speaking.

I've lived here since last January.

Contrast with Present Perfect Continuous. Use the Present Perfect Continuous to describe an action that started in the past and continues in the present, when you're focussing on the activity itself.

He's been playing tennis for three hours.

Use the Present Perfect Simple to describe an action that happened in the past but has the result in the present.

The post has come. There's a letter for you.

just, *yet* and *already*

Just means a short time ago. It usually comes between *has/have* and the past participle.

I've just seen Mariana.

Already shows that something happened sooner than expected. It usually comes between *has/have* and the past participle or at the end of the sentence.

I've already done the shopping.

Yet shows that the speaker expected something to happen before now. It is used at the end of negatives and questions.

Have you finished that email yet?

She hasn't replied to the invitation yet.

Questions

Direct questions:

There are two main types of direct questions:

Yes/No questions

Are you going to Danka's party on Saturday?

Wh- questions

Where did she learn to speak such good Spanish?

Subject questions are used when the question word (e.g. *who*) refers to the subject of the sentence. When a *wh-* word replaces the subject in a question we do not use the auxiliary verb.

The teacher told us to go. → *Who told you to go?*

Indirect questions:

Use indirect questions when you want to be polite (e.g. when you don't know someone).

Use the word order of positive statements.

Use *if* or *whether* for indirect *Yes/No* questions.

Can you tell me where the nearest bank is?

I'd like to know whether this bus goes to Oxford.

Making comparisons

Add *-er* and -est to form the comparatives and superlatives of:

one-syllable adjectives and adverbs

two-syllable adjectives and adverbs ending in *y*

Use *more* and *most* to form the comparatives and superlatives of two or more syllable adjectives and adverbs.

You can also use (*not*) *as* ... *as* to make comparisons.

I can't play the piano as well as Michael.

We can't use *very* to modify comparatives, but we can use the following:

for a small difference – *a bit, a little, slightly*

for a larger difference – *far, much, very much, a lot, quite a lot*

I'm feeling quite a lot better today.

Key vocabulary

Exploring

to have itchy feet   to be bitten by the travel bug   to go as an independent traveller   to experience culture shock   to go/be taken into uncharted territory   to wander around

Adjectives with *-ed* and *-ing* endings

fascinated/fascinating   daunted/daunting   challenged/challenging   petrified/petrifying   annoyed/annoying   disgusted/disgusting   inspired/inspiring   worried/worrying

Weather

cool   chilly   subzero temperatures   mild   scorching   to pour   to drizzle/drizzle   shower/showery   breeze/breezy   clear   overcast   bright   changeable

Verb phrases about moving/travelling

to emigrate   to live abroad   to move house   to leave home   to roam around   to set off   to see someone off   to be off

Expressions with *go*

to go away   to go on   to go for   to go back on   to go down with   to have a go at   to make a go of   to be on the go   to go without saying   to go to great lengths

1 Choose the correct alternatives.

Thanks for the party last week. I've really enjoyed/really enjoyed it.

1 I'*ve written/'ve been writing* eight emails all morning.
2 I'*ve seen/saw* a really awful film yesterday.
3 My brother is in France. He's been there *for/since* a week.
4 She's very well travelled. She's *been/gone* to more than twenty countries.
5 Billy's the nicest person I've *ever/already* met.
6 I live in a flat in London. I'*ve lived/lived* here for three years.
7 He'*s worked/been working* in the garden for hours and he's exhausted.
8 Would you like some coffee? I've *yet/just* made some.

2 Write sentences using the prompts. Use the Past Simple, Present Perfect Simple or Continuous.

I/stand/at this bus stop/forty minutes

I've been standing at this bus stop for forty minutes.

1 He/already/phone me/three times today.
2 We/go/to India/three weeks last summer.
3 I/just/see/a really fantastic musical.
4 You/hear/the news/yet?
5 I/decorate/the living room/all day.
6 I/know/my best friend/primary school.
7 You/ever/read/the *Lord of the Rings* books?
8 How long/you/study/English?

3 Complete the direct questions for the underlined answers.

Where did you go on holiday last year?

I went to Sardinia.

1 ____________ your motorbike?
I've had my motorbike for a week and a half.
2 ____________ at university?
She's going to study engineering at university.
3 ____________ ?
I think I'm about 1 metre 70 centimetres tall.
4 ____________ that box on the top shelf for me?
No, sorry, I can't reach it. I can only reach the second shelf.

4 Write indirect questions for the underlined answers starting with the words given and using the words in brackets.

Can I ask you where you went on holiday last year? (you go on holiday last year)

I went to Rio de Janeiro for carnival.

1 Can ________________ ? (this shop)
It closes at half past five.
2 I'd ________________ (can buy/theatre tickets here)
Yes, you can.
3 Would ________________ ? (you/finish your homework)
I'll definitely finish it by 12.00.
4 Can ________________ ? (the most interesting country/you ever visit)?
I'm not sure – either Japan or Russia.

5 Choose the correct alternatives.

I want to get to work earlier than/as yesterday.

1 My suitcase is *much/more* heavier than yours.
2 Tania got the *worse/worst* maths results in the whole class.
3 The exam wasn't as difficult *than/as* I'd expected.
4 You're the *most/more* helpful person I know.
5 You need to speak *quite/quiet* a lot louder than that.
6 People are far more *friendly/friendlier* here than in my country.
7 This one is *a/the* little more expensive than that one.
8 Which actor is the *better/best*: Brad Pitt or Leonardo DiCaprio?

6 One word is wrong in each sentence. Find the word and correct it.

1 We'll need an alarm because we're putting off very early in the morning.
2 He's desperate to go travelling. He's got really scratchy feet.
3 I'd really love to make a go with drama lessons.
4 I think I'm going down of a sore throat.
5 I'll give you a lift. That goes without speaking.
6 I experienced country shock at first and found it hard to get used to living in a new place.
7 I can't believe she went back to her word.
8 It was lovely having so many people to see me away at the station.

7 Excess

Lead-in

1 Discuss.

1 What can you see in each picture?
2 In what ways do you think they represent 'excess'?
3 In what other ways might people's lifestyles be described as 'excessive'?

2 7.1 Listen to three lifestyle descriptions. Do you think the things described are 'excessive'? Why/Why not?

3 **a** In pairs, discuss the meaning of the words in **bold**.

1 When was the last time you bought something really **extravagant**?
2 Do you think spending €100 on one meal is **excessive**?
3 If you could take one **luxury** to a 'desert island', what would it be?
4 Do you ever order **extra-large** portions in restaurants?
5 Do you think you were **spoilt** as a child? Why/Why not?
6 When was the last time you bought something you thought was **overpriced**?
7 Do you think the idea of having a 'self-cleaning' house in the near future is **far-fetched**?
8 Do you know anyone who would go on a **spending spree** to cheer him/herself up?

b Ask and answer the questions with a partner. How many of his/her answers are similar to yours?

7.1 Food for thought

Grammar countable and uncountable nouns
Can do describe how to prepare and cook a dish

Reading

1 Look at the photo and discuss.

1. How does the picture make you feel?
2. Do you eat a lot of fast food? Why/Why not? Do you think that the amount of fast food you eat is healthy?

2 **a** Read the text quickly and answer this question. According to the film-maker, what is the main message of the film?

SUPER SIZE ME

Three trips to McDonald's a day might be every little boy's dream. But the reality was a nightmare for Morgan Spurlock whose film Super Size Me documents his one-month existence on fast food and its disastrous consequences. So, if it was so awful, why did he do it? And does it work as a film?

The main basis of the film is that Spurlock promises to eat three McDonald's meals a day, every day, for a month. He must only eat food from McDonald's and every time an employee asks if he would like to 'super size' the meal, he must agree. 'Super sizing' refers to the fact that with this type of meal you get a considerably larger portion of everything. Instead of the normal burger, fries and a drink, you get an extra-large burger, extra-large fries, and an extra-large drink for only a very small price increase.

Spurlock admitted that the whole experiment ignored any sensible eating plan. He knew that by eating three McDonald's meals a day, he would be consuming more calories, fat, salt and sugar per meal than he needed. Before he started, three doctors certified that Spurlock was 183cm tall, weighed about 84kg and was in good health. Although both Spurlock and his doctors knew this diet was unhealthy, none of them were quite prepared for just how unhealthy it turned out to be. The changes in his body were horrifying. In the first week, he put on 4.5 kilos in weight and by the end of the thirty days he had gained nearly 14 kilos, bringing his total weight to a massive 98kg.

Weight gain was only one of the negative effects, however. When all three doctors saw the severe damage to his liver, they all recommended stopping the experiment after twenty days. Spurlock continued to follow the diet, however, because he wanted to show people what this kind of diet can do to you. And you begin to realise that the film could be a fast-forward picture of your life: in thirty days you get to see what could happen to you over twenty or thirty years of over consumption. You're on a path to heart disease, liver failure, high blood pressure, diabetes, depression and more.

'I think we need to take responsibility for ourselves,' says Spurlock. 'There also has to be some responsibility on the part of the fast food companies. McDonald's alone feeds 46 million people every day. They have an obligation to give their consumers information about exactly what they're eating.' Spurlock also focusses on the advertising and marketing of fast food products, especially to children. McDonald's markets to children through Happy Meals (a children's meal in a box including a free toy) and playgrounds in the restaurants. 'The playgrounds aren't there just for kids to come and play,' he says. 'You're only allowed into the playground when you've bought a burger or some fries or a Coke. It's an effective way of establishing a positive association in children's minds.'

It's the humour above all that makes this film work. Even towards the end of the month, when he admitted to feeling lethargic, depressed and smelly, the audience remain entertained by his sense of humour and upbeat style. Spurlock says that he hopes that the film is entertaining, but he also hopes that it encourages them to take better care of themselves. He says, 'I'd love people to walk out of the movie and say, "Next time I'm not going to 'super size'. Maybe I'm not going to go there at all. I'm going to sit down and eat dinner with my kids, with the TV off, so that we can eat healthy food, talk about what we're eating and have a relationship with each other."' Judging by critics and audiences alike, the film certainly does seem to work. Food for thought indeed.

b Read the text again and explain what each of these phrases means in its context.

1 'the reality was a nightmare' (l.3)
2 'to "super size" the meal' (l.17)
3 'ignored any sensible eating plan' (l.27)
4 'just how unhealthy it turned out to be' (l.39)
5 'recommended stopping the experiment' (l.50)
6 'a fast-forward picture of your life:' (l.57)
7 'an obligation to give their consumers information' (l.71)
8 'a positive association in children's minds' (l.87)
9 'his sense of humour and upbeat style' (l.95)
10 'have a relationship with each other' (l.108)

3 Discuss. Have you seen this film? What did you think of it? Would you like to see it? Why/Why not?

Grammar | countable and uncountable nouns

4 **a** Look at the underlined words in the examples in the Active grammar box. Is each one countable or uncountable?

b Divide the words in the box into three groups: countable, uncountable and those which can be both.

c For the words that can be both, discuss what the difference in meaning is.

You can say 'a coffee' when you're talking about a cup of coffee and you can say 'some coffee' when you're not saying exactly how much.

Active grammar

1 *He ate three McDonald's meals a day, every day, for a month.*
2 *He must only eat food from McDonald's.*
3 *I'll have sausage, beans and a black coffee, please.*
4 *If I drink coffee in the evenings, I can't sleep properly.*

food meal coffee diet burger meat sugar salt chicken bread chocolate fruit cake weather luggage paper trip travel equipment advice iron furniture business hair information news

COUNTABLE	UNCOUNTABLE	BOTH

see Reference page 101

5 What is the difference in meaning between *few/a few* and *little/a little* in these sentences?

1 a He's lucky. He's got *few* problems to worry about.
  b Things aren't going well. He's got *a few* problems.
2 a We must go. There's *little* time before the train leaves.
  b Stay and have a drink. We've got *a little* time before the show starts.

6 Complete the sentences with the correct word/phrase from the box.

much many a little a few bread lots lot some a great deal of piece slice

1 You haven't eaten _______ fries.
2 I only have _______ sugar in my coffee nowadays.
3 There is too _______ traffic in the city centre.
4 She gave me a _______ of paper with her address written on it.
5 He gave me _______ really good advice.
6 I've got _______ of bags to carry. Can you help me?
7 He's very lazy. He spends _______ time doing nothing.
8 I'll just have one _______ of toast please.
9 There were only _______ shops still open when I went out.
10 I've spent a _______ of time working with children.

7 Find the mistakes in eight of the sentences and correct them.

1 Do you spend lot of time doing exercise?
2 Have you given anyone a good advice recently?
3 How many sugar do you have in your coffee?
4 When was the last time you had piece of cake?
5 How often do you watch the news on TV?
6 How many fruits do you usually eat every day?
7 Do you like a very hot weather?
8 Do you ever use the Internet to get information?
9 When did you last go on an interesting travel?
10 When did you last buy some new furnitures?

Person to person

8 Ask and answer the questions in Ex. 7 with a partner.

Vocabulary | food and cooking

9 **a** Put these words into the correct place in the word map below.

a saucepan an oven sweet to bake
a cooker beef to scramble bitter
a frying pan salty to fry a peach
to roast cabbage to boil sour
a wooden spoon to grill savoury
parsley a plate

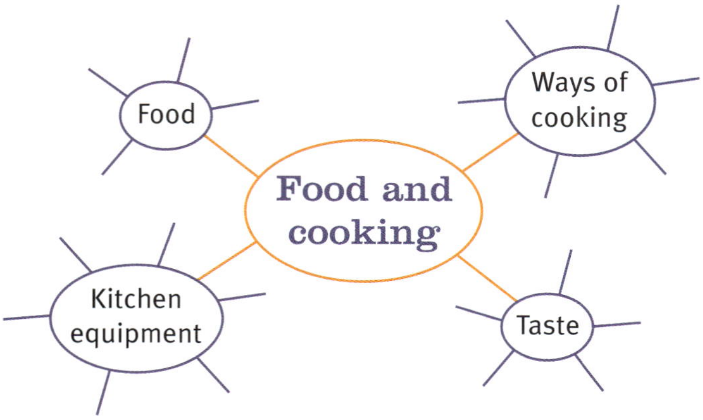

b What is the difference between:

1 a cook/a cooker
2 a vegetable/a vegetarian
3 a recipe/a dish
4 rare/raw
5 to stir/to beat
6 to slice/to chop/to grate

c Work in pairs. Add at least two more words to each group of words in the word map.

10 **a** Choose the correct alternatives.

1 Sushi is a Japanese dish made with *raw/rare* fish.
2 *Beat/Stir* the mixture slowly every five minutes.
3 Ugh! This soup is much too *savoury/salty*.
4 First, you *slice/chop* the onion into small squares.
5 I don't eat many cakes and biscuits. I find them too *sweet/sour*.
6 Fill a large saucepan with water and *bake/boil* the pasta for ten minutes.
7 Macaroni cheese is my favourite *dish/plate*.
8 The *cook/cooker* has broken. I need to buy a new one.
9 In Britain at Christmas, it's traditional to *bake/roast* a turkey in the oven.
10 Which vegetable shall we have today: *cabbage/parsley* or broccoli?

Pronunciation

11 **a** 7.2 With a partner, decide which syllable in each of the words below has the main stress. Then listen and check your ideas.

cooker

1 saucepan
2 oven
3 vegetable
4 vegetarian
5 bitter
6 savoury
7 carrot
8 sugar

b Now decide which syllable(s) in each of the words above you think is pronounced as a weak form /ə/. Listen again and check your ideas.

Speaking

12 7.3 Listen to someone talking about a traditional British Christmas dinner. Do you think you would enjoy this meal?

13 **a** Choose one of the things in the list below. Think about how it is prepared and cooked.

1 your favourite dish
2 the last meal you made for visitors
3 a traditional dish in your country
4 a dish you used to love as a child

b Tell other students what the dish is and how to prepare/cook it.

c Which of the meals you heard about would you like to eat most?

7.2 Buy, buy, buy

Grammar passives
Can do write a formal letter of complaint

Listening

1 Discuss. What can you see in the photos? How do you think they are connected?

2 7.4 Listen and check your ideas.

3 Listen again and decide if these statements are true (T), false (F) or we don't know (DK).

1. A friend of Andress found the bikini in her attic.
2. Andress said it was a difficult decision to sell the bikini.
3. Someone bought the bikini for $6100.
4. Six stormtrooper helmets were auctioned in London.
5. The owner made a profit of nearly $25,000.
6. Someone sold Britney Spears' chewing gum at a traditional auction.
7. The gum came with a guarantee to prove it was real.
8. Thousands of people put in bids for the gum.
9. One man in Texas bought his sons Christmas presents on eBay.
10. When he sold the presents again, he made $1000 profit.

4 Discuss.

1. Do you know anyone who collects things (e.g. pop memorabilia, old magazines, stamps, etc.)? What do you think of this kind of hobby?
2. What do you think of what the Texan father did?
3. Have you ever visited eBay or a traditional auction? What do you think of these ways of buying and selling things?

Vocabulary | verb phrases about money

5 What is the difference in meaning between the verb phrases in *italics* in each pair of sentences?

1. a Lots of people *bid* for the chewing gum on eBay.
   b That bag is very expensive. Why don't you try and *haggle* for it?
2. a These boots were only £30. I think I *got a bargain*.
   b I'd like to buy this T-shirt but it's slightly marked. Could I *get a discount*?
3. a You can *get a refund* within twenty-eight days if you are not completely satisfied.
   b *Get a receipt* just in case you want to take the CDs back.
4. a I'd love to get a new camera but I *can't afford* it at the moment.
   b It'll cost £10 to take a taxi – it's *not worth it*. Let's walk instead.

6 **a** Read the sentences and decide which of the phrases in Ex. 5 you could use for each one.

1. One man offered to pay £5000 for a small antique chair at an auction.
2. Ten CDs for only £50 – that's really cheap!
3. I asked if I could pay less, but the shop assistant said no.
4. I'd like to buy a motorbike but I haven't got enough money.
5. This DVD player broke after only a week. I'd like my money back, please.
6. I always try and negotiate a lower price with market traders.
7. The rent on that tiny flat is much too expensive.
8. Don't forget to keep the paper they give you when you buy something.

b Rewrite the sentences using the correct form of the verb phrase.

c 7.5 Listen and check your ideas.

Grammar | passives

7 **a** Look at the example sentences in the Active grammar box and answer these questions.

1 Which of the underlined verbs are active and which are passive?

2 For each pair of sentences, why would we choose to use the passive (not the active)?

b Check your answers by reading the rules of meaning A and B.

Active grammar

1 a *The bikini was bought for $61,000.*

b *Someone bought the bikini for $61,000.*

2 a *The bikini was bought by the American, Robert Earl, co-founder of Planet Hollywood.*

b *The American, Robert Earl, co-founder of Planet Hollywood, bought the bikini.*

Meaning

Use the passive when you want:

A to talk about actions, events and processes when who or what causes the action, event or process is unknown or unimportant. This is often the case in writing (or more formal speech)

B to put new information or longer expressions later in the sentence

Form

verb *to be* + past participle

c Read the rule of form in the box and complete the passive sentences below using the correct verb forms (in brackets).

Thousands of things are bought (buy) on eBay every day. (Present Simple Passive)

1 The car _______ (clean) at the moment. (Present Continuous Passive)

2 The stormtrooper helmet _______ (find) by chance at a second-hand sale. (Past Simple Passive)

3 The painting _______ (display) when I arrived at the auction. (Past Continuous Passive)

4 Some items _______ (buy) at auctions for absurdly high prices. (Present Perfect Simple Passive)

5 It was a piece of chewing gum which _______ (spit) out by Britney Spears. (Past Perfect Simple Passive)

6 Ridiculously high prices _______ (pay) for completely useless items. (Future Simple Passive with *will*)

7 The new shop _______ (open) by the mayor. (Future with *going to*)

8 It seems that almost anything _______ (buy). (Modals in the passive, e.g. *can*)

see Reference page 101

8 Complete the email with an appropriate active or passive form of the verbs in brackets.

Hi John

Just a quick message to tell you about an auction I was taken (take) to in London last week. I (1) _______ (persuade) to go by some friends of mine and although I wasn't very keen at first, I ended up having a great time. When we first got there we (2) _______ (give) a list of all the items in the auction and then we (3) _______ (have) some time to look at everything. Most of it was rock-and-roll memorabilia and there were some old records and things. I was a bit nervous about bidding for things at first, but soon got into it.

Anyway, to cut a long story short, I (4) _______ (buy) a large jukebox. It's really fantastic – and a real bargain I think. It (5) _______ (deliver) next week. But can I ask you a huge favour? You see, they said it (6) _______ (could/not/send) abroad to my house so I (7) _______ (give) them your address in London. I hope that's OK! I (8) _______ (arrange) for my uncle to pick it up from your place very soon, I promise. Then he'll look after it until I'm in London again in the summer. Don't worry, when it arrives, you (9) _______ (ask) to sign something but you won't have to pay anything. All the payment (10) _______ (sort) out already.

I'll phone soon to let you know the exact time of delivery.

All the best

Guiseppe

Speaking

9 Discuss with a partner what you would do in each of the situations below and why.

1. You have just been served a meal in a restaurant which is cold and very late to arrive.
2. You realise that you bought four CDs in a shop yesterday but you were charged for five.
3. You have just arrived at your hotel on holiday. The brochure said there was a swimming pool but it hasn't been finished.
4. Your new washing machine is broken and some wet clothes are stuck inside it.

10 a 7.6 Listen to the conversation and answer the questions.

1. Which of the situations in Ex. 9 is it?
2. How does the customer feel?
3. What solution is offered?

b Listen again and complete the How to box.

HOW TO ...

complain in a shop, restaurant, hotel, etc

Customer asks to speak to someone	*I'd like to speak to the* (1) _______ *, please.* *Could I speak to Customer Services, please?*
Manager/ Assistant asks what problem is	*Can I help you?* *Can I be of any* (2) _______*?* *What* (3) _______ *to be the problem?*
Customer says what problem is	*My washing machine has stopped completely and there's a load of washing stuck inside.* *Your computers were down and I couldn't get through.* *We have been waiting for over an hour for our main course.*
Manager/ Assistant apologises and offers a solution	*Oh, I'm very sorry about that, madam.* *I can only* (4) _______ *.* *We'll provide a* (5) _______ *free of any extra charge.* *Would you like a refund?*

c Add one sentence to each section in the How to box.

11 In pairs, choose one of the situations in Ex. 9. Do a roleplay in which the customer complains about the situation. Use the language in the How to box to help you.

Writing

12 Read the letter in the Writing bank on page 154 and do the exercises.

13 Choose one of the situations in Ex. 9 or one of your own ideas and write a formal letter of complaint. Use the paragraph plan to help you.

Paragraph 1: state briefly what you're complaining about

Paragraph 2: give details about your complaint

Paragraph 3: give further details about your complaint (if necessary)

Paragraph 4: say what you would like them to do

7.3 It's a dog's life

Grammar *have/get something done*
Can do talk about services

Reading

1 Discuss.

1 Do you have any pets? Did you use to have any pets when you were a child? If so, which ones? If not, why not?
2 What do you think are the main reasons why people keep pets? Do you think it is a good idea for children to have pets? Why/Why not?
3 What can you see in the photos?

2 Read the text quickly. Which of the things in the photos are mentioned?

Pet heaven?

In some parts of Europe and the USA, many pet owners see their cat or dog as a member of the family. In the UK, owners spend an amazing €4 billion annually on keeping their pets fit, well and entertained. In one survey, it was found that up to forty percent of owners said they bought gifts for their pets, including Christmas and birthday presents. Owners happily pamper their pets with increasingly lavish lifestyles, including toys, furniture, accessories and 'gourmet' food. There are also pet psychologists for those with problems, pet passports for those who want to travel and a whole range of services on offer. There are hundreds of retail outlets offering owners a vast array of products. But many pets have everything they could ever ask for (or bark for?). The question for many owners now is: what do you give to the pet that has everything? We asked some owners what their pet got for his or her last birthday …

Marion Dowdeswell and 'Pixie': Marion lives on her own in Edinburgh, UK with her dog, Pixie. 'Pixie really is my best friend,' says Marion. 'He's such a lovely dog and my constant companion. I'd be lost without him, so I think I just treat him like I'd treat anyone I love.' For his last birthday, Marion bought Pixie a bed costing over €300. She admits that it was too much money to spend on an animal. 'I know it's a bit over-the-top,' she says, 'but he does love it!' Marion says she doesn't only indulge him on his birthday. Last week, she got a set of 'doggie boots' to keep Pixie's paws warm and stop him from slipping on wet ground. 'Probably a luxury, but why not occasionally?'

Sylvia and Brad Phillips and family and 'Beauty': The Phillips family from California, USA, acquired Beauty three years ago when some friends emigrated. 'We didn't really know much about dogs then, and at first we didn't know how it would work out,' says Sylvia. 'But right from the start, she just made our family complete and the kids adore her. They're always finding new things to buy for her. She probably is spoilt but it's fun.' Last year, they got her a present they were really excited about: a necklace made of fake pearls which cost about €70. 'She doesn't really wear it because it seems to irritate her, but we took some great photos!' says Sylvia.

Claudette and Pierre Leroi and 'Mignon': Claudette and Pierre live in Paris with their Yorkshire terrier, Mignon. Because Mignon is a longhaired dog, Claudette says that it's necessary to take her to the hairdresser regularly. 'I take her to the beauty parlour once a week to have her fur done. I don't think it's a luxury really.' Mignon has it washed and brushed and sometimes cut and even curled. On special occasions, like her last birthday, for example, Mignon had the fur from the top of the head pulled back and tied as a ponytail, while the rest of her fur was cut short. 'She looked so cute – like a little Barbie doll,' says Claudette. She gets the dog anaesthetised to do these things so that she stands still for long enough, but Claudette thinks it's worth it.

So, is all this pet indulgence gone mad? Or is it simply spoiling a valued member of the family?

3 **a** Read the first paragraph again and decide if these statements are true (T), false (F) or we don't know (DK).

1 British owners spend €4 billion on their pets every year.
2 One quarter of owners buy their pets presents.
3 More pets than before have psychological problems.
4 Some owners have a problem knowing what to buy for their pets.

b Read the rest of the text. Which of the following apply to which pet or pets (or none of them)?

1 his/her owner buys him/her clothes
2 his/her owner wants to make him/her look nice
3 he/she provides friendly company for his/her owner
4 his/her owner takes him/her on expensive holidays
5 his/her owner knows he/she is overindulgent
6 his/her owner takes him/her to the hairdresser
7 his/her owner buys him/her toys and dolls
8 his/her owner was ignorant about pets initially

4 Discuss. Do you think pets should be treated like a member of the family? In general, what is the attitude to pets in your country?

Grammar | *have/get something done*

5 **a** Complete examples A–C in the Active grammar box using *had*, *have* and *gets*. Then look at the text again to check your answers.

Active grammar

A *I take her to the beauty parlour to* (1) _______ *her fur done.*
B *On her last birthday, Mignon* (2) _______ *the fur from the top of the head pulled back and tied as a ponytail.*
C *She* (3) _______ *the dog anaesthetised so that she stands still at the hairdresser.*

Form *have* (or *get*) + object + _______

Meanings

1 In examples A–C, is this structure (with *have* or *get*) used to talk about a) doing something ourselves or b) arranging for something to be done by somebody else?
We can also use this structure:
2 with *have* or *get*, to talk about things that happen to us, and
3 with *get* only (not *have*), to mean 'finish doing something'.

D *I had my bag stolen on my way home from work.*
E *She got her fingers caught in the car door.*
F *As soon as I get this essay written, I'll take the dog out.*

b Complete the rule of form with the correct part of speech.

c Look at rule 1 and answer the question.

d Look at rules 2 and 3. Then match each rule with the correct examples D–F.

see Reference page 101

6 Find the mistakes in six of the sentences and correct them.

1 I've never had my hair dye.
2 I've had my house broken into several times.
3 I never my house have decorated – I do it myself.
4 I haven't had my eyes testing for ages.
5 I've got a lot of things to get doing by this weekend.
6 I have dry-cleaned some of my clothes every month.
7 I really need to have my hair cut soon.
8 I'd like to get my photo took by a professional photographer.

Person to person

7 Discuss.

1 Are any of the sentences in Ex. 6 true for you? Tell another student and change the others so that they are true.
It's true I haven't had my eyes tested for ages. I think I should have it done soon because my eyes hurt when I use a computer.
2 What things do you have done regularly? Why? What things can you have done in your neighbourhood?
I have my car cleaned inside and out once a month! I know it's extravagant but I hate doing it myself.

Vocabulary | animal expressions

8 **a** With a partner, divide the animals in the box below into six groups.

eagle, duck = birds

~~eagle~~ horse dog whale spider bull fish bat fly ~~duck~~ cat bear

b Add at least three more words to each of your groups.

9 **a** 7.7 Label the parts of the animals in the pictures using the words in the box. Then listen and check your answers.

fur feathers paws hooves claws tail wings whiskers fins horns beak

b Which of the underlined vowel sounds in the words in the box have the same sounds as each other? Listen again and check.

c In pairs, describe an animal using the words in the box. Your partner should guess which animal it is.

A: *This animal's body is covered in fur. It has four paws and it wags its tail when it's happy.*

B: *A dog!*

10 **a** Complete the expressions in *italics* by writing the name of one animal in each.

1. It's true she paid over £300 for one pair of shoes. I didn't just hear it from someone else – she told me herself. It was *straight from the ______'s mouth.*
2. It's my job to tell him he's failed his exam. I've got to tell him but I feel really bad about it. I'll just have to *take the ______ by the horns* and do it.
3. My eyesight has got much worse. I can't read this price label at all. I need glasses for most things nowadays. *I'm as blind as a ______* without them!
4. My boss was in a bad mood with everyone yesterday. He shouted at anyone who went near him. He *was like a ______ with a sore head.*

b 7.8 Listen and check your answers.

11 **a** What do you think the expressions mean? Read the sentences again and discuss in pairs.

b Match the expressions 1–4 in Ex.10a with the correct definition a–d below.

a) to have very bad eyesight
b) to be in a bad temper and extremely irritable
c) 'first hand' information from the original source
d) to confidently deal with a difficult or dangerous situation

c Choose two of the expressions and tell other students about a person or situation using them.

d Do you have similar expressions in your language?

7 Vocabulary

Prefixes

1 **a** 7.9 Listen and match the people with items A–D. One of them cannot be used.

A Someone annoying
B Someone completely 'over-the-top'
C Something to be proud of
D Something embarrassing

b Listen again and make brief notes about each story.

c Retell each story with your partner.

2 **a** Look at the tapescript on page 158 and find a word to match with each definition below.

Story 1

1 to sleep more than you had intended – *oversleep*
2 to think or guess something is less than it is
3 a former employer

Story 2

4 to go back to studying again and learn new skills
5 to be able to speak two languages equally well
6 describing a company that has offices, factories, etc. in many different countries

Story 3

7 not usual or normal
8 very big
9 describing a way of speaking that sounds uninterested because it's on one note

b Look at the words from Ex. 2a and write the appropriate prefixes in the table.

PREFIXES	MEANINGS	EXAMPLES
1 *mono*	one/single	*monolingual*
2	twice/two/every two	
3	many	
4	more than	
5	less than	
6	former	
7	again	
8	very	
9	not	

c Read the rule about hyphens. Then write one more example of your own for each prefix in the table above.

Hyphens: We use hyphens (-) with some prefixes, including *extra-* and *ex-*. Check in a dictionary if you are unsure.

3 **a** Complete the sentences below with the most appropriate word from the box. Not all the words can be used.

monologue monolingual bicycle
biannual multimedia multipurpose
overtired overworked undercooked
underpaid ex-girlfriend ex-husband
reheat rewrite extra-small
extra-strong uncomfortable unnecessary

I always feel slightly uncomfortable and silly wearing a hat.

1 The company holds a big _______ conference, so the next one will be in six months' time.
2 When you go camping, what you need is a good _______ knife that does everything.
3 You'll need to use some _______ packaging so that it doesn't get torn in the post.
4 Be careful that the food is hot all the way through and never eat _______ meat.
5 I think nurses are _______ especially considering the amount they get paid.
6 I've only studied English in my own country where the classes are all _______ .
7 The teacher has asked me to _______ my essay because I misunderstood the question the first time.
8 I still get on well with my _______ even though I don't see her much nowadays.

b 7.10 Listen and check your answers.

4 **a** Work with a partner. Choose something to talk about from the list in Ex. 1a. Prepare to tell your story using as many of the words in Exs. 2a and 3a as you can.

b Listen to other students' stories. Which of the items in the list do you think each of the stories you heard was about?

7 Communication

Can I help you?

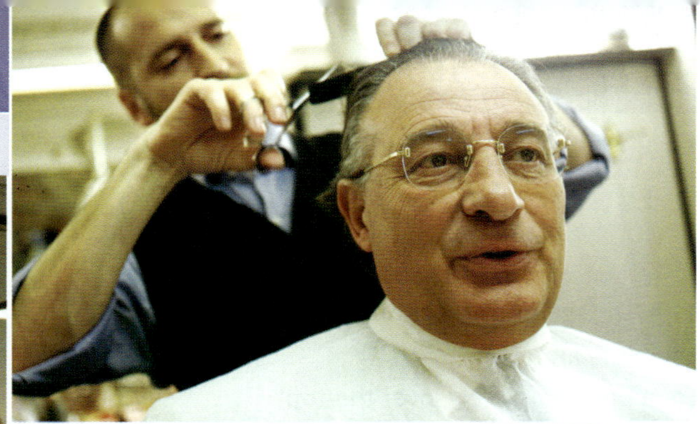

1 **a** In pairs, complete the word maps for each of the places in the pictures. Include as many words as you can which are related to each place.

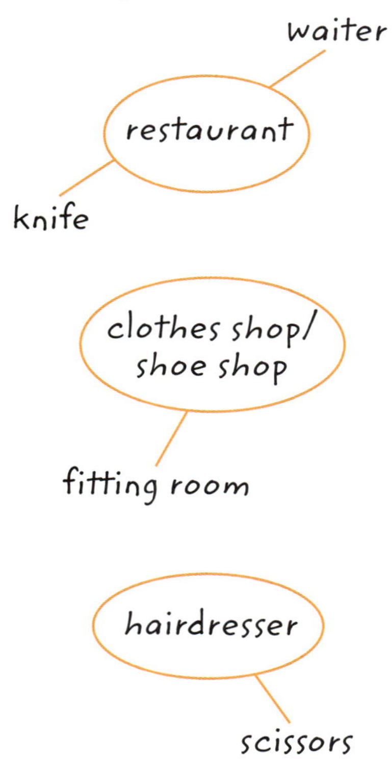

b Compare your words with other students.

2 **a** Which of the sentences would you expect to hear in a) a restaurant, b) a shoe shop, c) a hairdresser?

1 I'd like to try these on, please.
2 I'll have the grilled tuna, please.
3 Just a cut and blow-dry?
4 I've got black in size 38, but not in 39.
5 Rare, please.
6 I'd also like some highlights done.
7 A bottle of the house red, please.
8 They look really nice on you. How do they feel?
9 I'd like to book an appointment.
10 We're offering all customers an Indian head massage.
11 We booked a table for two in the name of Morrison.

b 7.11 Listen to three conversations and number the sentences in the order you hear them.

3 **a** In pairs, choose one of the situations from the listening. Look at the tapescript on page 158 and underline any important phrases.

b Roleplay the situation using the ideas from the listening and your own ideas.

4 **a** Look at the table and note down some more things that people complain about in the three places.

RESTAURANT	SHOE/CLOTHES SHOP	HAIRDRESSER
Food is undercooked *Service is slow*	*Shoes are dirty* *Button is missing*	*Cut too short* *Dyed wrong colour*

b In pairs, choose a different place and decide on one or two things to complain about. Roleplay the situation.

Countable and uncountable nouns

Countable nouns are words like *banana*, *hotel*. They can use a singular or plural form of the verb.

That's a lovely hotel!

Uncountable nouns are words like *food*, *information*, *equipment*. They use a singular form of the verb.

There isn't much food left.

Common uncountable nouns:

accommodation, advice, behaviour, bread, equipment, food, furniture, health, information, knowledge, luggage, news, research, salt, spaghetti, traffic, travel, trouble, water, weather, work

Common nouns which can be countable or uncountable:

chicken, chocolate, coffee, egg, glass, hair, iron, paper, room, space, time, wine

You can use: *a/an*, *few*, *a few*, *some*, *any*, *many*, *a lot of*, *lots of*, before countable nouns.

I haven't roasted any potatoes.

You can use: *little*, *a little*, *some*, *any*, *much*, *a lot of*, *lots of*, before uncountable nouns.

There wasn't much traffic this morning.

few/a few and *little/a little*:

Few and *little* (without '*a*') are used to talk about negative ideas.

She's got few friends and is quite lonely.

He's got little money and can't afford a new car.

A few and *a little* are used to talk about more positive ideas.

I've got a few biscuits left. Would you like one?

Could I have tea with a little milk, please?

Passives

We can use active constructions when the subject is the person or thing that does the action.

I bought a really fantastic party dress on eBay.

We can use passive constructions:

when who or what causes the action is unknown or unimportant

when we want to put new information or longer expressions later in the sentence

We often use passive constructions in writing or in more formal speech. The passive is common in news stories, scientific and academic writing.

The dog was found three days after it went missing.

Also use the passive when the object of the active sentence is the main focus. Use *by* to say who did the action.

A Picasso painting was sold by a wealthy businessman last week.

We can use the passive in any tense and with modal verbs.

Form verb *to be* + past participle

We haven't been given the exam results yet.

have/get something done

Form *have* (or *get*) + object + past participle

Use the structure *to have* (or *get*) *something done*:

to talk about arranging for something to be done by someone else

I have my hair dyed once every six months.

to talk about things that happen to us or to describe an 'experience'

I had my bike stolen last week.

There is another use of *get* + object + past participle (NOT *have*) which is used to mean 'finish doing something'.

I need to get my homework done.

Key vocabulary

Excess

extravagant excessive a luxury extra-large
to spoil someone overpriced far-fetched
to go on a spending spree

Food and cooking

a saucepan a frying pan a wooden spoon
an oven a cooker a cook a plate a dish
a recipe sweet savoury bitter salty sour
rare raw to bake to roast to scramble to fry
to grill to boil to stir to beat to slice
to chop to grate beef cabbage parsley
a peach a vegetable a vegetarian

Verb phrases about money

to bid for something to haggle for something
to get a bargain to get a discount
to get a refund to get a receipt
to be able to afford something to be worth it

Animals and animal expressions

dog cat bull horse bear bat fish whale
duck eagle fly spider fur feathers paws
hooves claws tail wings whiskers fin horns
beak straight from the horse's mouth
to be as blind as a bat
to be like a bear with a sore head
to take the bull by the horns

Prefixes

oversleep undercooked ex-boss retrain
bilingual multinational unusual extra-large
monotonous

7 Review and practice

1 Choose the correct alternatives.

Is there a/any bread in the cupboard?

1 Could you give me *an/some* information about train times please?
2 I've got two large pieces of *luggage/luggages*.
3 How *many/much* furniture have you got in your living room?
4 The news *is/are* always so depressing.
5 He's been doing *a/some* research into global warming.
6 There were only *few/a few* people there when I arrived.
7 I'd like *a/some* slice of toast with jam and an orange juice, please.
8 Can I give you *an/some* advice about revising for your exam?

2 Complete the sentences using the correct tense of a verb from the box in the passive form.

catch charge deliver employ include open repair send

1 Service _______ in the bill so you don't need to leave a tip.
2 I _______ some flowers yesterday but I don't know who they're from.
3 The goods that you ordered _______ next Friday.
4 My car broke down last week. It _______ at the moment.
5 Don't use the medicine if the packet _______ already.
6 It's unlikely that the robbers _______ .
7 I was annoyed because we _______ for a bottle of wine we didn't have.
8 She was sacked after she _______ by that company for over fifteen years.

3 Look at part of Tilly's diary and imagine that today is Tuesday and it's 1.30p.m. Write sentences about what she *had done*, *is having done* and *will have done*.

She had her living room decorated yesterday.

1 ________________
2 ________________
3 ________________
4 ________________
5 ________________
6 ________________
7 ________________
8 ________________

Monday

10.30a.m. Decorator (living room)
Pick car up from garage (fit new tyres)
Delivery of new cooker (after 5p.m.)

Tuesday

Haircut (& highlights) 9.15a.m.
Carpet fitters (living room) – between 1 and 2p.m.
Take watch to repair shop – don't forget!

Wednesday

Eye test (optician on High Street) 10.00a.m.
Window cleaner (a.m.)
Don't forget to take coat to dry-cleaners

4 Choose the correct alternative.

1 I don't really like cooked carrots. I much prefer them *rare/raw/roast*.
2 I've decided to bid *from/for/at* that table I told you about.
3 £60 is too much for that bag. It's really not *value/afford/worth* it.
4 I won't believe he's got the job until I hear it straight from the *cat's/bull's/horse's* mouth.
5 I'm taking my dog to the vet because he cut his *hoof/paw/claw* on some broken glass.
6 The sound on this CD is really strange. Take it back and get a *discount/refund/receipt*.
7 Before you roast potatoes, you should *bake/beat/boil* them for ten minutes.
8 She's like a *bat/bear/bull* with a sore head today. She's already shouted at me twice.

5 Complete the words with the most appropriate prefix.

1 The children need an early night. They are ____tired and rather irritable.
2 It all took a lot longer than I expected. I ____ estimated the time by several hours.
3 She talks in such a boring and ____tonous voice that I just fell asleep.
4 I've been a teacher for ten years but I've decided to ____train as a computer technician.
5 We've decided to have a school reunion every two years and make it a ____ennial event.
6 The classrooms are extremely modern and have all the latest ____media equipment.
7 When you ____heat food, you need to make sure that you get it hot enough.
8 She's got a very ____usual name. I wonder where it comes from.

8 Success

Lead-in

1 In pairs, describe the photos and answer the questions.

1. What do you think the people all have in common?
2. What do you think they had to do to achieve their success?

2 **a** Complete the sentences with the words/phrases from the box in the correct form. Use a dictionary if necessary.

best-seller	succeed	go under	have had their day	have a go	give up	up to scratch

1. If the business doesn't start making money by the end of the year, it will probably ______ and have to close.
2. His book's been an instant ______ . Everybody's talking about it.
3. Just because you failed this exam doesn't mean you should ______ . You can always re-take it in October.
4. I think these reality TV shows ______ . No one's very interested in them anymore.
5. You know what they say: 'If at first you don't ______ – try, try, try again!'
6. I'm afraid the work you've done on the house really isn't ______ . You'll have to redo a lot of it.
7. I'm not sure that pushing the car will help start it, but you can ___ .

b 8.1 Listen and check your answers.

3 Tell another student about the last time you felt you achieved something special.

8.1 Lead or follow?

Grammar *It's time/I'd rather/I'd better*
Can do describe different types of people

Reading

1 Discuss.

1 Is leadership a natural-born talent or a learned skill?
2 What qualities does a successful leader need?
3 In what different situations do people need to work together as a group?
4 Does every group need a leader? Why/Why not?

2 Read the text quickly and match the questions above with the correct paragraphs.

3 Read the text again. Are these statements true (T), false (F) or we don't know (DK).

1 Being able to work in a group is one of the most important life skills.
2 Groups of people doing social activities generally don't need leaders.
3 Members of leaderless groups often stop attending.
4 Antonio Carluccio thinks he is a natural-born leader.
5 Good leaders are often slightly afraid of their role.
6 Good leaders should do more work than the other group members.

Are YOU a successful leader?

The Successful Leadership Trust – our company specialises in training you to be a successful leader for whatever situation you're in.

A ...?

Almost nothing we do in this world is done in isolation. At work or at play, you'll find yourself in groups, working with other people: your team at work, a meeting with colleagues, your family, a holiday with friends, a group of students working together, a day out walking in the mountains, a group of neighbours wanting to make changes. It is now recognised that being able to work successfully with other people is one of the major keys to success, partly because we need to do it so often.

B ...?

In almost every situation where you're in a group, you will need a skilled leader. All groups need leaders and all successful groups have good leaders. Groups without leaders or with weak leaders almost always break down. Members of a leaderless group often begin to feel dissatisfied and frustrated. Time is wasted and the tasks are not achieved. There are often arguments and tensions between people as there is nobody to keep the goals clear. Some personalities dominate and others disappear. Often group members begin not to come to meetings in order to avoid more disharmony.

C ...?

Some people are natural leaders. The celebrity chef, Antonio Carluccio says, 'True leaders are born and you can spot them in kitchens. They're people who combine toughness, fairness and humour.' Although a lot of people agree that there are some natural-born leaders, most people now recognise that leadership can also be taught. Our professional and experienced staff can train almost anyone how to be a successful leader. Good leaders don't make people do things in a bossy, controlling way. You can learn how to involve everyone, encouraging the whole group to work towards a common goal.

D ...?

Our training courses use activities and techniques to develop a range of qualities which are necessary to be a good leader. Self-confidence is vital and being able to overcome your own fears about being a leader. Successful leaders also need to be calm and intelligent. They need to be able to work out good strategies and make sound judgements under pressure. Lastly, and probably most importantly, good leaders need to be sensitive, sociable and be able to get on with a wide range of people. Good leadership is essentially the ability to influence others and good leaders allow all members of the group to contribute.

4 Discuss. Do you agree with the quotes? Why/Why not?

'The art of leadership is saying no, not yes. It is very easy to say yes.' Tony Blair

'The most important thing about successful leadership is knowing how to get on with people.' Teddy Roosevelt

'Don't tell people how to do things, tell them what to do and let them surprise you with their results' George S. Patton

Grammar | *It's time/I'd rather/I'd better*

5 8.2 Listen to the work appraisal interview and decide which of the sentences best summarises the main points.

1 He's doing well in his role of team leader but would like some more training
2 He's finding his role of team leader difficult and thinks he needs some training
3 He's interested in becoming a team leader but would like some training first

6 a 8.3 Complete sentences 1–4 in the Active grammar box. Then listen and check your answers.

Active grammar

1 *I feel that it's _______ I moved on now.*
2 *I think I _______ you did the first course.*
3 *I _______ not wait for two months.*
4 *I _______ get your name on the list immediately.*

A **Form** *It's time* + subject + _______
Meaning to talk about when you should have done something already or at least started it

B **Form** subject + *would rather* + object + _______ (+ *than* ...)
Meaning to talk about what you'd prefer someone else to do

C **Form** subject + *would rather* + _______ (+ *than* ...)
Meaning to talk about what you'd prefer to do

D **Form** subject + *had better* + _______
Meaning to talk about something when it is advisable to do it (in the present or future)

b Complete the rules of form by writing *past tense* or *infinitive*.

c Look at the sentences 1–4 again and explain what each one means. Read the rules about meaning to help you.

see Reference page 115

7 a Complete the dialogue. Use *It's time, 'd rather* or *'d better* and the correct form of the verb in brackets.

Anna: Hi, Will. How did your appraisal go?

Will: It went well, thanks. My boss thinks (1) _______ (have) more responsibility and maybe became a team leader.

Anna: Oh that's good. How do you feel about that?

Will: I'm pleased because I was thinking of looking for a better job in another company, but (2) _______ (stay) here if I can.

Anna: It would be great if you were our team leader. (3) _______ (be) in charge than someone we don't know.

Will: Thanks. Anyway, (4) _______ (go) because I've got a meeting in five minutes. See you later.

b 8.4 Listen and check your answers.

Person to person

8 a Write three sentences about you starting with *It's time* ...

It's time I tidied up the living room.

It's time I got in touch with my brother.

It's time I changed my job.

b In pairs, compare your sentences with another student. Ask your partner to tell you more details about his/her sentences. Try and include *I'd better* and *I'd rather* in your answers.

Vocabulary | describing personality

9 **a** Work in A/B groups. Use a dictionary to find out the meanings and pronunciation of the five adjectives in your group below.

GROUP A	GROUP B
outgoing	easy-going
open	selfish
proactive	witty
opinionated	manipulative
single-minded	headstrong

b Work in A/B pairs.

1 Tell each other about the meaning and pronunciation of the five words in your group.
2 Add some adjectives which have a) opposite meanings and b) similar meanings to the ones in the box.

open → reserved (opposite)

headstrong → determined (similar)

c Compare the adjectives you added with other students.

10 8.5 Listen to ten people describing different people they know. For each one write an adjective from Ex. 9 which you think describes him/her best.

1 *easy-going*

11 **a** Think of three people you know who you can describe using some of the adjectives in Ex. 9.

b Tell your partner about each person, giving examples of how he/she behaves which show why you've chosen those adjectives.

My sister is a very headstrong person. She really wanted to travel around South America on her own. Everyone tried to persuade her not to because it was dangerous but she decided to do it anyway and ...

c Which of the qualities from Ex. 9 do you think successful people usually have, and which can stop you being successful? Give reasons.

I think that most successful people are very determined and single-minded but if you are too headstrong it could go against you because ...

12 **a** Match the expressions in the box with the correct picture. In pairs, say what you think each one means.

1
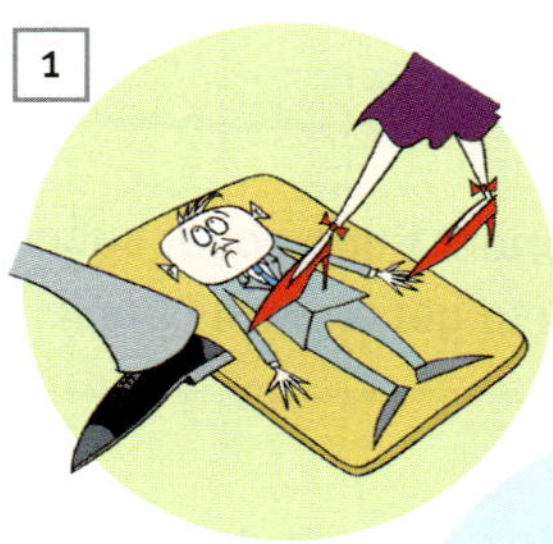
2

3

4

5

be the centre of attention   be a party animal
be a complete doormat   be down-to-earth
be really high maintenance

b Do you have any similar expressions in your language?

13 **a** Talk about yourself and the different sides of your personality. First, think about how you behave in different situations using the ideas in the box and your own ideas.

leading a discussion at work or school
giving a presentation at work
making a complaint in a shop or restaurant
talking about yourself in a job interview
performing on stage
being in a crowd of people at a party
cooking for a small group of friends
playing a team game (e.g. football)
organising a group of children

b Work in pairs and tell each other about the different sides of your personality in different situations.

I think I'm generally an outgoing person in social situations like a party. I like being the centre of attention and I'm quite witty sometimes! I can be shy too, though, especially at work if I have to speak in public or chair a meeting – I just clam up.

8.2 Winners

Grammar reported speech
Can do report and describe what people say to you

Listening

1 Discuss.

1 Match each photo above with the most appropriate feeling in the box below. What do you think is happening/has happened in each case?

> completely ecstatic
> absolutely devastated
> totally single-minded

2 Can you remember any sporting moments that you've watched (or been involved in) when someone has felt in similar ways?

2 8.6 Listen to part of a radio programme and answer the questions.

1 What proportion of sportspeople use sports psychologists to help them with their mental attitude?
2 What are the main purposes of the Haka war dance used by the New Zealand All Blacks rugby team?

3 Listen again and write one sentence summarising the speaker's main points about each of the following:

1 self-belief
2 negative thoughts
3 personal lucky 'routines'

4 Discuss. Do you (or does anyone you know) have lucky routines, superstitions or lucky charms for things like sport, exams, special events, travelling, etc.?

Vocabulary | adjectives and intensifiers

5 **a** Look at the underlined adjectives in the table. What is the difference in meaning between gradable and non-gradable adjectives?

Gradable adjectives	*He missed an important goal.*
	He is a big success as a racing driver.
Non-gradable adjectives	*He missed a vital goal.*
	He is a huge success as a racing driver.

b Match the gradable adjectives in 1–4 with the correct non-gradable adjectives a–d. Use a dictionary if necessary.

1 happy	a) starving
2 upset	b) ecstatic
3 hungry	c) exhausted
4 tired	d) devastated

6 **a** Read the rules A and B. Then look at the sentences and decide if one or both intensifiers are correct.

A We can use intensifiers *very, really* and *extremely* with gradable adjectives to make the meaning stronger.
B We can use intensifiers *really* and *absolutely* with non-gradable adjectives to make the meaning stronger.

1 Kelly Holmes must be *really/absolutely* ecstatic about her success.
2 A(n) *extremely/very* big sports centre near here has just opened.
3 If you want to get to the top in athletics, it's *really/extremely* vital to get yourself a professional trainer.
4 Whenever he plays football, he comes back *really/absolutely* filthy.
5 She was *absolutely/extremely* exhausted at the end of the race.
6 I love running. I'd be *really/very* devastated if I had to give it up.

b 8.7 Listen and check your answers.

7 Think of a true story about you that relates to one of the phrases in the box in Ex. 1. Tell your partner what happened.

I couldn't believe it when I won the prize for best actor. I was completely ecstatic!

Grammar | reported speech

8 **a** 8.8 Listen and complete the sentences and questions.

Direct speech

1 ________ to be the last player onto the pitch.
2 ________ the race easily.
3 ________ to train ________ .
4 ________do it by thinking about something different.
5 Why ________ so negative?
6 ________ help ________ ?

b Compare the reported speech in the Active grammar box with the direct speech above. Find examples of the changes 1–6 and write them in the box.

Active grammar

Reported speech

Andy Cole said (that) he wanted to be the last player onto the pitch.

She said (that) she had won the race easily.

He told me (that) he wasn't going to train that day.

I told him (that) he could do it by thinking about something different.

I asked him why he was feeling so negative.

She asked me if I would help her the following day.

1 Tense changes, e.g. go → went: *want → wanted*
2 Modal verb changes, e.g. *can* → *could*: ________
3 Subject pronoun changes, e.g. *I* → *he*: ________
4 Object pronoun changes, e.g. *me* → *him*: ________
5 Time reference changes, e.g. *now* → *then*: ________
6 Word order changes, e.g. *were they going* → *they were going*: ________

Rules

A We can use *that* after both *say* and *tell*, but it isn't necessary.
B We don't use an object after *say*.
C We must use an object after *tell*.
D We use a question word when reporting *Wh-* questions.
E We use if when reporting *Yes/No* questions.
F We sometimes ignore the rule that changes the tense or modal verb back. This can happen if the situation is still true, or for dramatic effect when telling a story.

see Reference page 115.

9 Read the rules A–F in the box and decide if these sentences are correct or not. Correct the ones which are wrong.

1 He said that he was totally devastated about the result.
2 She told me that she couldn't come to training this evening.
3 He told me he's training three times a week at the moment.
4 She said him she had taken up basketball the previous January.
5 I told them I was going to be late and that they should start without me.
6 I asked her she wanted to come round and watch the tennis.
7 He asked me why I went to a sports psychologist.
8 She told me she wants to move away from sport and further her career elsewhere now.

10 **a** Check you understand the meanings of the verbs in **bold** in the sentences below.

*Nobody needed to **remind** him to focus on the goal.*

*She **admitted** feeling totally out of control.*

*He **explained** that he wanted to compete in the Olympics.*

*I **promise** to go swimming at least three times a week.*

*I **suggested** talking to a sports psychologist.*

*They **decided** to buy tickets for the football match.*

*My trainer **warned** me that the training would be very hard.*

b Write the verbs in **bold** from Ex. 10a in the correct place in the table.

VERBS	CONSTRUCTIONS
say,	verb + (*that*)
tell,	verb + object + (*that*)
ask,	verb + object + infinitive
	verb + infinitive
	verb + gerund

11 Report these statements starting with the words given.

1 'I broke the window yesterday when I kicked a ball through it by mistake.'
He admitted ...

2 'Why don't we try the new Italian restaurant when we go out on Friday?'
He suggested ...

3 'I think I'll stay in tonight because I'm completely exhausted.'
She decided ...

4 'I'm going to buy my girlfriend some flowers as a way of saying sorry.'
He told ...

5 'Are you going to book tickets for the cinema or are you going to just turn up?'
She asked ...

6 'You really mustn't be late for your interview this afternoon.'
She warned ...

7 'Please all bring your homework to me by 9.00 on Monday morning.'
The teacher reminded ...

8 'I'll pay you back all the money I owe you by tomorrow.'
He promised ...

Person to person

12 Choose A or B below and follow the instructions.

A

1 Write notes about three things that you've seen or heard in the news in the last week. Make notes about when and where you saw or heard each story and details of each story.
TV news /yesterday/interest rates up by one percent ...

2 Then tell your partner details of the news stories you've seen or heard.
'On the news yesterday, they said that interest rates were going to go up by one percent ...'

B

1 Write notes about three things that three different people have said to you in the last twenty-four hours. Make notes about the time, the person and his/her actual words.
10.30 this morning/Marianne/'Why don't we go out for lunch today?'

2 Then tell your partner what the three people said, giving details.
'At 10.30 this morning, Marianne suggested going out for lunch today.'

Speaking

13 **a** Look at the photos. Discuss what you think is happening in each one.

b Think about someone who has helped you to succeed in something. Make notes using the questions below to help you.

1 What were you trying to do? And when?
2 Who helped you?
3 What did he/she suggest that really helped?
4 What did you learn from this person?
5 How did you feel when you succeeded?

14 **a** Tell other students about the person who helped you succeed. Make short notes about other students' experiences.

b Report back to the class about the most interesting story you heard about.

Lifelong learning

Successful language learning

A successful language learner is generally someone who:

- is willing to make mistakes
- wants to get his/her message across
- finds as many opportunities to practise as possible
- doesn't worry about words he/she doesn't understand

1 Which of the characteristics above apply to you?
2 Do you know anyone who is a very successful language learner? What kind of person is he/she?

8.3 Tot.com

Grammar *hard* and *hardly*
Can do write report of survey findings

Reading

1 Look at the photo. Discuss.

1. At what age should children learn how to use computers?
2. How do you feel about how much children use computers in your country?

2 Read the article. What does Dr Ryde think the advantage of sending children to his school is?

TOT.COM

Every week, a group of British pupils file into class to start their lessons, turn on their computers and obediently follow their teacher's instructions. For an hour, they are taught mouse techniques, keyboard skills, and reading and writing, using the computer. However, these are toddlers, hardly out of nappies. (A) ______ .

At Ryde College they take the idea that 'It's never too young to start' very seriously indeed. Since the college opened in 1982, more than a thousand pupils have achieved exam results at an earlier than usual age.

The college was founded by Dr Ronald Ryde, a former university lecturer, now aged seventy. (B) ______ . Word spread around the neighbourhood and Dr Ryde soon had to move to a special centre to cope with the demand for his services. To the man who happily puts seven-year-olds in for GCSEs, the 'Technology for Toddlers' classes were the next logical step. (C) ______ . Aside from the actual lessons, parents are also encouraged to get the children to practise their new skills at home.

The parents of these young computer whiz kids have no qualms about giving their children a head start. Kevin Mills, forty-four, enrolled his son, Piers, a year ago, just before his second birthday, after he showed an interest in playing with a computer at home.

Elick Harding, a marketing manager and father of Safiya, another of the toddler students, admits his daughter is not always in the mood to sit still and learn but says her vocabulary and reading skills are now streets ahead of other children her age. (D) ______ .

Whereas toddlers are tutored during the day, the older children attend either in the evenings until as late as 9p.m. or at weekends. So, there is an issue about when they get to run around and climb trees like their friends. (E) ______ . Last year parents Teeta and Kaushik Radia, whose son, Krishnan, became the youngest child ever to get a GCSE in Information Technology, aged just six, complained that Ryde College pushed young children into sitting exams for the publicity.

Dr Ryde remains unrepentant. 'I would argue that it's a crime to hold children back. (F) ______ . All of us here are committed to education, not publicity.' Dr Ryde sees his college not as a hothouse for brilliance – he claims there is no great secret to their success other than small class sizes and traditional schooling methods – but rather as a way to make up for the time wasted in normal state secondary schools. 'All too often the first years in secondary are lost years and teachers waste them getting all the children up to the same level.'

Glossary
GCSE = General Certificate of Secondary Education. National exams in all subjects, usually taken at age sixteen.

3 **a** Each of the sentences 1–6 comes from the article. Read the article again and decide where each one should go.

1 'She can count up to thirty, has an excellent vocabulary and has gained so much confidence through her classes.'
2 Introduced last year, they are aimed at giving the eighteen-month to three-year-old pupils a head start in writing, reading and communication using the computer.
3 There is also the question of why these children need to take additional exams, especially at such a young age.
4 Next term, they will move up a class to begin instruction in computer science, just months after they have celebrated their fourth birthdays.
5 The only thing we are exploiting is their ability to learn.
6 He started offering home classes after he helped his son, Mike to pass a computer GCSE at the age of fourteen, rather than the normal sixteen.

b Read the text again through from beginning to end, to check your answers.

4 Find these words in the article. Write a short definition for each one. To help you a) decide if they are nouns, verbs or adjectives, b) look at them in the context of the words before and after them.

file (l.1) – verb: to walk in line

1 nappies (l.7)
2 former (l.14)
3 spread (l.15)
4 cope (l.17)
5 qualms (l.24)
6 head start (l.24)
7 mood (l.31)
8 hothouse (l.48)

5 Discuss. What are the advantages and disadvantages of pushing children to study intensively and take exams early?

Grammar | *hard* and *hardly*

6 **a** Look at examples 1–3 in the box and decide if the words in **bold** are adjectives or adverbs.

Active grammar

1 *Studying every weekend for my exams was **hard** work.*
2 *The children are encouraged to work **hard** for their exams.*
3 *The pupils in the college are **hardly** out of nappies.*

Hardly means almost not or very little. It is often used with *any(thing/one/where*, etc.) and *ever*. It is not used with negative words (~~I hardly never eat chocolate~~).

4 *I'm very tired this morning. I hardly slept last night.*
5 *I have hardly any money. I must go to the bank.*
6 *She hardly ever comes to visit us. Just once or twice a year.*

b Look at examples 4–6 in the box . Explain the meaning of each one in other words (not using *hardly*).

see Reference page 115

7 Complete each of these sentences with *hardly* and a verb from the box in the correct form.

know	say	believe
walk	change	have

1 I'm very busy at the moment. I ______ any time to go to the gym.
2 Are you ok? You ______ a word during dinner.
3 Doesn't Tom look amazing? He's ______ at all since we were at school.
4 I don't understand why that woman from the office was so friendly. I ______ her.
5 Her leg is hurting her a lot. She says she can ______ at the moment.
6 I was shocked when she told me he had left. I could ______ it.

8 Decide if each of the sentences is correct. If not, correct it.

1 I can hardly hear you. Could you speak up, please?
2 She needs to study hard if she is going to pass her exam.
3 He's eaten anything hardly all day.
4 We tried very hard to finish the report but there wasn't enough time.
5 Hardly anybody I know is going to Sarah's party.
6 We've got hard any milk left.

Person to person

9 Complete the sentences so they are true for you. Compare your answers in pairs.

1 The last time I studied hard ...
2 At school/work, I hardly ever ...
3 Recently, I've hardly been to any ...

Speaking

10 Read the questions below and make a note of your answers.

1 What are the three most important things that help children to do well at school?
2 Which three subjects should children spend most time studying at school?
3 What are the most important qualities of a good teacher?
4 What are the three most important things that help people to do well at work?
5 Which three things should people get most training in for work?
6 What are the most important qualities of a good manager?

11 a Look at the How to box. Add one more way of giving opinions and one more way of justifying opinions.

HOW TO ...

Give your opinion

Give your opinion	***I believe*** *small class sizes are crucial ...* ***As far as I'm concerned*** *maths is the most important subject ...*
Justify your opinion	*... **because** the teacher can spend more time with each child.* *... **for several reasons; firstly,** you need maths for lots of things in everyday life ...* ***If*** *a teacher is approachable, **then** children will feel able to ask questions.*

b Ask other students the questions in Ex. 10 and note their responses. When answering, use the How to box to help you.

c Make notes of the main findings of your survey.

1 a good teacher
small classes
modern technology

2 Maths
English
I.T.

3 caring
knowledgeable
keep control

4 feeling appreciated
good environment
good salary

5

6

Writing

12 Look at the report in the Writing bank on page 155 and do the exercises.

13 Discuss with other students which words or phrases in the report might be useful in other similar reports.

14 Write a report on one of the topics in Ex. 10 in 120–140 words. Divide it into separate paragraphs.

8 Vocabulary

Phrasal verbs with three parts

1 Match the phrasal verbs in *italics* with the correct meanings a–j below.

1 We'll never *catch up with* them. They're too far ahead.
2 They stole £1m and *got away with* it.
3 Don't walk so fast! I can't *keep up with* you.
4 They're *putting* her *in for* her Grade 8 piano exam this year.
5 Have you *come up with* any new ideas for the advertising campaign?
6 I'd like us to *cut down on* the amount of TV we watch.
7 I've always *looked up to* my grandmother. She's an amazing person.
8 I'm *looking forward to* seeing my sister's new baby at the weekend.
9 How do you *put up with* the noise of the traffic outside your bedroom window?
10 We want to *make up for* all the time she wasted in her first year at secondary school.

a) to think of, suggest
b) to think you will enjoy
c) to move at the same speed
d) to formally apply to do something
e) to tolerate
f) to reduce
g) to respect, admire
h) to reach the same place
i) to compensate for
j) to escape punishment

2 **a** Complete the sentences with one of the phrasal verbs from Ex. 1 in the correct form.

1 You need to ______ how much salt you have in your food.
2 If none of us says anything to the police, we'll probably ______ it.
3 We're really ______ moving back to New Zealand. It'll be especially great to see all our friends.
4 I can't ______ his constant criticism anymore. I've decided to move out.
5 The increase in salaries isn't ______ the rise in the cost of living. People's disposable income is getting less and less.
6 She's ______ a transfer to the London office to be nearer her parents.
7 I think I've ______ a rather good solution to our problem.
8 The delicious food more than ______ the slow service.
9 All her students ______ her. She's an amazing teacher.
10 I had to run to ______ you. You walk incredibly fast!

b 8.9 Listen and check your answers.

c Listen again and decide which part of each phrasal verb is stressed.

3 **a** Which of the following sentences are correct?

1 You won't catch up with them.
2 You won't catch up them with.
3 You won't catch them up with.
4 I'm looking my holiday forward to.
5 I'm looking forward my holiday to.
6 I'm looking forward to my holiday.

b What does this tell you about the grammar of this kind of phrasal verb?

4 Discuss.

1 Is there anything you are really looking forward to doing over the next few weeks? If so, what?
2 Is there anything you are trying to cut down on at the moment? If so, what and why?
3 Are there any things in everyday life that you find difficult to put up with, e.g. mobile phones? If so, what?
4 Is there anyone that you really look up to? If so, who and why?
5 Are there any kinds of crime that you think are easy to get away with? If so, which and why?

8 Communication

Radio phone-in

1 Discuss.

1. What can you see in the picture above?
2. How often do you listen to the radio?
3. What different kinds of radio programmes do you know?

2 **a** 8.10 Listen to the extracts from a radio phone-in. What is the reason for each person's call?

b Listen again and decide what advice you would give each caller and why.

3 Discuss.

1. Do you ever listen to this kind of radio programme? Why/Why not?
2. Who/Where do you usually go to for advice about problems?

4 **a** Work in A/B groups. Decide on some interesting problems for a radio phone-in.

b In A/B pairs, take it in turns to roleplay phoning a radio phone-in programme and asking for advice.

It's time/I'd rather/I'd better

It's time …

Form *It's time* + subject + past tense

Meaning 'It's time I did something' is used to mean 'I should have done something already or at least started it'.

It's time you did your homework.

I'd rather …

Form subject + *would rather* + object + past tense (+ *than* ...)

Meaning 'I'd rather you did/didn't do something' is used to talk about what you'd prefer someone else to do.

I'd rather you didn't smoke in here.

Form subject + *would rather* + infinitive (+ *than* ...)

Meaning 'I'd rather do/not do something' is used to talk about what you'd prefer to do.

I'd rather not spend all day lying on the beach.

I'd better …

Form subject + *had better* + infinitive

Meaning 'I'd better do/not do something' is used to talk about something when it is advisable to do it (in the present or future).

I'd better mend that window as soon as I can.

Reported speech

Use 'reported' or 'indirect' speech to tell people what somebody said or thought.

Make the tense of the verb one 'step' further back into the past.

'I want to go out.' → *She said (that) she wanted to go out.*

Modal verbs also change.

'Can you help me paint the kitchen?' → *She asked me if I could help her paint the kitchen.*

Subject and object pronouns change.

'I will give it to you soon.' → *He said he would give it to me soon.*

References to particular times change, e.g.

'The books will be delivered tomorrow.' → *She said the books would be delivered the next day.*

Word order changes, e.g.

'What are you doing at the weekend.' → *He asked me what we were doing at the weekend.*

Use *if* (or *whether*) when reporting *Yes/No* questions, e.g.

'Did you enjoy the film?' → *He asked me if I had enjoyed the film.*

Reporting verbs

Say and *explain* are followed by verb + (*that*).

She explained that John was ill and couldn't come.

Tell is followed by verb + object + (*that*).

He told us we needed to show identification.

Ask, remind and *warn* are followed by verb + object + infinitive.

We reminded him to post the letter.

Promise and *decide* are followed by verb + infinitive, e.g.

We decided to stay at home and watch TV.

Admit and *suggest* are followed by verb + gerund.

He admitted liking her a lot.

Hard and hardly

Hard as an adjective means firm and difficult to cut or break.

The mattress is quite hard.

These plums are too hard to eat.

Hard as an adverb means using a lot of effort or force, e.g.

She's been working hard all day.

Hardly is an adverb which means *almost not* or *very little*.

I hardly know the people in my class.

Hardly is often used with *any*(*thing/one/where*, etc.) and *ever*.

We hardly ever go out in the evening.

Key vocabulary

Success

best-seller succeed go under have a go have had their day give up be up to scratch

Personality

proactive headstrong opinionated manipulative selfish single-minded open easy-going witty outgoing to be the centre of attention to be a party animal to be a complete doormat to be really high maintenance to be down-to-earth

Adjectives/Intensifiers

happy – ecstatic important – vital big – huge upset – devastated hungry – starving tired – exhausted very really extremely absolutely

Phrasal verbs with three parts

catch up with get away with keep up with put in for come up with cut down on look up to look forward to put up with make up for

8 Review and practice

1 Find the mistakes in six of the sentences and correct them.

I'd better wrote your phone number down before I forget it. → write

1 I'd better went to the shops before they close.
2 Had you rather I didn't say anything to your boss?
3 Isn't it time you told him how you really feel?
4 I'd rather not working this weekend if at all possible.
5 Would you better take a raincoat in case it rains?
6 I'd rather you paid me back in cash than by cheque if that's OK.
7 What's that smell? I think it's time you get the cake out of the oven.
8 I'd rather took just hand luggage on the plane than a large suitcase.

2 Complete the sentences using the past.

Zoe/say/can't remember/where/leave/keys. → Zoe said she couldn't remember where she had left the keys.

1 Tony/ask/I like/play/tennis/this weekend.
2 They/tell/best time/visit Egypt/be/in January or February.
3 Helen/say/not know/what time/firework display/start.
4 He ask/me when/I want/go/see/the London Eye.
5 My boss/tell/I have to/make/presentation/at sales conference/in March.
6 The newspaper/say/one/our athletes/fail/drugs test.

3 Choose the correct alternative in each case.

He told (me)/to me that he was going to be at least twenty minutes late.

1 She promised *to do/doing* all her homework before she went out to see her friend.
2 Can you explain *me/to me* exactly how this DVD recorder works?
3 They decided *to sell/selling* their house and move to the country.
4 My doctor suggested *taking/to take* a week off work.
5 They warned *us/to us* that the weather conditions would make walking in the mountains quite dangerous.
6 Will you remind me *to go/going* to the post office this afternoon?
7 He admitted *being/be* wrong about the time of the train.

4 Complete each of the following gaps with *hard* or *hardly*.

1 I'm going to work really ______ on my maths from now until the end of term.
2 We ______ have any time to see friends at the moment. Life is just too busy!
3 I could ______ believe it when she said they were going to get married!
4 It will be a long, ______ climb to the top of that hill.
5 ______ anyone came to opening night of the restaurant. It was very disappointing.
6 If you look ______ , you can just see Michael on the other side of the car park.

5 Unjumble each of the words in *italics* in the sentences below.

1 She loves being the centre of *nnaoiettt*. She wants everyone to be talking about her.
2 He's terribly *doopitninae*. He really thinks that his own opinions are the only ones which are worth listening to!
3 Tara got all As in her final school exams. She's absolutely *ccttiase*!
4 She finally *ducdecees* in persuading him to go to the police.
5 We're really looking *rrwfdoa* to visiting my brother in Australia. It'll be the first time we've been out there.
6 My brother's very *goginuto*. He really enjoys being with friends and meeting new people.
7 He's spent a lot of money getting his new car up to *hctsacr* before the big race.
8 I told her not to take her driving test yet but she's very *narthesdog* and insisted on doing what she wanted.

9 Crime

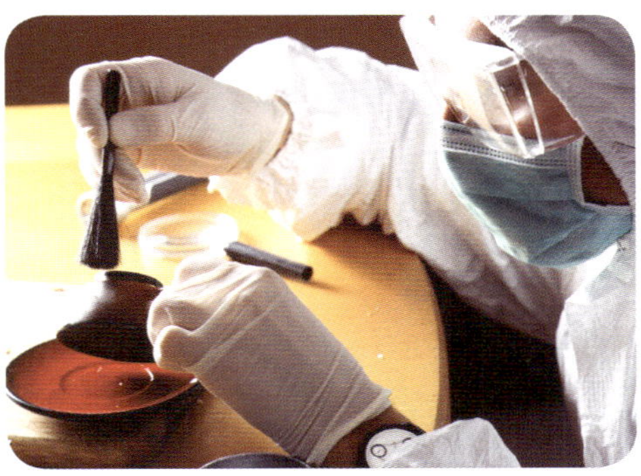

Lead-in

1 a How are the photos connected to the topic of 'crime'?

b Think of words and expressions connected with crime and the law. Write them in the appropriate columns.

LAW COURT	CRIME	CRIMINAL	EVIDENCE	PUNISHMENT
a judge	*robbery*	*thief*	*fingerprints*	*community service*

2 Explain these newspaper headlines. Use a dictionary if necessary.

1 Local MP stopped for speeding

2 **Cyber crime up by 50%**

3 **Overcrowded prisons slammed in new report**

4 **Chaos in fraud case after witness intimidation**

5 Suspended sentence for teacher in road rage incident

6 **Keen cop gives out record number of fines**

3 Do you think crime is increasing or decreasing where you live? Are there any particular types of crime which are a special problem in your area?

9.1 Legal madness

Grammar sequencing devices, e.g. *After* + *-ing*
Can do tell a funny story

Vocabulary | law and insurance

1 Match the words/phrases 1–10 to the appropriate definitions a–j.

1 insurance	a) officially decide in a court of law that someone is guilty of a crime.
2 premium	b) an amount of money that you pay for insurance
3 fraud	c) when you pay a company money and they pay the costs if you are ill, have a car accident, etc.
4 to file (a claim)	d) give a legal punishment to someone who is guilty of a crime
5 to sue (someone)	e) the crime of deliberately making something burn, especially a building
6 to guarantee	f) start a legal process to get money from someone who has harmed you in some way
7 an appeal	g) make an official statement that you are going to do something, especially in a court
8 arson	h) promise that something will happen or be done
9 to convict (someone of)	i) when someone deceives people to get money
10 to sentence (someone to)	j) when someone asks a higher court to change the decision of a lower court

2 **a** Complete the sentences with the words/phrases from Ex. 1 in the correct form.

1 She plans to ______ the hospital after they gave her the wrong operation.
2 Bailey was ______ to three years in prison for his part in the robbery.
3 We lost the case this time but there's going to be an ______ . We will never give up.
4 I'm afraid that the cost of the annual ______ has gone up again. They say it's because of the number of claims last year.
5 My neighbour has been ______ of shoplifting but luckily he doesn't have to go to prison.
6 Does this ______ plan cover things that are stolen from me while I'm on holiday?
7 Can you ______ that this TV will be delivered before Christmas? It's very important.
8 They don't think the fire was an accident. They think it was ______ .
9 Ted's wife has ______ for divorce. He's very upset about it.
10 He's been arrested and charged with ______ . Apparently, he pretended that an expensive painting had been stolen to get the insurance money.

b 9.1 Listen and check your answers.

3 Discuss.

1 Imagine someone buys a coffee in a fast food restaurant. They then spill the hot coffee on themselves and are burned. Should they sue the fast food company?
2 What different things do people insure? Have you ever heard about anyone insuring something strange?
3 Do you know any famous cases of fraud? If so, what happened?

Listening

4 **a** You are going to listen to a story about a crime involving cigars. Before you listen, suggest what the story might be using as many of the words in Ex. 1 as possible.

b 9.2 Listen to the story and compare your ideas.

5 Listen again. Put these sentences in the order in which they happen in the story.

1 The lawyer is arrested.
2 The insurance company refuses to pay.
3 He makes a claim against the insurance company.
4 The lawyer is sentenced to jail.
5 He smokes the cigars.
6 The insurance company pays the lawyer.
7 He insures the cigars against fire.
8 The lawyer sues the insurance company.
9 A lawyer buys some rare cigars.

6 **a** Listen to the story again. Which of the following expressions do you hear?

1 Go on ...
2 The way it goes is that ...
3 Fancy that.
4 Fair enough.
5 What on earth for?
6 Pull the other one.
7 You're kidding!
8 Cross my heart.

b Find the expressions in the tapescript on page 160. Discuss in groups what you think each expression means.

Grammar | sequencing devices

7 **a** Look at the examples in the Active grammar box. Then, complete the structures A and B by writing the correct part of speech for each one.

Active grammar

Having cashed the cheque, the lawyer was arrested.

After cashing the cheque, the lawyer was arrested.

Use the following two forms to describe the order of events in a story.

(Clause 1)	(Clause 2)
A: *Having* + ___ ,	Past Simple
B: *After* + ___ ,	Past Simple

see Reference page 129

b Which clause comes first in the order of events?

8 Complete the sentences by writing the correct form of a verb from the box.

stay read promise do go win

1 After ______ to the bank a number of times, the robbers felt they understood all the security systems.
2 Having ______ to pick his friend up from the police station, Terry completely forgot.
3 After ______ extremely well in his first year exams, we were very surprised when he said he wanted to stop studying law.
4 Having ______ some excellent reviews of the new P.D. James murder mystery, I wanted to get a copy to take on holiday with me.
5 Having successfully ______ her case against her old employer for wrongful dismissal, she decided to go out and celebrate.
6 After ______ at the office until midnight to prepare her report for the judge, she decided to give herself the next day off.

9 **a** Think about three things that happened to you last week and what you did after each one.

b Tell another student the first thing and see if they can guess what you did next. Then, tell them if they were right or not.

A: *After doing my English homework ...*
B: *... you watched a film on TV?*
A: *No. I collapsed on the sofa and fell asleep!*

Speaking and reading

10 Work in pairs. Student As look at the pictures for Story 1 below. Student Bs look at the pictures for Story 2 on page 146. The pictures make a story. With another student, work out the story.

Story 1

11 Check your ideas by reading the story. (Story 1 is on page 145, Story 2 is below).

Story 2

An ambitious burglar broke into a vast mansion on millionaires' row at Bel Air, Los Angeles. He went through the house room by room, putting anything of value that he could see and carry in the large bag he'd brought with him. Having completely filled his bag, he decided it was time to leave.

He started to realise that he wasn't sure of the way out but moved on quickly, through a large dining-room, past an indoor gym and through another room filled with exotic parrots. By now he was beginning to panic. Then, having run through a large library and a small room full of art, he began to get quite desperate.

He ran up a small circular staircase to what seemed to be a large bedroom. He knocked on the door and went in. The owners of the house had been asleep in bed but sat up in fright only to find a traumatised burglar desperate to find his way out of the maze of rooms. After giving him detailed directions, they phoned the police, who arrived minutes later and escorted the relieved burglar to the safety of a nearby police station.

12 **a** Prepare to tell another student your story using the expressions in the How to box.

HOW TO ...

tell a funny story

Check you remember all the important information.	*A lawyer bought some rare cigars.* *He insured them against fire.*
Check you know the key vocabulary	*cigar, to insure*
Introduce the story	*Did you hear the story about the man who stole a parrot?* *Have you heard the one about the robber who fell asleep?*
Keep the funny part until the very end.	*... and so can you believe it? He was sentenced to twenty-four months in jail and a $24,000 fine.*

b In A/B pairs, show your partner your pictures and tell him or her the story. Include the structures *Having* + past participle and *After* + present participle as appropriate.

9.2 It's a mystery!

Grammar past modals of deductions *must/might/can't have done*
Can do speculate about past events

Grammar | *must/might/can't have*

1 Look at the pictures. What do you think the person is doing?

2 9.3 Listen to the conversation. What do the people say is happening in the photos?

3 Read the examples 1–3 below, then complete the rules A–C.

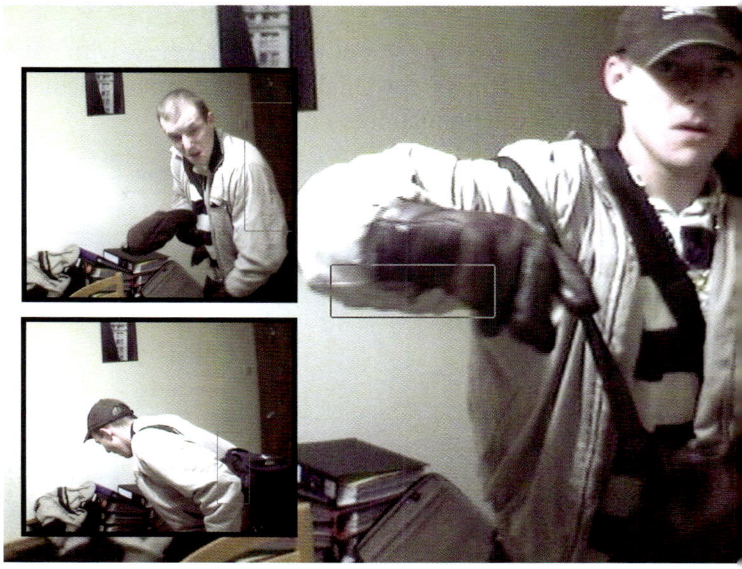

Active grammar

1 *He must have fixed up some kind of security camera.*
2 *He might have done it before.*
3 *He can't have realised he was being caught on camera.*

A Use ______ ______ + past participle to say that you think something is possible in the past.
B Use ______ ______ + past participle to say that you think something is not possible in the past.
C Use ______ ______ + past participle to say that you are certain about something in the past.

see Reference page 129

4 Choose the correct alternative in each sentence.

1 They *must/might/can't* have got into the house through a window. They were all locked.
2 He *must/might/can't* have told my parents that I was caught shoplifting but I hope he didn't.
3 The judge *must/might/can't* have liked you. It's unusual to only get a suspended sentence in this kind of case.
4 They *must/might/can't* have sacked him because he was lazy. He was one of the hardest working people in the company!
5 Don't be negative. She *must/might/can't* have passed her English test. We will only know when we get the results.
6 She *must/might/can't* have left very quietly. I didn't hear her go.
7 She *must/might/can't* have had a bad meeting with the Marketing Director. She's been in a terrible mood ever since.
8 He *must/might/can't* have arrived yet because he promised to phone us the minute the plane landed.

5 **a** Complete the sentences using *must/might/can't have* and an appropriate verb from the box.

go forgot drop tell finish be leave spend

1 We don't know who took the money. There were lots of people in the office during the day and it ______ any of them.
2 I wonder why Pete didn't turn up to do his community service. He ______ about it. I reminded him yesterday.
3 I'm not sure where Jo is. She ______ round to Sally's. They're working on a school project together.
4 How did you know about the surprise party? Someone ______ you!
5 You ______ all your birthday money already. You got nearly £100!
6 I ______ my keys at home. I remember feeling them in my jacket pocket when I got on the bus.
7 She ______ her homework yet. She only started it at 9 o'clock.
8 I've lost one of my gloves. I ______ it on the way to work.

b 9.4 Listen and check your answers. Pay attention to the pronunciation of *must/might/can't have*. How is *have* pronounced each time?

6 9.5 Listen to the extract from a radio news programme. How did the police find the photos from Ex. 1?

Vocabulary | compound adjectives

7 Combine a word from column A below with a word from column B to make compound adjectives. Check in a dictionary if necessary.

1 *single-minded*

A	B
1 single-	a) minute
2 one-	b) aged
3 middle-	c) time
4 left-	d) called
5 home-	e) minded
6 last-	f) made
7 part-	g) new
8 so-	h) consuming
9 time-	i) way
10 brand-	j) handed

8 **a** Complete the sentences with the compound adjectives from Ex. 7.

1 Apparently, she said that the computer and TV that were stolen were ______ when in fact they were several years old.
2 They arrested a ______ man for joy-riding last night. It's surprising because joy-riders are usually in their teens.
3 In his interview for inspector he came across as very ______ which is exactly what we want. We need someone who will get things done.
4 He said he just wanted a ______ ticket to Alicante which is what made me a little suspicious.
5 I'm doing some voluntary work with young offenders. I really like it but it's quite ______ . It's taking up most of my weekends at the moment.
6 It was a ______ decision to go to Paris but I'm really glad we did. After all the hassle of the court case we needed a break.
7 The fact that the thief was ______ was a vital clue that helped the police catch him. They found some specially designed scissors in his flat.
8 The ______ expert for the defence was very vague in his answers. I'm not sure it was really his specialist area.
9 I'm starting work as a ______ community police officer in January. It's Monday and Friday mornings which is perfect for me.
10 You must try a piece of this ______ chocolate cake. One of the prisoners made it in the cookery class.

9 Discuss.

1 Do you consider yourself to be a single-minded person? Why/Why not?
2 When is someone 'middle-aged' do you think?
3 What things in your life are particularly time-consuming? Can you do anything about this?
4 Are you a 'last-minute' kind of person? If so, give some examples.
5 Have you ever had a part-time job? If so, what was it? Did you enjoy it?
6 Do you think home-made cooking is always the best?

Reading

10 Work in pairs. How many different ways can you think of to steal $200,000?

11 Read the article and briefly summarise how D.B. Cooper managed to steal $200,000.

D.B. Cooper

At 2p.m. on 24th November 1971, a middle-aged man of average height, dressed in a dark suit, white shirt, dark glasses and a black tie, handed a $20 note to a clerk at the Portland airport, asked for a one-way ticket and then boarded Flight 305 for Seattle. Identifying himself as Dan Cooper, he carried only a briefcase. Just before take-off, he handed the flight attendant a note. Watching her put the note in her pocket, he said quietly, 'Miss, you'd better look at that note. I have a bomb.' The message demanded $200,000 and four parachutes – by 5p.m. To remove any final doubts, Cooper opened his briefcase and showed the flight attendant sticks of dynamite, attached to wire and a battery. As the plane circled over Seattle, the pilot, William Rataczak, quickly learned he was not dealing with an amateur. This man was totally single-minded. With the confidence of an army commander, Cooper told Rataczak that after the money and parachutes had been delivered, he wanted him to head south from Seattle, fly no higher than 10,000 feet and leave the rear door open.

The plane landed in Seattle and by 7p.m, it had refuelled and the parachutes and money were on board. The plane took off again a few minutes after 7.30p.m. Then Cooper carefully collected all his cigarette ends, made sure he had all his handwritten notes and strapped the money bag to his body using cords he cut from one of the parachutes.

At 8.12p.m, 'we felt a little bump and the air pressure changed,' Rataczak said. And that was the last fix on D. B. Cooper. The Air Force had sent up two F-106 fighter planes to chase the Boeing 727 and try to keep Cooper's parachute in sight but they were too fast and had to keep making giant S-curves in the sky. For the next few weeks, hundreds of federal agents, helped by Army troops, searched around the area under where Cooper jumped. A small submarine also searched nearby Lake Merwin. But they found nothing. In fact there was no concrete evidence of any kind until February 1980 when an Oklahoma boy, having a picnic with his family on the shore of the Columbia River, came across a waterlogged bag containing 294 mouldy $20 notes. The serial numbers matched those on the notes given to D.B. Cooper. This find got the FBI's attention. Helicopters flew over the area, squads of agents dug up the shore, searching for more notes, Cooper's body or parachute but again, nothing.

D.B. Cooper entered the history books as an authentic American legend. 'There's a good reason for this,' says Larry Goldfine, a Seattle lawyer who was sitting on Flight 305 that day. 'It was the first skyjacking for money and then the skyjacker disappeared without a trace. No one was hurt and it all happened right under the noses of the FBI'. Most people think D.B. got away with it. The Cooper of the legend has the coolness of a Steve McQueen or Clint Eastwood. In the end, no one has ever worked out just who he was – or is. In his enduring anonymity, he has inspired three books, a play, a film, a song and thousands of D.B. Cooper bars and restaurants. Perhaps the ultimate tribute is the annual 'D.B. Cooper Days' festival in the tiny Washington town over which Cooper was thought to have parachuted. There's a D.B. Cooper look-alike contest (lots of forty-ish men in dark suits and dark glasses), and half-a-dozen parachutists make a jump.

12 Read the article again and answer these questions.

1 What did D.B. Cooper take with him onto the plane?
2 What did he want?
3 How did Rataczak realise he was not dealing with an amateur?
4 At what time did the plane take off for the second time?
5 At what time did D.B. Cooper jump from the plane?
6 Why couldn't the fighter planes follow D.B. Cooper?
7 Who took part in the official search for D.B. Cooper?
8 What single clue did they get?
9 Why has the case of D.B. Cooper captured the popular imagination?
10 What different things have been done to commemorate what D.B. Cooper did?

13 Find three examples of compound adjectives in the text.

14 Discuss.

1 What do you think of what D.B. Cooper did?
2 How do you think he got away with it?
3 Do you understand why some people admire what he did?
4 Do you know any stories about famous criminals from your country?

9.3 Sherlock or not?

Grammar	relative clauses
Can do	write an article

Reading

1 **a** Discuss with other students.

1 What do you know about Sherlock Holmes?
2 Was he a real person?
3 Why and when was he famous?

b Now read the text and check your ideas.

The Real Sherlock Holmes

Was Sherlock Holmes a real person? Not exactly, but Dr Joseph Bell, the man who inspired the character of Sherlock Holmes, shared many qualities with the famous detective. Arthur Conan Doyle, the writer and creator of Holmes, met Dr Bell in 1877 at the University of Edinburgh Medical School. Conan Doyle was studying to be a doctor and Bell was one of his professors.

Bell was thirty-nine years old when Conan Doyle first attended one of his lectures. He is said to have walked with great energy. His nose and chin were angular and his eyes twinkled with intelligent humour. Bell, who was a brilliant doctor, liked writing poetry, playing sport and bird-watching.

By the end of Conan Doyle's second year Bell had selected him to serve as his assistant. Being on a ward with Bell, where he had plenty of opportunity to observe, only increased Conan Doyle's admiration for the great doctor. Amongst other things he was able to witness Dr Bell's remarkable ability to quickly deduce a great deal about the patient.

Dr Bell observed the way a person moved. The walk of a sailor, who had spent many years at sea, varied greatly from that of a soldier. If he identified a person as a sailor, he would look for any tattoos that might assist him in knowing where their travels had taken them. He trained himself to listen for small differences in his patients' accents to help him identify where they were from. Bell studied the hands of his patients because calluses or other marks could help him determine their occupation.

Conan Doyle published the first Holmes story in 1887. His innovation in creating a character that would appear over and over in a series of self-contained stories meant that Holmes's popularity grew with each instalment. Soon the character was so beloved that people refused to believe he wasn't a real person; letters addressed to 'Sherlock Holmes, Consulting Detective' arrived daily at Baker Street and Scotland Yard, each begging him to take on a real case.

2 Read the text again and complete the notes.

The Real Sherlock Holmes
Person who Sherlock Holmes was based on: *Dr Joseph Bell*
Relationship to Conan Doyle: (1) ______
Where/When met Conan Doyle: (2) ______ , (3) ______
Dr Bell's hobbies: poetry, (4) ______ , (5) ______
Things Dr Bell observed about patients: the way they moved, (6) ______ , their accents, (7) ______
Date first Holmes story published: (8) ______
Letters for Sherlock Holmes sent to: (9) ______

3 Read the text again and find words that mean:

1 to give someone the idea for something (para. 1)
2 very good, intelligent, skilful (para. 2)
3 part of a hospital where patients stay (para. 3)
4 new idea, method, etc. that is used for the first time (para. 5)
5 to ask for something in an urgent or anxious way (para. 5)

4 Discuss.

1 What new information have you learned about Sherlock Holmes?
2 Do you think you are observant like Dr Bell? Would you be a good witness in a crime situation?
3 Would you be interested in being a police detective? Why/Why not?

Grammar | relative clauses

5 Read the information in the Active grammar box and decide which of the examples 1–5 contain 'defining relative clauses' and which contain 'non-defining relative clauses'.

Active grammar

1 *Dr Joseph Bell was the man who inspired the character of Sherlock Holmes.*
2 *Bell, who was a brilliant doctor, liked writing poetry, playing sport and bird-watching.*
3 *Bell was thirty-nine years old when Conan Doyle first attended one of his lectures.*
4 *Being on a ward with Bell, where he had plenty of opportunity to observe, only increased Conan Doyle's admiration for the great doctor.*
5 *Conan Doyle, whose Sherlock Holmes novels were enormously popular, died in 1930.*

Defining relative clauses

The underlined part of the sentence is essential to the meaning of the sentence.

Commas are not used to separate the clauses.

Who and *which* can both be replaced by *that*.

Non-defining relative clauses

The underlined part of the sentence gives us extra information. This clause can be removed without affecting the central meaning of the sentence.

Use commas at the beginning and end of these clauses unless they end the sentence.

Who and *which* cannot be replaced by *that*.

see Reference page 129

6 Join these pairs of sentences to make one sentence.

The police still haven't found the man. He stole my bag.

The police still haven't found the man who stole my bag.

1 John's been my best friend since school. He's helping me start a new business.
2 My current flat needs redecorating. I've been in it for a couple of years.
3 Tamsin's going to Australia for the winter. Her parents emigrated there last year.
4 My neighbour has given me his old computer. I've always liked him.
5 The family at the end of the road are thinking of moving. Their dog barks constantly.
6 Tina's car is up for sale. She's had it for years.

7 Complete the sentences in a way that makes sense.

1 Where are the jeans which ... ?
2 That's the pop star who ...
3 She's the little girl whose ...
4 I'd like to find a place where ...
5 I think that's the couple whose ...
6 We went to a shop where ...
7 Wasn't it your father who ... ?
8 She bought the mobile phone which ...

Person to person

8 Tell another student three interesting things about you. Begin like this:

Libya is the place where I was born. My mother was an English teacher there.

1 X is the place where ...
2 Y is the person who ...
3 Z was the time when ...

Listening

9 **a** 9.6 Listen to an interview with an ordinary American whose name is 'Sherlock Holmes'. First, discuss with another student:

1. Why do you think he has this name?
2. What do you think are the possible consequences of having a name like this?

b Listen and check your ideas.

10 Listen again and explain the significance of the following things in the interview:

1 *This is what the American Sherlock Holmes likes to be called.*

1. The name 'Holmes'
2. The original Conan Doyle stories
3. A favourite literary figure
4. The question 'Where's Dr Watson?'
5. TV magicians
6. The mother of an old family friend
7. $7000
8. His torch and magnifying glass

11 Discuss.

1. How do you feel about your name? Does it mean something? Were you named after someone in your family or someone famous? If so, who and why?
2. What reasons do people have for changing their names? Do you know anyone who has changed his/her name? If so, why did he/she do it?
3. In Britain, women often take their husband's surname when they get married? What do you think about this?

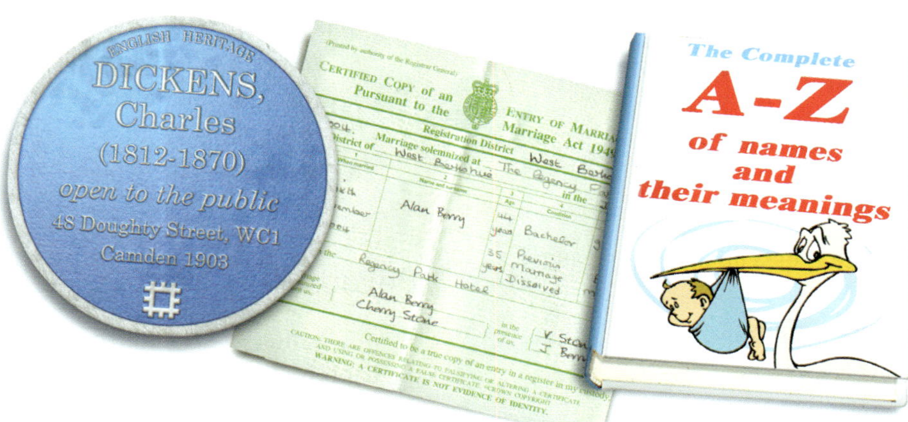

Writing

12 Read the article in the Writing bank on page 155 and do the exercises.

13 9.7 You are going to write an article about a famous crime.

1. Listen and make notes from this description of how Nick Leeson broke the Barings investment bank.
2. Decide on the main points for your article.
3. Organise your ideas into paragraphs.
4. Write your article in 100–150 words. (Check the important points about writing articles from Ex. 12.)
5. Read your article through. Is it interesting and easy to read? Make any necessary changes.

9 Vocabulary

Newspaper headlines

1 Discuss.

1. Do you ever read English newspapers?
2. What is the purpose of a headline?
3. Do you ever have problems understanding headlines? Why?

2 **a** Match the words 1–12, with the meanings a–l. Use a dictionary if necessary.

A	B
1 aid	a) strong request
2 axe	b) affect badly
3 back	c) explosion
4 bid	d) leave, resign
5 blast	e) essential, vital
6 blaze	f) cut, remove
7 quit	g) dispute, conflict
8 clash	h) attempt
9 drama	i) tense situation
10 hit	j) support
11 key	k) help
12 plea	l) serious fire

b In pairs, discuss what you think the two headlines above might mean.

3 Choose the most likely alternative in each headline.

1. *Key/Plea* witness receives death threat
2. IBM *axes/bids* top managers
3. Guests escape hotel *clash/blaze*
4. School governors *back/quit* teacher
5. Chat show host fight *drama/key*
6. Police and students *clash/hit*
7. BT *bids/pleas* for US communications network
8. General *quits/aids* top job

4 Discuss. Would you be interested in reading articles with the following headlines? Why/Why not? What do you think each one might be about?

1. **Interest rate cut boosts exports**
2. **Prince and model to wed**
3. **Leading bank in sex discrimination case**
4. **Man. Utd. crash to defeat in Cup match**
5. **MP spy drama**
6. Riddle of 2nd Van Gogh painting
7. **Butler quits the Palace**
8. **Cape Town bids for Olympics**
9. **Bomb blast in northern India**
10. **Votes scandal in California**

5 Discuss.

1. Do you read newspapers/magazines often? If so, which ones? Why do you like them?
2. Do you read the whole paper/magazine or just certain parts? If so, which parts?
3. Do you think newspapers are the best way of getting the news in your country?
4. Which are the most popular newspapers in your country? What are the main differences between them?

9 Communication

Mind benders

1

A police officer was sitting on his motorcycle at a red traffic light when two teenagers in a sports car drove by him at 50 mph. He did not chase them or try to apprehend them.
Why not?

2

A man was driving alone in his car when he came off the road at high speed. He crashed through a fence and went down a steep slope before the car plunged into a fast flowing river. As the car slowly settled in the river, the man realised that his arm was broken and that he could not release his seat belt and get out of the car. He was trapped in the car. Rescuers arrived two hours later, yet they found him alive.
How come?

3

A man rode into town on Friday. He stayed for three nights and then left on Friday.
How come?

4

Bobby lives with his parents in London. Last week, while his parents were out, Bobby's neighbour Susie came round to spend the evening. At 8 o'clock precisely she went out to buy some cigarettes from the corner shop five minutes walk away. One minute after she left, two men burst into the house and, ignoring Bobby, took the TV set, the stereo and a computer. Bobby had never seen the men before and they had no legal right to remove the equipment – yet he did nothing to stop them. In fact, he didn't even act surprised by their behaviour.
How come?

5

A man leaves hospital and begins to walk home. On his journey he passes a phone box which begins to ring. Instead of answering it he punches the air and runs all the way home cheering. **Why?**

6

When a fire broke out in an airplane, a panicking passenger opened the emergency hatch and threw himself out, even though he had no parachute.
How was it that when the rescue services found him, he was alive and well and without injury?

1 Try and solve the lateral thinking problems above. Follow these instructions:

1. Read each of them and make a note of any vocabulary which stops you understanding them.
2. Ask other students and/or check in a dictionary to find out the meaning of the unknown vocabulary.
3. Work with another student. Discuss ideas you have to explain each of the problems.

2 Now choose the one you are most interested in and read the explanation for it. (1 page 147; 2 page 145; 3 page 146; 4 page 146; 5 page 147; 6 page 145).

1. Make two *Yes/No* questions to ask about each of the other problems.
   Was the policeman asleep? Were the teenagers invisible in some way?
2. Ask other students who know the explanations for the other problems your questions.
3. With the additional information, suggest explanations for each of the other problems.
   The teenagers might have been the policeman's children.

Sequencing devices

Use *Having* + past participle or *After* + present participle to show the order of events when telling a story or describing a series of events.

Having discussed the problem for several hours, we decided to go out for something to eat.

After explaining to her boss why she needed a raise, she told him that she was thinking of leaving the company.

Other examples with a similar structure include:

Before painting the room, she had to strip off the old wallpaper.

On entering the room, he noticed that all the windows were open.

While cleaning the room, she discovered a locked diary.

Must/Might/Can't have

Use *must* to say that you believe something is certain.

Use *might* to say something is a possibility.

Use *can't* to say that you believe something is not possible.

For the past, use *must/might/can't have* + past participle. This is the same for *I/you/he/we/they*.

You must have enjoyed your holiday in Australia.

I think I might have left my wallet in that shop.

She hasn't phoned me so she can't have got my message.

You can use *may* instead of *might* and *couldn't* instead of *can't*.

She may have stopped to get some petrol

They couldn't have gone swimming. They didn't take any towels.

May/might have + past participle can also refer to the present or future.

I'll give him a call but he may have left by now.

By this time next year I might have moved to Brussels.

Relative clauses

Defining relative clauses

Defining relative clauses define or identify the person, thing, time, place or reason. They cannot be left out.

Tim is the teacher who I told you about.

That's the street where I grew up.

No commas are used before and after the defining relative clause.

That can be used instead of *who* or *which*.

The woman that/who I share an office with has been in the company for years.

The relative pronoun can be left out if it is the object of the verb in the relative clause.

Simon bought the jacket (that/which) we saw when we went shopping last weekend.

Non-defining relative clauses

Non-defining relative clauses give extra information which can be left out.

Commas are used before and after non-defining relative clauses unless they end a sentence.

Who and *which* cannot be replaced by *that*.

I've lent my new bike, which I really like, to my brother.

Cairo, where I lived for several years, is a fascinating city.

Key vocabulary

Crime

robbery thief fingerprints community service speeding fraud witness intimidation road rage

Law and insurance

premium fraud to file (a claim) to sue (someone) to guarantee appeal arson to convict (someone of) to sentence (someone to)

Conversational expressions

Go on ... The way it goes is that ... Fancy that. Fair enough. What on earth for? Pull the other one. You're kidding! Cross my heart.

Compound adjectives

middle-aged one-way single-minded left-handed home-made last-minute part-time so-called time-consuming brand-new

Newspaper headlines

aid axe back bid blast blaze quit clash drama hit key plea

9 Review and practice

1 **Join the following pairs of sentences. Use *After* + present participle or *Having* + past participle.**

She arrived at the office early. She worked hard and fast all morning.

Having arrived at the office early, she worked hard and fast all morning.

1. She travelled for hours to get to the village. She thought she should stay there for at least a couple of days.
2. He saw his neighbour struggling with a lot of heavy bags. He offered to help her.
3. She came first in her university exams. She was approached by a top firm of lawyers.
4. She took home an injured cat she had found by the side of the road. She felt she had to keep it.
5. He saw a young man take a CD without paying. He told the security staff.
6. He spoke to his father. He told his boss he wanted a raise.
7. They got a long letter from their cousin. They decided to go and see him.

2 **Complete the second sentences so that they mean the same as the first. Use *must/might/can't* with the verb in brackets.**

I don't believe she got an 'A' in her exam.

She ______ . (get)

She can't have got an 'A' in her exam.

1. It is possible he stayed late at the office.
   He ______ . (stay)
2. There's no chance that I left my gloves in the car.
   I ______ . (leave)
3. I'm sure she's shown me her holiday photos at least ten times.
   She ______ . (show)
4. It's not possible that she's finished all her homework already.
   She ______ . (finish)
5. I have no doubt that they were really pleased to win the competition.
   They ______ . (be)
6. There's a chance my letter got lost in the post.
   My letter ______ . (got)

3 **Add commas as necessary to the sentences.**

David Gray who wrote the song *White Ladder* is performing in Paris this weekend.

David Gray, who wrote the song White Ladder, is performing in Paris this weekend.

1. I'm afraid I lost the book which she lent me.
2. I'm going to spend a few days in Seville where I first met Raquel.
3. These are the apples which I picked from the tree in my garden.
4. The young man who I spoke to has promised to give me a refund.
5. We decided to stay at the Regina Hotel which some friends had recommended to us.
6. Tim whose job involves a lot of travelling has offered to let us use his flat for a few weeks.

4 **Find the mistakes in four of the sentences and correct them.**

1. Steve works for a small company makes kitchen equipment.
2. I think the name of the film that I'd like to see is *Collateral*.
3. Did you hear exactly that he said?
4. The demonstration, had been going on for several days, is finally over.
5. Isn't that the place where you grew up?
6. My sister, that speaks French and Italian fluently, wants to be an interpreter.

5 **Complete the sentences with one of the words from the Key vocabulary section on page 129.**

I'm going to get a <u>part-time</u> job working in a local newsagents. It's just three days a week.

1. I remember being forced to write with my right hand as a child even though I was obviously ______ .
2. Government ______ gives boost to troubled steel industry.
3. They say I have to pay a fine for travelling without a ticket but I'm going to ______
4. We're going to try and get a ______ deal with a local travel agent. Apparently there are some real bargains.
5. **A:** If you come to my place, I'll cook dinner.
   B: ______ enough. Shall I bring some wine?
6. Can you believe it? My DVD recorder stops working after thirteen months and the ______ is for one year!
7. Mystery ______ at chemicals factory injures three workers. Arson suspected.

10 Mind

1

2

3

Lead-in

1 Discuss.

What is happening in each photo? How are they connected?

2 **a** In pairs, match the quotes below with pictures 1–3 and explain what you think the phrases in *italics* mean.

'Walking on hot coals is a question of *mind over matter*.'

'Politicians often rely on the *power of persuasion* to make people vote for them.'

'I gave up eating all sweet things using nothing but *willpower*.'

b In what situations have you used a) mind over matter, b) the power of persuasion and c) willpower?

3 **a** 10.1 Listen to six people answering questions 1–6. Make brief notes about their answers.

1 Do you ever *have premonitions*? Do you take them seriously?
2 Have you ever *had a feeling of déjà vu*? What happened?
3 Are you someone who is usually able to *trust your intuition*?
4 Do you know anyone who uses *his/her sixth sense* a lot?
5 Have you ever *been unconscious*? What happened?
6 Do you think you have any *subconscious fears*?

b In pairs, write a short definition for each of the phrases in *italics* in the questions above. Then, compare your definitions with the definitions in an English–English dictionary.

c Ask and answer the questions with a partner.

10.1 Look into my eyes

Grammar	reflexive pronouns
Can do	ask about and give your own beliefs and opinions

Reading

1 **a** Discuss.

What sort of problems do hypnotists help people with?

b Read the text quickly and answer the questions .

1 What problems are mentioned in the text?

2 How do you think the writer feels about the hypnotist Paul McKenna: sceptical, impressed, indifferent or nervous?

Their lives in his hands

He is a modern-day guru. The rich and famous all turn to him when they are in need of help. Christa D'Souza meets Paul McKenna, the hypnotist with hidden powers.

It is early in the afternoon in West London and the office of Paul McKenna Productions is bustling with activity. McKenna himself is a small, mousy man and when I arrive he is talking animatedly on the phone. On the shelves around the office, I notice boxes marked 'smoking', 'motivation' and 'flying' amongst others. McKenna eventually puts the phone down, apologises and then, noticing me looking at the boxes, politely wonders whether I am frightened of flying. 'Yes, that's why I'm here,' I admit. Already, I feel in awe of this man.

Paul McKenna has an eclectic band of followers, who come to him with a wide range of problems and phobias, from fear of flying to depression. He has worked with many famous people, including actors, rock stars, sportspeople and even royalty. He doesn't charge his clients for their treatment, but asks them to make a donation to a charity of his choice. Besides, he doesn't need to charge them; he has his incredibly successful TV career, with programmes like *The Hypnotic World of Paul McKenna*. His two-year contract with one television station is said to be worth about £2.5 million.

McKenna is more than just a hypnotist, however. He has become a new-style guru and many of his clients now turn to him instead of their doctor or psychiatrist. He is fascinated by phobias and is constantly getting clients with problems that their doctors just can't do anything about. Recently he saw a woman who thought her fingernails were turning into knives. Her doctors were completely at a loss to know what to do but amazingly McKenna cured her with just one half-hour session. 'I can see why people come to me,' he says. 'If you use the traditional approach, it sometimes takes six months.'

This is how it works. When the client gets there, McKenna sits them in the chair I'm sitting in. He will then hypnotise the client by having him or her fix on a point on the ceiling. After a while the 'natural relaxation of trance' sets in, the eyes close and McKenna then talks to the client. One exercise that he uses on sportspeople involves them resisting pressure from his arm. You hold your arm out straight and try to keep it there while McKenna pushes it downwards. First, you do it while thinking about something nasty (like a bad day at the dentist) and then while thinking about something nice (like a relaxing holiday you had). Oddly, it's thinking the nice thoughts that makes you stronger. I tried it, and it really works. The difference really is amazing.

I asked McKenna to put me into a trance. Initially I resisted and resisted, rather as you do just before being given a general anaesthetic, but soon found myself, not exactly 'under', but completely relaxed. One of his clients said of McKenna, 'He hypnotised me down the telephone. It gave me a really good feeling, like when you've done strenuous exercise and you feel great.' I know exactly what she means. And I'll definitely be back.

2 **a** Read the text again and decide if these statements are true (T), false (F) or we don't know (DK).

1 The writer is frightened of flying.

2 His clients give money to a charity that McKenna specifies.

3 Some clients go and talk to McKenna every week.

4 He hypnotises people by looking into their eyes.

5 The writer enjoyed being hypnotised by McKenna.

b Write a paragraph of about 75 words summarising the main points from the text.

c Read your partner's paragraph. Did you include the same points?

3 Discuss.

1 What is your reaction to Paul McKenna and what he does?
2 Have you (or has anyone you know) had any experience of being hypnotised? Give details.
3 Would you like to be hypnotised? Why/Why not?
4 If you were going to be hypnotised, what would you ask for help with?

Grammar | reflexive pronouns

4 Complete the reflexive pronouns 1–6 in the Active grammar box.

Active grammar

	SUBJECT PRONOUNS	REFLEXIVE PRONOUNS
Singular	I	(1) ________
	you	*yourself*
	he	(2) ________
	she	*herself*
	it	(3) ________
Plural	we	(4) ________
	you	(5) ________
	they	(6) ________

A A common use of reflexive pronouns is to talk about actions where the subject and object are the same person. The reflexive pronoun is essential to the grammar of the sentence.

He started to teach himself to be a hypnotist.

B We can also use reflexive pronouns for emphasis, when we mean 'that person or thing, and nobody or nothing else'. The reflexive pronoun is not essential to the grammar of the sentence, but is added for emphasis.

McKenna himself is a small, mousy man with glasses.

5 **a** Match the examples 1–6 with the correct rule A or B in the Active grammar box.

1 I cut myself while I was cooking.
2 Emily herself said she's not very good at maths.
3 They blamed themselves for the accident.
4 I spoke to the boss himself.
5 You should put yourself in my position and try to understand.
6 She didn't go to the hairdresser; she cut her hair herself.

b Which one of these sentences is grammatically incorrect and what do the other two sentences mean?

1 We taught ourselves how to play tennis.
2 We taught each other how to play tennis.
3 We taught us how to play tennis.

see Reference on page 143

6 Complete these sentences with *each other*, reflexive pronoun (*myself*, *themselves*, etc.) or object pronoun (*him*, *us*, etc.).

1 I ________ have never been hypnotised but I know people who have.
2 My best friend and I often know what ________ are thinking.
3 A friend gave ________ a book about acupuncture for my birthday.
4 I'm so forgetful – I'm always locking ________ out of my house.
5 People in Britain usually give ________ presents at Christmas.
6 I'd like to speak to the doctor ________ , not the receptionist.
7 The teacher taught ________ to meditate by thinking about our breathing.
8 The people in my family talk to ________ a lot.

Person to person

7 **a** Do you agree with these statements? Make brief notes about your views.

1 Most people can cure themselves of a phobia (e.g. fear of spiders) or an addiction (e.g. smoking) without getting help from a professional.
2 One of the best ways of learning is being with other students and teaching each other.
3 Parents should be punished for persistent child truancy, as well as the children themselves.

b Compare your views with other students. Do you agree with each other?

Listening

8 10.2 Listen to three people talking about Paul McKenna and hypnosis. Which statement best summarises each person's opinion. One statement cannot be used.

1. He/She has benefited personally from hypnosis.
2. He/She admires McKenna for what he has achieved.
3. He/She thinks that going to hypnotists is often a waste of money.
4. He/She thinks it's good but doesn't understand how it works.

9 **a** Listen again and complete these verb phrases about belief and opinion.

1. *I reckon* he's probably genuine myself.
2. *I'm in* _______ *of* just accepting it if it works for you.
3. *I've always* _______ *that* people like Paul McKenna are just good showmen.
4. *I have my* _______ *about* how much he can actually do for people in the long-term.
5. *I'm* _______ *that* hypnosis has any effect at all.
6. *I'm* _______ people paying for a service and getting nothing real in return.
7. *I* _______ hypnosis actually works for anyone.
8. *I'm* _______ that it was the hypnosis that helped me.
9. *I* _______ I would've left my job by now.

b Answer the questions about the meaning of the verb phrases.

1. Which two verb phrases mean: I feel almost certain that something is true?
2. Which three verb phrases mean: I think that something may not be true or is unlikely to happen?
3. Which two verb phrases mean: I think something is true or is likely to happen?
4. Which one verb phrase means: I agree with and support a plan, idea or system?
5. Which one verb phrase means: I disagree with and am opposed to a plan, idea or system?

Pronunciation

10 Listen again and repeat the sentences paying special attention to the pronunciation of the phrases in Ex. 9a.

11 Rewrite the sentences using the words in brackets.

1. My view has always been that there is life on other planets. (believed)
2. I think that ghosts don't really exist at all. (doubt)
3. I had a very strong feeling that I knew what she was thinking. (convinced)
4. I agree with people trying all sorts of different treatments. (favour)
5. I think that some people have supernatural powers. (reckon)
6. I am not sure about the existence of UFOs. (doubts)
7. I disagree with paying someone for a service I don't understand. (against)
8. I think it's unlikely that anyone can predict the future. (sceptical)

Speaking

12 In pairs, discuss your views about some of the topics in the box. Use the How to box and the verb phrases in Ex. 9.

hypnosis vegetarianism marriage
military service smoking in public places
ghosts telepathy Internet chat rooms

HOW TO ...

ask about other people's views

What are your views on ...?
What do you think of ...?
Are you for or against ...?
How do you feel about ...?
Do you have any strong feelings about ...?

13 **a** Choose a topic from Ex. 12. Prepare to talk for one minute about your views. Use the notes below to help you.

1. Say what experience you have of the topic and/or why it interests you
2. Say arguments in favour or any positive points about the topic
3. Say arguments against or any negative points
4. Say your conclusion and/or summarise your personal views

b Listen to other students give their talks. Which of the views you heard were similar to yours?

10.2 Persuasion

Grammar gerunds and infinitives
Can do write the arguments for and against a point of view

Listening

1 Discuss.

1 What are the people in each picture doing?
2 What do you think their aim is in each case?
3 What different techniques are they using to achieve their aim?

2 10.3 Listen to an extract from a radio programme and decide which two of these things are being discussed: a) advertising, b) politicians, c) supermarkets.

3 Listen again and complete the notes.

> **Persuasion**
> 1 Where persuasion takes place: *television, ...* ______________
> 2 Large amounts of money spent on: ______________
> **Supermarkets**
> 3 Two ways to relax customers: ______________
> 4 Why reward cards are good for supermarkets: ______________
> **Advertising**
> 5 Two types of advert: ______________
> 6 Adverts for cleaning products: ______________
> 7 Most powerful adverts: ______________
> 8 Adverts for luxury cars: ______________
> 9 Adverts which use famous people: ______________

4 Discuss.

1 What do you think about the ways that supermarkets persuade you to buy more things or visit more frequently?
2 How much do you think you are influenced by advertising?
3 Can you describe an advert that you particularly like or that has stuck in your mind? Why do you like it or why do you think you've remembered it?

Vocabulary | advertising

5 Choose the correct alternatives.

1 Have you got any favourite *advertising/advertisements*?
2 What are three of the best-known *target markets/makes* of clothing in your country?
3 Would you like to work in *commercial break/marketing*?
4 Do you think you would be good at thinking up *commercial breaks/slogans*?
5 What do you usually do during *commercial breaks/marketing* on TV?
6 Have you ever bought anything through a *target market/classified* ad?
7 Which film has had a lot of *classified ads/hype* recently?
8 What do you think the *hype/target market* is for eight-seater 'people-carrier' vehicles?

Pronunciation

6 **a** 10.4 Listen to these three words and mark where the main stress is. Is it on the same syllable or not?

1 advertising
2 advertisement
3 advert

b Choose four of the questions in Ex. 5 to ask and answer with a partner.

Grammar | gerunds and infinitives

7 **a** Look at the verbs in **bold** in sentences 1–5 in the Active grammar box and choose the correct alternatives.

b 10.5 Listen and check your answers.

c Write the verbs in **bold** in the correct place in the Active grammar box.

Active grammar

1 They **persuade** us *buying/to buy* things we may not want.
2 We **carry on** *using/to use* reward cards at the same supermarket.
3 Adverts for clothes often **want** *making/to make* us feel that we belong.
4 I **try** *resisting/to resist* buying expensive designer clothes but it's difficult!
5 You could **try** *leaving/to leave* your credit card at home if you don't want to spend so much.

verb + gerund	*carry on*
verb + infinitive	
verb + object + infinitive	
verb + gerund OR verb + infinitive with a different meaning	

8 **a** Check the meaning of the verbs in the box. Then, write them in the correct place in the Active grammar box. Use a dictionary if necessary.

advise agree allow arrange avoid encourage hope practise regret remember stop suggest

b Look at these pairs of sentences. What is the difference in meaning between the underlined parts in each pair?

1 a The TV remote control wouldn't work so I tried changing the batteries.
b I tried to change the batteries in the remote control but I couldn't open it.
2 a Did you remember to buy some shampoo when you were out?
b I remember buying some more shampoo but now I can't find it.
3 a I regret to tell you that you failed your final exam.
b I regret telling her that I failed my final exam.
4 a The news was on but we stopped watching when the adverts came on.
b We were having lunch but we stopped to watch the news.

see Reference page 143

9 Complete the second sentence in each pair, so it has the same meaning as the first. Use between two and four words including the word in **bold**.

As a rehearsal, I gave the speech in front of a mirror.
practised
I practised giving the speech in front of a mirror.

1 'Why don't we go to the cinema?' he said.
suggested
He _______ to the cinema.

2 'You really should get a job in advertising,' she said to me.
encouraged
She _______ a job in advertising.

3 I made an attempt to speak to her on the phone but she was out.
tried
I _______ to her on the phone but she was out.

4 'OK. I'll give you a lift to the airport,' he said.
agreed
He _______ me a lift to the airport.

5 I used to come here when I was a child.
remember
I _______ here when I was a child.

6 'If I were you, I'd see a doctor,' he said.
advised
He _______ see a doctor.

7 We drove the long way so we wouldn't get stuck in traffic.
avoid
We drove the long way to _______ stuck in traffic.

8 'Go on! Buy the jeans and the boots! They're so cheap,' she said to me.
persuaded
She _______ the jeans and the boots.

Person to person

10 Talk to different students in the class and find someone who ...

- ... was allowed to watch as much TV as he/she wanted as a child
- ... regrets not learning to play a musical instrument as a child
- ... has arranged to do something exciting this weekend
- ... hopes to travel to a different continent next year
- ... remembers what they were doing on 31st December 1999
- ... has tried to give up smoking

Writing

11 **a** Discuss the statement in pairs. Do you agree? Why/Why not?

Advertising on TV during children's programmes should not be allowed.

b The sentences in the box are taken from an essay. Complete the table with the correct paragraph number 1–4.

Paragraph 1: Introduction – general statement about the issue
Paragraph 2: Arguments in favour of the statement
Paragraph 3: Arguments against the statement
Paragraph 4: Conclusion – briefly summarise your opinion

Paragraph 2	A Firstly, companies know that children can be persuaded to want things very easily.
	B Finally, it is important to remember that many children enjoy watching advertisements and finding out what is available in the shops.
	C In conclusion, I think it is the parents' responsibility to control how much television their children watch.
	D In this essay, I will consider the question of whether companies should be allowed to advertise to children on television.
	E On the other hand, it is not only the companies who have responsibility for what children watch.
	F On balance, I am convinced that companies should be banned from advertising to children, especially on television.
	G Another reason why they should not be allowed to advertise to children is that they are using children to make their parents spend more.
	H This is an important issue and there are strong feelings on both sides of the argument.

12 Choose a topic for your essay using one of the statements below or something else you feel strongly about. Write down arguments in favour and against your statement.

1 teenagers should not be allowed to wear designer clothes or shoes at school

2 small, local shops are better for the community than large supermarkets

3 background music and TV screens should be banned in public places, e.g. cafés, waiting rooms, shops, etc.

13 **a** Write an essay about your statement. Use the plan and the language in the table in Ex. 11b and your notes to help you.

b Read another student's essay. Do you agree with his/her final conclusion? Why/Why not?

10.3 Brave New World

Grammar *if* structures (2)
Can do talk about your regrets and resolutions

Reading

1 Read the short text below and answer the questions.

1. What is the matter with Bernard Marx?
2. Why is this a problem for him in his world?

2 Read the extract and answer this question: What are the babies learning while they are asleep?

1. what different types of work they could choose to do in the future
2. how to get on well with other children
3. how to be happy with their future role in society

Aldous Huxley wrote *Brave New World* in 1932. It remains one of the most powerful science fiction stories ever.
It is set in a future where peace and good health are compulsory but love and parenthood are obsolete. Thinking for yourself, being an individual and being unhappy are not allowed. Babies are produced and 'brought up' scientifically in 'Hatchery and Conditioning Centres'.
But one of the main characters, Bernard Marx, refuses to be happy and to fit in. He is haunted by the feeling that there must be more to his life than this.

'Silence, silence,' whispered a loud speaker. 'Silence, silence,' repeated other loudspeakers at intervals along the corridor. The students and even the Director himself, without thinking, obeyed the voices and walked on the tips of their toes. They were Alphas, of course, but even Alphas have been well conditioned. 'Silence, silence.' The air of the fourteenth floor was heavy with the whispered command.

The Director carefully opened a door. They entered a room where the light was very low. Eighty little beds stood in a row against the wall. All that could be heard was light regular breathing and a continuous hum like the sound of very faint voices speaking softly at a great distance.

A nurse stood up as they entered.
'What's the lesson this afternoon?' the Director asked quietly.
'Elementary Class Consciousness,' she answered.
The Director walked slowly down the long line of beds. In each one lay a child asleep. Eighty little boys and girls with pink, healthy faces lay there softly breathing. There was a whisper under every bedcover. 'Elementary Class Consciousness, did you say? Let's have it repeated a little louder by the loudspeaker.'

At the end of the room a loud speaker hung on the wall. The Director walked up to it and pressed a switch.

'... all wear green,' said a soft but very distinct voice, beginning in the middle of a sentence, 'and Delta Children wear light brown. Oh no, I don't want to play with Delta children. And Epsilons are even worse. They're too stupid to be able to read or write. Besides, they wear black, which is such an ugly colour. I'm so glad I'm a Beta.'

There was a pause, then the voice began again.

'Alpha children wear grey. They work much harder than we do, because they're so clever. I'm really very glad I'm a Beta, because I don't work so hard. And then we are much better than the Gammas and Deltas. Gammas are stupid. They all wear green, and Delta children wear light brown. Oh no, I don't want to play with Delta children. And Epsilons are even worse.'

The Director pushed back the switch. The voice sank to the faintest of whispers which could just be heard from beneath the eighty bedcovers.

'They'll have that repeated a hundred and twenty times three times a week for thirty months while they are sleeping, then they go on to a more advanced lesson. Sleep-teaching is the most powerful force of all time in social education. The child's mind becomes these suggestions and the total of these suggestions is the child's mind. And not only the child's mind. The adult's mind too, all his life long. The mind that thinks and desires and decides. But all these suggestions are our suggestions!' The Director almost shouted in his enthusiasm. 'Suggestions from the State.'

(Extract from: *Brave New World* by Aldous Huxley, Penguin Readers, Level 6)

Vocabulary | ways of speaking

5 **a** Work in A/B groups. Look at the words/phrases in the table. Using a dictionary, find the following: a) the meaning, b) the pronunciation, c) an example sentence.

GROUP A	GROUP B
to whisper	to mumble
to shriek	to interrupt
to blurt out	to speak your mind
to be lost for words	to have a word with

b In A/B pairs, tell each other the meaning, pronunciation and example sentence for each word/phrase.

6 **a** Complete the quotes with the correct form of the words/phrases from Ex.5.

1 'I told a colleague that I'd been using one of those self-help CDs to help deal with my stress. Then, in the middle of a meeting with some other colleagues, he suddenly _______ everything I'd told him. Honestly, I _______ – I was so shocked I didn't know what to say.'
2 'I went to the cinema last weekend and the people behind me were _______ to each other throughout the whole film. They didn't seem to notice that they were annoying everyone else. In the end, my friend _______ them and they stopped, but by that time the film was nearly over.'
3 'My cousin has been staying with me for the last week. I must say she's quite irritating. She's really loud and every time I say anything she _______ with laughter. The other thing she does is constantly _______ people when they're in the middle of a conversation. I don't mean to be horrible but I'll be really glad when she goes!'
4 'I did my first presentation at work yesterday and it was OK. But at the end one of my colleagues told me that I had been _______ and he couldn't really hear me. He's the kind of person who isn't afraid to _______ and I was a bit upset at first. I suppose it's useful feedback though.'

b 10.6 Listen and check your answers.

7 Choose three of the words/phrases from Ex. 5a. Tell your partner about different situations in which you or someone else spoke in each of these ways.

3 Read the text again and write the question for each of these answers.

1 Because the loudspeakers were whispering 'Silence'.
Why were the students walking quietly along the corridor?
2 They heard children breathing and the sound of quiet voices talking.
3 They looked healthy with pink faces.
4 Because he wanted the students to be able to hear what the loudspeakers were saying to the children.
5 Epsilons.
6 Betas.
7 360 times.
8 When they're thirty months old.
9 It means that the child learns to think in exactly the way he/she is taught.
10 The fact that the suggestions are all controlled by him and the State.

4 Discuss.

1 What do you think of the extract ? How does it make you feel?
2 What kind of world does the book describe? Do you know of any other books or films that depict futuristic worlds?
3 Do you think that people in our world are conditioned to do certain things?

Grammar | *if* structures (2)

8 **a** Match the examples 1–3 with the correct uses A–C in the Active grammar box.

1 *If parents always speak two languages to their children, they become bilingual.*

2 *If she works really hard, she'll pass her exams.*

3 *If I won a lot of money, I'd give up my job.*

b Now match examples 4–6 with the correct meanings D–F.

4 *If she had studied harder, she would be at university now.*

5 *If she didn't study as hard as she does, she would have failed the test.*

6 *If he had memorised his verbs, he wouldn't have failed the test.*

Active grammar

Uses

A First conditional: to talk about future possibility

B Second conditional: to talk about present or future unreal or imagined situations

C Zero conditional: to talk about things that always happen

D Third conditional: to talk about past unreal situations with a past result

E A mixed conditional: with an '*if* clause', referring to the past and a main clause referring to the present/future

F A mixed conditional: with an '*if* clause', referring to the present/future and a main clause referring to the past

Modal verbs (*can*, *could*, *might*, etc.) can be used in First, Second, Third and mixed conditionals instead of *will* and *would*.

Form:

a) First conditional = *If* + Present Simple, *will* + infinitive

b) ______________ = *If* + Past Simple, *would* + infinitive

c) ______________ = *If* + Past Perfect, *would have* + past participle

d) ______________ = *If* + Present Simple, Present Simple

e) ______________ = *If* + Past Perfect, *would* + infinitive OR *If* + Past Simple, *would have* + past participle

9 **a** Look at the rules of form a–e in the Active grammar box and write the correct type of conditional next to each one.

b Look at the examples and choose the correct alternatives from rules 1 and 2 below.

If you talk to babies a lot, they will learn to speak quickly.

Provided you talk to babies a lot, they will learn to speak quickly.

Unless you talk to babies a lot, they won't learn to speak quickly.

1 *unless/provided* has a similar meaning to *if*.

2 *unless/provided* means *if not*.

see Reference page 143

10 What type of conditional is each sentence? Correct the grammar mistake in each one.

1 If I had more time, I'll go and study English abroad.

2 If parents shouted at their children, they become aggressive.

3 I speak English fluently now if I'd learned it as a child.

4 I usually remember vocabulary, provided I'll write it down.

5 If you'll repeat a word enough times, you'll probably remember it.

6 If I'd attended more lessons, I would passed my exams.

7 I'd have a better job if I passed my exam.

8 If a student reads books in English, his/her vocabulary improved.

Person to person

11 Which of the sentences in Ex. 10 apply to you or do you think are true? Tell a partner.

Speaking

12 **a** Look at the sentences in Ex. 10. Which of them could be:

1 regrets

2 resolutions

b Think about your language learning or your school/work life. Make a note of one or two of your regrets and your resolutions using *if* structures.

c Compare your lists with a partner. Have you got any of the same resolutions?

10 Vocabulary

Commonly misspelt words

1 **a** Discuss these questions.

1. How many basic spelling rules do you think there are in English?
   a twenty-five
   b sixty
   c ninety
2. How many different ways do you think there are for spelling the sound /iː/?
   a at least five
   b at least eight
   c at least twelve
3. What do you think the *Spelling Society* in Britain wants to do?
   a simplify English spelling
   b encourage correct spelling
   c go back to old spelling rules

b Read the text and check your answers.

There are ninety basic spelling rules in English and eighty-four of these have exceptions! For some sounds, there are no clear rules at all and identical sounds can be spelt in several different ways. For example, the sound /iː/ can be spelt as in: seem, team, theme; sardine, protein, thief, people, he, key, ski, debris, quay.

The Spelling Society in Britain thinks that the English spelling system should be simplified. They say, for example, that we should spell the sound /iː/ simply as 'ee', e.g. peeple, and save learners a lot of time and effort. Until then, however, it's just a question of lots of learning and testing!

2 Choose the correct spelling for each pair of words?

1. beleive/believe
2. intelligence/intelligance
3. subconscious/subconsious
4. psychologist/pyschologist
5. dout/doubt
6. existance/existence
7. successful/successfull
8. responsability/responsibility

3 **a** Find the 18 common spelling mistakes in the email and correct them.

Dear Emine

Hi. How are you? I'm having a grate time. All the people I've met have been very genrous. Of course, I'm still a foriener here and it felt wierd at first, but I'm begining to feel more at home now. The wether is definately very changable – and it rains a lot! So that feels like home!

I've now got my accomodation sorted out. I'm living in an intresting part of town with lots of restraunts and a good libarry round the corner. Everything is very close so it's not really nessasry to go to school by bus. I usally walk, although I occasionly get a lift with some freinds in there car.

I'm going to send a seperate email to Mum and Dad. But say 'hi' to Murat from me. I'll write again soon.

Lots of love, Melisa

b Compare with a partner. Do you agree?

4 **a** 10.7 Listen and say which of these questions the student does NOT talk about.

1. Why is important to spell accurately?
2. Why is it difficult to spell accurately in English?
3. Are there any words that you particularly like or dislike the spelling of?
4. What are some of the ways you use to remember how to spell words?

b Discuss the questions with other students.

Lifelong learning

Spelling test

Can you add any more tips to this list?

- use a dictionary to check spelling
- keep a notebook of words you find difficult to spell
- choose ten words to learn how to spell every week. Ask a friend to test you.
- use a computer spell-check

10 Communication

How does your mind work?

Albert Einstein

William Shakespeare

Madonna

Nelson Mandela

Buddha

1 Discuss.

1 What do you know about each of the people in the photos?

2 Whose approach to life do you think is most similar to yours? In what ways?

2 **a** Do the quiz and make notes about your own answers. Use the ideas in the boxes and your own ideas.

b Now do the quiz with your partner and make a note of his/her answers.

1 What would you most like to spend your time doing when you're on holiday?

> playing sports   doing nothing
> reading a good book   doing a puzzle book
> talking to local people

2 When you're learning a language, which of these appeals to you most?

> analysing grammatical rules
> speaking without worrying about mistakes
> immersing yourself totally in the country where the language is spoken

3 Which one of these would you be most keen on doing as part of your work?

> working together in a team
> writing a story or poem
> doing scientific research
> doing something practical   being outdoors

4 When you're in a group, which one of these are you most likely to do?

> wonder what other people are thinking
> be the 'entertainer' who keeps the mood high
> speak on behalf of the group
> take control of any money or number issues
> keep the group focussed on reaching its goal

5 Do any of these statements describe you? If not, write one which does.

> I enjoy dancing.
> I like trying to figure people out.
> I like telling stories.
> I'm interested in science.
> I enjoy a good discussion.

6 Which of these jobs would you like to do most?

> politician   artist   journalist   lawyer
> psychologist   teacher   astronaut   nurse

3 Compare your notes with the descriptions on page 147. Then discuss these questions.

1 Which description do you think you are most like?

2 Which description do you think your partner is most like?

3 Do you and your partner think/learn in a similar or a different way?

Reflexive pronouns

Singular: *myself/yourself/himself/herself/itself*
Plural: *ourselves/yourselves/themselves*

We use reflexive pronouns to talk about actions where the subject and object are the same person. The reflexive pronoun is essential to the grammar of the sentence and would not make sense without it.

I cut myself while I was cooking.

We can also use reflexive pronouns for emphasis, when we mean 'that person or thing, and nobody or nothing else'. In this case, the reflexive pronoun is not essential to the grammar of the sentence, but is added for emphasis.

They built that house themselves.

Gerunds and infinitives

Some verbs are followed by particular structures. The following verbs are some of the most common ones for each structure.

Verb + gerund: enjoy, avoid, imagine, consider, finish, miss, practise, involve, carry on, suggest

Does the job involve working in the evenings?

Verb + infinitive: want, seem, offer, decide, hope, afford, agree, arrange, promise, refuse, manage

He offered to give me a lift into town.

Verb + object + infinitive: persuade, convince, encourage, allow, advise

I encouraged her to work as hard as she could.

Verb + gerund OR verb + infinitive – with a different meaning: remember, regret, try, stop, go on

I stopped talking to Sam. (I was talking to Sam and then I stopped)

I stopped to talk to Sam. (I stopped what I was doing and started talking to Sam)

If structures (2)

If structures or conditional sentences generally have two clauses. The '*if* clause' can come first or second. When the '*if* clause' is first, we need a comma at the end of the clause.

Use the First Conditional to talk about future possibility.

If + Present Simple or Present Continuous or Present Perfect, *will/could/should/might/may/going to* + verb or Present Continuous or Imperative

If you're going to the party tomorrow, I'll see you there.

Use the Second Conditional to talk about present or future unreal or imagined situations.

If + Past Simple/Past Continuous, *would/could/should/might* + infinitive

He'd be much more healthy if he didn't smoke.

Use the Third Conditional to talk about past unreal situations with a past result.

If + Past Perfect, *would have/could have/should have/might have* + past participle

If you hadn't been so rude, he wouldn't have walked out.

Use the Zero Conditional to talk about things that always happen.

If + Present Simple, Present Simple

If you heat ice, it melts.

Use Mixed Conditionals:

with an '*if* clause' referring to the past and a main clause referring to the present/future

If + Past Perfect, *would* (or *'d*) + infinitive

If we hadn't missed the plane, we'd be in Spain now.

with an '*if* clause' referring to the present/future and a main clause referring to the past

If you didn't want to come to the theatre tomorrow, I wouldn't have bothered getting you a ticket.

We can use modals in the First, Second, Third and Mixed Conditionals.

If you see James, you should invite him to the party.

If I had studied harder, I might have passed my exam.

Key vocabulary

The power of the mind

willpower, mind over matter, the power of persuasion, to have a premonition, to have a feeling of déjà vu, to trust your intuition, your sixth sense, to be unconscious, subconscious (fears)

Belief and opinion

to reckon, to suspect, to doubt, to have your doubts about, to be sceptical that, to have always believed that, to be convinced, to be in favour of, to be against

Advertising

advertisement, classified ad, commercial break, advertising, marketing, target market, slogan, make, hype

Speaking

to whisper, to shriek, to mumble, to blurt out, to interrupt, to speak your mind, to have a word with, to be lost for words

Commonly misspelt words

accommodation, beginning, believe, changeable, definitely, doubt, existence, friend, foreigner, great/grate, generous, intelligence, interesting, library, necessary, occasionally, psychologist, responsibility, restaurants, separate, subconscious, successful, there/their/they're, usually, weird, weather/whether

1 Complete each sentence using the correct form of a verb from the box. Use a reflexive pronoun where necessary.

relax feel blame enjoy express meet hurt concentrate burn

They are blaming themselves for the accident, but it wasn't their fault.

1 Don't touch the iron. You'll _______ .
2 I _______ very disappointed when I found out I'd failed my driving test.
3 She's a good speaker. She _______ very clearly.
4 You've worked hard today. You should sit down and _______ now.
5 Jack's gone to the doctor because he _______ while he was playing football this morning.
6 My boss and I are going to _______ for lunch tomorrow.
7 Thank you for the party. We really _______ .
8 I _______ as hard as I could on the maths lesson, but I still couldn't understand it.

2 Find the mistakes in six of the sentences and correct them.

The manager agreed giving my money back. → to give

1 We encourage all students doing some voluntary work.
2 I've arranged visiting my grandparents on Saturday.
3 I couldn't avoid hitting the dog as it ran out in front of my car.
4 I remember to go to the park every day after school when I was a child.
5 He persuaded me joining the new gym with him.
6 My teacher suggested to learn ten new spellings every week.
7 Please will you stop talking for a minute.
8 He advised to have us an early night before the exam.

3 Complete the sentences with the correct form of the verbs in brackets. There is sometimes more than one correct answer.

If we don't go and see Jane, she 'll be (be) really upset. (or ... she might be ...)

1 If you _______ (not go) to bed late last night, you wouldn't be so tired.
2 You'd feel a lot better if you _______ (do) more exercise.
3 Dogs _______ (behave) very well if you train them properly.
4 If I _______ (bring) enough money, I would have paid for your dinner.
5 He'll miss the beginning of the film if he _______ (not arrive) soon.
6 If you _______ (press) that button, you get cold water.
7 What _______ (you/do) if you lost your passport?
8 I _______ (lie) on a beach now if I'd booked that holiday.

4 Complete the sentences with the correct form of the words in the box. Three of the words cannot be used.

hype ~~déjà vu~~ premonition slogan make interrupt shriek convince blurt intuition mumble reckon

I was sure I'd seen her before. I had a strong feeling of déjà vu.

1 I'm _______ that recycling is essential for helping the environment.
2 Don't believe all the _______ about that new film. It's not much good.
3 Can you let me finish what I'm saying without _______ me all the time?
4 I _______ he knows something that he's not telling us.
5 The surprise was spoilt because he _______ out the whole plan before I could stop him.
6 Don't worry about other people. Trust your _______ and do what you want.
7 I don't really care what _______ of jeans I wear as long as they're comfortable.
8 I'm not going in a car today. I had a _______ about being in a car accident.

5 Find the misspelt words in six of the sentences and correct them.

1 I'll definately see you tomorrow evening.
2 Finding cheap accomodation in London is very difficult.
3 Having children is an enormous responsability.
4 We went to a great new restaurant yesterday.
5 Could you put the sandwiches in seperate bags please?
6 Have you seen there new house?
7 I can't believe how rude the waiter was!
8 My sister is an extremely sucessful designer.

Communication activities

Lesson 9.1 | Ex. 11, page 120

Story 1

At 5a.m. one September morning two would-be robbers from Edmonton in Canada, raided a small petrol station in Vancouver. After locking the attendant in the toilets, they made their getaway with a few hundred dollars. Coming from Edmonton, they didn't know their way around Vancouver and twenty minutes later they drove up at the same petrol station to ask directions.

The attendant, Mr. Karnail Dhillon, having just escaped from the toilets, was alarmed to see the two robbers coming into the shop again. "They wanted me to tell them the way to Port Moody," he said. "I guess they didn't recognise me or the petrol station."

He was just calling the police when the pair came back again to say that they couldn't get their car to start. While they were waiting for a mechanic to help them, the police arrived and arrested them.

Communication 9 | Ex. 2, page 128

6 **Explanation**

The airplane was on the ground when he leapt.

Communication 9 | Ex. 2, page 128

2 **Explanation**

The water in the river only came up to the man's chest

Lesson 6.2 | Ex. 13b, page 81

Student B

Camel trips at

Price: $160 per person per night

Where?

Dakhla Oasis is about 850km from Cairo. The hotel is situated at the top of pink cliffs which surround the oasis below. Within the oasis, there are beautiful fields and gardens full of grapes, olive trees, date palms, figs, apricots and citrus fruits. Beyond the oasis, there are the incredible sand dunes of the Sahara Desert.

Accommodation

Dakhla has 32 large rooms all with private bathrooms. The rooms are simply but tastefully furnished in the local style. They all have fans and also heaters for the cold winter nights. Some rooms have a terrace with spectacular views of the nearby mountain range. The restaurant serves delicious local food including the traditional 'falafel'.

Activities

There are camel trips and walking tours available from half a day to 3-plus days. These go across the sand dunes of the desert and also up into the mountains. The guides will help you set up the tents and prepare a delicious barbecue dinner on the campfire with homemade bread, baked in the sand.

Lesson 9.1 | Ex. 11, page 120

Story 2

Communication 9 | Ex. 2, page 128

3 **Explanation**

He was riding a horse called "Friday" ...

Communication 9 | Ex. 2, page 128

4 **Explanation**

Because Bobby was only 9 months old ...

Communication 6 | Ex. 3a, page 86

You love your creature comforts

You love your holidays but you prefer a touch of home wherever you go. Creature comforts mean a lot to you. Trekking through the desert with a camel for company is probably not your idea of a great holiday. You prefer a complete rest and lots of sun.

You love a touch of adventure

You're a bit of an adventurer compared to some holidaymakers. You hate lying around sunbathing, but prefer something different, such as white-water rafting. However, you also prefer to sleep in a nice bed in a good hotel after a hard day's adventure.

You love to be independent

You're a true independent traveller who probably avoids package holidays and is rarely seen on a Greek island or the Costa del Sol. You love exploring far-flung countries and mixing with the locals. And you've probably got cupboards full of photos and interesting souvenirs.

You're a real explorer

You have the spirit of a Stanley or Livingstone – a real explorer who loves to get lost in places where no tourist has gone before. You love meeting the locals, hate bumping into anyone who speaks your language and don't mind sleeping in the open with the local wildlife for company.

Communication 9 | Ex. 2, page 128

1 **Explanation**

The teenagers were travelling on the road that crossed the road that the police officer was on. They drove through a green light.

Communication 10 | Ex. 3, page 142

Types of thinkers/learners

Linguistic: They like to think in words and use complex ideas. They are sensitive to the different sounds and meanings of words and enjoy the process of learning a foreign language.

Logical-mathematical: They like to understand patterns and the relationships between things. They are good at thinking critically and problem-solving. They like to analyse and understand the rules.

Interpersonal: They like to think about other people and are often peacemakers. They are aware that different people have different views on life and probably have lots of friends.

Existential: They like to spend time thinking about philosophical issues and don't like to be bothered with trivial questions. They are always asking questions provoking discussions and debates.

Kinaesthetic: They like to think in movements and find it difficult to sit still for long. They are interested in fitness and health and they learn best when they are physically involved.

Lesson 6.2 | Ex. 13b, page 81

Student A

Bird watching in Mexico at

Yucatan Ecolodge

Price: $100 per person per night

Where? Yucatan Ecolodge is a 5-hour drive from Cancun airport and is surrounded by beautiful coconut trees with wonderful views of the Gulf of Mexico. The whole area is famous for its incredibly varied plant and animal life, especially birds.

Accommodation Stay in a comfortable bungalow with a veranda as well as bedroom, sitting room and bathroom. There are fans but no air conditioning. Meals are served in our main building – half board including tasty Mexican breakfast and 4-course candle-lit dinner. There is a lot of delicious fresh food and seafood available. There is also a bar, a games room and a swimming pool for you to enjoy.

Activities A variety of tours are available including bird watching tours, trips to the famous caves in the area and moonlight safaris. There is also a small Natural History Museum, offering an overall view of the flora and fauna surrounding the hotel.

Communication 9 | Ex. 2, page 128

5 **Explanation**

The man had just been cured of deafness, and the ringing phone is final proof that it has been a success.

6 Bhutan

Michael Palin started his career in TV as part of the team behind the comedy series *Monty Python*. Various other comedy programmes and films followed including the film, *A Fish called Wanda*. More recently he has become well-known for his BBC travel programmes. These include *Around the World in 80 days*, *Pole to Pole*, *Sahara* and *Himalaya*. In this latest project, he travels the full length of the Himalaya from the Pakistan-Afghan frontier through India, Nepal, Tibet and Yunnan to China, before re-crossing the mountains to Assam, Bhutan and Bangladesh. The whole journey took six months of hard travelling and he even met the Dalai Lama in Tibet who recognised him from his *Monty Python* days!

Monty Python

A Fish Called Wanda

Himalaya

1 Look at the photos and read the information above.

1. Are you interested in watching travel programmes on TV? Why/Why not?
2. Are you surprised that Michael Palin became a travel show presenter?
3. What do you think makes a good travel show presenter?

2 How much do you know about Bhutan? In pairs choose the correct alternatives to complete the sentences.

1. Bhutan is situated between:
   A China and India B China and Russia
2. Most Bhutanese people wear:
   A western clothes B Bhutan national costume
3. The population of Bhutan is about:
   A one million B five million
4. National Park covers about:
   A 25% of the country B 45% of the country
5. The King of Bhutan says the most important thing is:
   A Gross National Product B 'Gross National Happiness'
6. Bhutan has many areas and buildings devoted to:
   A Hinduism B Buddhism
7. Tourists in Bhutan have to pay a minimum of:
   A $75 a day B $200 a day
8. The main link between the east and the west is:
   A a road B a river
9. The main influence on Bhutan's climate and culture is:
   A the rivers and sea B the mountains

3 Watch the film extract and check your answers.

4 Discuss.

1. Did you enjoy watching this extract? Why/Why not? Does it make you want to watch more of this series?
2. Do you think Michael Palin is a good travel show presenter? Why/Why not?
3. Would you like to be involved in making travel programmes like this one?
4. If you had the chance to travel for six months as part of a travel programme like this, where would you go and why?

7 Vikings

The Vikings lived over one thousand years ago and came from Denmark, Norway and Sweden. They were mostly farmers, but some worked as craftsmen or traders. The Viking Age – or Dark Ages as they were known – began in Britain about 1200 years ago in the 8th century AD and lasted for 300 years. At the time of the invasions, Britain was mostly inhabited by the Anglo-Saxons who were terrified of these fierce people.

There are people in Britain today (and in Europe and the US) who are fascinated by the Vikings and their whole way of life. Many of these people are members of 'Re-enactment Societies' and they spend their spare time living exactly as the Vikings did. They go to great lengths to be as accurate as they can about every detail including clothes, food and battles. Although some people may regard this type of hobby as excessive, for the 'Re-enactors' it is a fantastic way of spending their free time.

1 Look at the pictures and discuss these questions with other students.

1 What you know about the Vikings?
2 What do you think a 'Re-enactment Society' is?

2 Read the information above and answer these questions.

1 What did you learn about the Vikings that you didn't know before?
2 What do you think people enjoy about being part of a 'Re-enactment Society'?

3 Watch the film extract and answer the questions .

1 Which of the reasons below for doing this hobby are mentioned?

it's fun to dress up   it brings history to life   it's very friendly
it's a way of making money   it's good exercise

2 Do the re-enactors try to hurt each other when they are fighting? Why/Why not?
3 What are the two main reasons for creating the Viking village?
4 One man says that he knows some people who '... seem to take it a bit far.' What example does he give?
5 Where do the re-enactors get the costumes from?
6 What does the blacksmith say about the tools he makes?
7 What jobs does the film mention that some of these people do in their 'real lives'?

4 Discuss.

1 Do you think that being a member of one of these societies is 'excessive'? Why/Why not?
2 Many other 'Re-enactment Societies' exist for different periods in history (e.g. World War I, The American Civil War, The Roman Invasion of Britain). If you were going to join (or start up) a 'Re-enactment Society', which one would it be? Why?

8 The secrets of success

1 Which of the jobs in the box below are represented in the photos?

> a milliner a web consultant a quantity surveyor a card maker street performers an Indian takeaway owner an Internet entrepreneur

2 Discuss.

1 What are the biggest challenges of starting up your own business?
2 If you had the chance to start up your own business, what would it be? Why?

3 Watch the film and number the following quotes in the order you hear them.

- I did some market research on it. ☐
- I've an annual turnover of £70,000. ☐
- Always believe in yourself. ☐
- I'm very passionate about my work. ☐
- Last year I decided to set up my own business. ☐
- We've been very lucky and very successful. ☐
- We've been going for two and a half years now. ☐

4 Having watched the film, can you remember the seven secrets of success? Complete the sentences below using the words in the box.

> boss give help idea customer partner passionate

1 Stay __
2 Get some __
3 Be your own __
4 Have a good __
5 Choose your __
6 Know your __
7 Don't __ up

5 Discuss.

1 Which three tips above do you think are the most important?
2 Can you add one other?
3 What are the advantages and disadvantages of working for yourself rather than working for someone else? Which would you rather do? Why?

9 The Bullion Robbery

The Lavender Hill Mob

The Italian Job

The Sting

Ocean's Twelve

1 Look at the pictures. Have you seen any of these films? Which well-known actors are in them? What is the connection between them all?

2 Watch the film extract from *The Lavender Hill Mob* and decide if the following statements are true (T) or false (F).

1. There are 211 bars of gold in the van.
2. Mr Holland says he is going to Paris on holiday.
3. Mr Holland stops the van because he says he is worried about another car.
4. The man on the bicycle tells the van driver that one of his lights is broken.
5. The pavement artist jumps in the van and pushes the van driver out.
6. The robbery takes place near Queen Elizabeth Street.
7. Mr Holland is part of the criminal gang.

3 Imagine you are Mr Holland. Tell another student the whole story from your point of view.

4 Discuss.

1. Do you know of any famous robberies?
2. What happened?
3. Why are they famous?
4. Were those responsible ever caught?

10 Yes, Prime Minister

Yes, Prime Minister and *Spitting Image* are two of Britain's most well-known political satirical TV series. In different ways they both make fun of key political characters and the political system.

In *Yes, Prime Minister*, Jim Hacker (new elected Prime Minister) attempts to make various bold changes but these generally come to nothing, thanks to the manoeuvring of his manipulative Cabinet Secretary, Sir Humphrey, who opposes action or change of any sort.

In *Spitting Image*, famous characters in British and international life were re-created in the form of latex puppets, which – in the manner of newspaper political cartoons – grossly exaggerated that person's most obvious facial or personality characteristic.

1 Look at the pictures and read the information above. Then, discuss these questions with other students.

1 Do you have any political satirical TV programmes in your country? Do you find them funny? Why/Why not?

2 Do you think programmes like this are a good thing? Why/Why not?

2 Watch the extract from *Yes, Prime Minister*. What does the TV producer, Godfrey, say about the following:

glasses face suit hair eyes nose

3 Discuss with other students.

1 What advice would you give to a politician who was making a political broadcast?

2 Have you seen any TV debates between politicians? Who did well? Who didn't? Why?

Writing bank

Informal emails

Lesson 6.1 | Ex. 13, page 78

1 Read the email. Which of the following best summarises Maisie's experience?

1. She's about to finish an interesting course.
2. She's nearly at the end of an exciting holiday.
3. She's coming to the end of her time at university.
4. She's about to leave a job she's been doing for a long time.

Name, date and email address are included at the top, so don't write them in the main part of the email

From: Maisie Ryland

Date: 07.12.05 19:34

To: leila@hotmail.co.uk

Subject: elephant orphanage

Attach: elephant2.JPG (285 KB)

Use an informal greeting with or without the person's name

Hi Leila

Wow! Where do I start? Did I tell you about this amazing project I'm doing before I go to university? I've been on holiday in Sri Lanka for three months working in an elephant orphanage! It's the first time I've been anywhere like this – and although I was a bit daunted at first, now I love it!

Use informal language, including contractions (e.g. *I've*), informal words and exclamation marks

We don't work all the time – there's plenty of time to have a real holiday too. It's been great to experience a different culture and to see the places I've only read about in books. The best bit is meeting so many friendly people and it's fascinating being so close to the elephants. I'm attaching a photo of me washing one of the babies!

I've only got ten more days to go. I'm looking forward to seeing you all, but I don't want to leave this place.

See you soon!

Lots of love,

Maisie

Writing skill | punctuation

2 **a** Look at the email again and find examples of the following:

1. an exclamation mark
2. a question mark
3. an apostrophe
4. a dash
5. a full-stop
6. a comma

b Match the punctuation (1–6) above with the correct explanations (A–F) below.

A Used to show the end of a sentence

B Used at the end of a sentence, to show it is a question

C Used at the end of a sentence, often to show excitement, surprise or other strong emotions

D Used in writing to show pauses in speech especially in lists, between adjectives and around clauses

E Used to show missing letters in contractions and with the possessive 's'

F Used in informal writing, to add an extra thought or idea to a sentence

Useful phrases

Opening phrases	*Hi Leila/Hello Leila/Hi/Hello/Dear Leila*
Giving news	*Did I tell you about ...?* *It's the first time I've ...* *It's been great to ...*
Attaching photos	*I'm attaching a photo of ...* *I'm sending you a photo of ...*
Closing phrases	*I'm looking forward to seeing you ...* *Lots of love, Maisie/Best wishes, Maisie/* *All the best, Maisie*

Formal letters

Lesson 7.2 | Ex. 12, page 95

1 Read the letter and answer the questions.

1 What are the three problems the customer is complaining about?
2 What does she want?

Write the name and/or title and address of the person you are writing to.

Write your address here. Don't write your name.

Write the date here.

55, Chestnut Avenue
Bristol, BS8 2JH

15th February 2006

Customer services
Film Express
214, Nightingale Lane
London, WC1 2AA

Dear Sir/Madam

I am writing to complain about two DVDs I bought recently from your company on the Internet and about how I was treated by a member of staff when I phoned to complain.

Firstly, I ordered them on 6th January and I was promised they would arrive in three days but they weren't sent to me for over two weeks. Then, when they arrived and I opened the box, I was shocked to see that one of them was broken, as they clearly hadn't been packaged properly.

Secondly, when I phoned to complain, I was very disappointed by the way in which I was treated. The member of staff who I spoke to was extremely rude and did not offer me any form of refund or replacement.

I would be grateful if you could send me a replacement DVD (Kill Bill 2) as soon as possible, or if this is not possible, I would like a full refund of my money. Thank you for your help with this matter.

Yours faithfully

Diana Jones

Diana Jones – customer number: FE3428890/3

email: jonesd@hotmail.co.uk

Use *Dear Sir/Madam* if you don't know the name of the person you are writing to. Use *Dear Mr/Mrs Smith* if you know the name. Put a comma (,) after the name, not a colon(:)

Use *Yours faithfully* if you don't know the name of the person you are writing to. Use *Yours sincerely* if you know the name.

Use formal language. Don't use contractions (I would like... NOT: I'd like)

Include any relevant reference numbers and email addresses at the end of the letter

Writing skill | formal and informal language

2 Look at the letter again. Is the language used formal or informal? Give two examples from the letter.

3 Mark the sentences formal (F) or informal (I).

1 It would be great to hear from you soon.
2 I would be grateful if a full refund could be sent as soon as possible.
3 I look forward to hearing from you at your earliest convenience.
4 Love, Jenny
5 I'm writing to tell you about something I bought recently.
6 Dear Ms. Harrison,
7 I am writing with reference to the service I received at your restaurant last week.
8 Dear Anna,
9 You know how I feel about all this, don't you?
10 Yours sincerely, Julio Manzanares
11 I am sure that you will understand why I feel so annoyed about this situation.
12 Could you give me the money back please?

Useful phrases

First lines	*I am writing with reference to ...* *I am writing to complain about ...* *I am writing in order to ...*
Ways of complaining	*I was promised that ... but ...* *I was shocked to see/find that ...* *I was very disappointed by ...* *The goods clearly hadn't been packaged properly and were damaged.* *The service I received was not of the standard I would expect from your company.*
Last lines	*I would be grateful if you could send me a full refund/a replacement as soon as possible.* *I would like a full refund/a replacement.* *I look forward to hearing from you at your earliest convenience.* *Thanks you for your help with this matter.* *Thank you in advance.*

Reports

Lesson 8.3 | Ex. 12, page 112

1 Read the report. Which of the topics in Ex. 10, page 112 is it about?

Writing Skill | paragraphs

2 What is the purpose of each paragraph in the report? Can you give them a short heading?

Useful phrases

Introduction	*This report gives the results of .../is intended to ...*
Reporting results	*Approximately 70% of all those who took part in the survey ...*
Conclusion	*From this survey it is clear that ...*

Divide your report into appropriate paragraphs.

Use formal language

State facts. Don't give personal opinions until the conclusion.

The first few years in school are possibly the most significant for any child. Consequently, the quality and attitudes of their teacher are of extreme importance. This report gives the results of an informal survey into the necessary qualities of teachers of young children.

Approximately 70% of all those who took part in the survey said that they thought the most important thing was that these teachers should care about the children. 60% also referred to the need for classes to be varied and interesting in order to keep the childrens' interest. 20% mentioned the importance of good discipline.

From this small survey it is clear that there is strong feeling that primary school teachers need to be carefully selected for their caring attitudes and creative teaching ability.

Articles

Lesson 9.3 | Ex. 12, page 126

1 Find five different pieces of information between the article and the interview in Ex. 9, page 126.

Writing Skill | referencing words

2 a Find these underlined words in the text and say what they refer to.

1 there (l.3)	4 it (l.11)
2 they (l.7)	5 she (l.13)
3 this (l.9)	6 them (l.18)

b How can using referencing words like those above improve a text?

Useful phrases

Interest your reader	*Oddly enough ...* *To my surprise ...* *Unbelievably ...*
Give examples	*There was a time when .../On one occasion ...*
Give your opinion	*As far as I'm concerned ...* *In my opinion ...*

Think of an interesting title.

The American 'Sherlock Holmes'

Deep in the heart of the United States of America, far from Baker Street in London, lives a man called 'Sherlock Holmes'. In May of this year, I tracked him down <u>there</u> and had the chance to ask him a few questions that I'd been wondering about.

Give some background or context to the title.

It turns out that Holmes's parents - (he prefers to be called 'Sherlock' by his friends and family) – were great lovers of the work of Conan Doyle. He has memories from his earliest childhood of how <u>they</u> used to read the stories to him. And apparently, they always knew that if they were going to have a boy, they would give him <u>this</u> name. They wanted him to feel special.

Use informal language.

Early on Holmes used to get quite angry about people's reactions to his name but he says he's more relaxed about <u>it</u> now. There was a time in San Francisco when a shop assistant looked at his I.D. card and thought he must be the real, original Sherlock Holmes. <u>She</u> looked like she'd seen a ghost.

Give examples of the points you make to interest your reader.

Oddly enough, Holmes says that people look to him sometimes to solve problems or mysteries. Luckily, he's done some magic himself, so he understands how some of the tricks on TV are done. On one occasion the police called him to help <u>them</u> out with a case they couldn't solve. Fortunately, he was able to find some clues on a computer which helped to work out what had happened to the missing person.

Meeting the American 'Sherlock Holmes' was quite an experience. I'm not sure that I would want to be named after such a famous person but from what I saw he has coped with it extremely well. As far as I'm concerned, parents need to think long and hard about the consequences of the names they give their children for their future lives!

Express your opinion.

Unit 5 Recording 6

W=Woman

W: Well ... where shall I start? Well ... the basic story is that a girl, Catherine, is left a box by her mother, who died when she was a baby. Catherine discovers the box when she's 31, the same age as when her mother died. Inside the box are 11 objects, like a red hat, a map of part of England and so on ... all of them meaningless at first, but when Catherine begins to examine each object, she finds new truths not only about her mother but also about herself. Through these objects Catherine finds that her mother was not the sweet and innocent woman that everyone likes to remember her as.

So, what did I think of it? Well ... overall ... I really enjoyed it – it's a really interesting idea for a story – and I thought it was very well-written. Not only that but there are lots of aspects of Catherine's life that I can totally relate to – different events, feelings and thoughts which so accurately mirror my own life that I found myself constantly underlining parts of the text.

However, sometimes I found it a bit slow. I wanted to know about the objects and it seemed to take ages to work out what they were all about. Still ... apart from that one small thing ... it was very easy to read and I'd certainly recommend it.

Unit 5 Recording 7

W=Woman

W: Well first of all it's very important to make sure that your time capsule container is going to last for a very long time ... obviously! So, it mustn't rust, it mustn't leak and it must be very hard-wearing. We were told to avoid any kinds of plastics and go for a material like aluminium or stainless steel.

We put in various books, newspapers and photographs ... all of which I still think were a good idea. With books and papers, it's important to make sure they're printed on the highest quality paper – so they don't deteriorate any faster than absolutely necessary.

One mistake we made was to put in colour photographs. I mean, photographs are very good information carriers across time and cultures ... but apparently, black and white photographs are much more stable and long-lasting than colour prints ... so that's something worth bearing in mind.

The other thing which we should have thought about was that some kinds of technology become redundant. We put in an old video tape and they probably won't be able to view that when the capsule finally gets opened. So, it's probably best not to include any items that require any technology or equipment to use ... other than eye and hand.

Finally, and again, pretty obviously I guess, do make sure that the outside of the capsule is clearly labelled using a permanent marker pen ... saying what it is and any necessary instructions.

Unit 6 Recording 1

W=Woman

W: I was about 25 and I'd been working at the same company for five years. A friend showed me his photos of an amazing holiday he'd had in Central America. One photo in particular really struck me. It was when he went diving and saw the most beautiful fish you've ever seen! I began to have itchy feet and wanted to leave work and do something exciting. I'd never been out of Europe before then and I was a bit worried about going straight into uncharted territory! I mean, I didn't know anything about countries so different and far away from mine. So, I decided to go to Spain first, to learn a bit of Spanish and get used to being away from home. I went as an independent traveller on my own, because I really wanted to do it all by myself. I spent a month wandering around the town where I was living and learning Spanish and loving every minute! I was bitten by the travel bug then and wanted to explore lots of other places. About six months later, after saving up some money, I went off to Guatemala, feeling very confident and pleased with myself. The first two months were difficult and I experienced real culture shock, I think. It seemed that everything was different. Lots of things went wrong too, like I was robbed twice, I couldn't find anywhere to live and I was really homesick and missed my family like mad! So I had a bit of a bumpy ride to start with, but after a while, I found a job teaching English, made some friends and started to really enjoy myself. In fact, I grew to love it so much I stayed there for three years!

Unit 6 Recording 5

1 The summer is generally hot and very <u>humid</u> and quite uncomfortable. It's often overcast too and there is no <u>breeze</u> to cool things down. It's very different in the winter, when it's <u>cool</u> and the sky is <u>clear</u>.
2 I'm not so keen on <u>mild</u> weather – when it's not really hot or cold. I much prefer it when the weather is quite dramatic. Like when you get <u>scorching</u> days and then it suddenly <u>pours</u> for hours. Or when it's hot in the day and then you get <u>subzero temperatures</u> at night.
3 The weather is very <u>changeable</u>. In the summer, the days are often <u>bright</u> but can be <u>showery</u> and the nights are sometimes <u>chilly</u> but not very cold. In the winter, it seems to <u>drizzle</u> a lot and the sky is often grey.

Unit 6 Recording 6

P=Presenter J=Jamie W=Woman M=Man

P: Hello everyone. I think we'll make a start as it's 7.30 already. Let me introduce Jamie. He's our 'Bhutan expert' ... He's spent a substantial amount of time in this amazing country and I'm sure he'll be able to help you with whatever queries you may have.

J: Hello. Thank you. Well, I'll do my best ... Please feel free to ask whatever you want and if I can't answer anything . Well, I'll say so!! ... So, fire away ...

W: Err... yes ... when is the best time to go?

J: Well, in the winter it can be up to about 15c in the daytime but you often get subzero temperatures at night. There is a lot of snow in winter, which can make travelling difficult. It's hot in the summer, sometimes really scorching, but it's often very wet too. In my experience, the best seasons to visit are spring and autumn. Spring is beautiful with wonderful flowers and lovely sunny days. And autumn is fantastic too with mild weather and clear views of the Himalayas ... Yes?

M: What activities do you recommend?

J: One of the most popular activities for visitors to Bhutan is to go trekking in the Himalayas. The high mountains and deep valleys are truly spectacular and you can sometimes walk for several days before coming to the next village. You'll see a huge variety of plant life ranging from dense forest to tiny mountain flowers. I've been many times ... You won't be disappointed, I can assure you!

M: Thank you.

W: Excuse me ... I'd like to know whether we need to take anything special.

J: Ah yes, good question. The changeable climate means that you will need an assortment of clothes, including rain gear and good walking boots. The sun can be very strong especially up in the mountains, so you'll need a hat and sunglasses. I'd also recommend warm clothes for the evenings ... it can get pretty chilly, even in summer.

M: Would we need to carry all our equipment on a trek?

J: No. Trekking is done in organised trips and they provide yaks to carry your luggage. They also carry the food and camping equipment, which is all provided. I've always found them very well-equipped and helpful.

M: and who goes with the trekking group? I mean do they provide a guide?

J: Oh yes ... There's always a guide who speaks English and a cook and other assistants to help make the trek run smoothly. They're all very friendly ... you really don't need to worry about getting lost or anything ...

W: Could I ask you what the food is like?

J: Mmm ... interesting, yes. The Bhutanese eat a lot of meat, dairy foods, vegetables and rice. The national dish is a fabulous chilli pepper and cheese stew called Emadatse. In fact, chillis are very common in Bhutan and you'll find that a lot of their dishes are flavoured with spicy chilli peppers. I love the food, I must say.

M: I'm thinking of going in the autumn. Do you know if there are any interesting festivals at that time?

J: Well, yes, this year there are, although the dates of festivals vary according to the moon. The most popular one for tourists is held in Thimphu, the capital and this year it's in October. People dress in their colourful, traditional clothes and there is a lot of music and dancing, including the masked sword dances. All the festivals are important religious events for the people to offer thanks to their gods.

M: I've seen pictures of strings of flags in the mountains. Can you tell me what they are?

J: Yes, they are prayer flags. As I said, the Bhutanese people are very religious and they use the flags as a way of communicating with the heavens ...

Unit 6 Recording 7

1 When I'm abroad I always have a go at speaking the language.
2 We're going away for the weekend. Could you look after our cat?
3 Don't worry. It goes without saying that I'll meet you at the airport.
4 There's something going on in the city centre. It's full of people.
5 Although they argue a lot, they want to make a go of their marriage.
6 I promise I won't go back on what I've said.
7 Can you help with dinner please? I've been on the go all day.
8 Your teacher can't be here today. She's gone down with a bad cold.
9 I couldn't decide which kitten to go for. They were all gorgeous.
10 He went to great lengths to make sure he was totally prepared for the interview.

Unit 7 Recording 1

1 Sharon Osborne has reportedly spent over €180,000 on cosmetic surgery and she says it was worth every penny. Her weight fell from 102 to 54 kilos, after surgeons dramatically reduced the size of her stomach, forcing her to eat much less than before. She then had multiple operations to remove excess flesh from her face, neck, stomach and other areas of her body.
2 Craig Flatman is a teenager known to his friends as 'Jam Boy'. Since early childhood, he has refused to eat any form of meat, fish, fresh fruit or vegetables. Instead, for the last 11 years, he has had five rounds of jam sandwiches a day, plus 1 litre of milk. Doctors are confused, however, as he is over 1.8 metres tall, weighs a healthy 70 kilos and has no fillings in his teeth.
3 Sir Christopher Gent was the boss of the mobile phone empire Vodafone for 17 years. While in the job, his salary increased hugely, rising to a massive £2.9million in his last year. Now, he lives off his Vodafone pension which totals £10.4million – meaning that he can expect an annual pension of around £662,000 for the duration of his retirement.

Unit 7 Recording 3

W=Woman

W: Well, we have a really big meal on Christmas Day in our family. It's lovely but we always end up eating too much and feeling too full! Our traditional Christmas dinner is roast turkey, roast potatoes, carrots, parsnips, gravy and cranberry sauce, followed by Christmas pudding of course. I suppose some people in Britain probably have slightly different things, but that's what we have. I love it! My favourite bit is the roast potatoes ... and there is a particular way of cooking them to make them taste really delicious. First, you peel them and boil them for a short time – about 5 minutes, or 10 minutes maximum. Then you cover them in flour. Then, you put them on a tray in the oven but the important thing is that the oil on the tray is very hot and that you roast them in a very hot oven ...

Unit 7 Recording 4

P=Presenter

P: And now, news of more celebrity items and film memorabilia going under the hammer ... In the last few years, some items have hit the headlines as they have been sold at auctions for absurdly high prices.
You'll probably remember that back in 2001, the white bikini worn by Ursula Andress in the James Bond film Dr No was put up for auction. The actress reportedly decided to sell the two-piece after she discovered it in the attic at her home. Andress is now in her sixties, but she shot to fame when she played the first 'Bond girl' in the first James Bond film in 1962. The bikini was bought for a huge $61,000 by the American, Robert Earl, co-founder of Planet Hollywood.
More recently, one of the six stormtrooper helmets used in the original Star Wars films was sold at an auction in London. It was put up for auction after it was found by chance at a second-hand sale and bought for just $75. The lucky owner ended up getting around $25,000 for it!
Of course, traditional auctions are not the only way to bid for things. Thousands of people now buy and sell things on eBay, the popular Internet auction site. And sometimes the most incredible things go for extraordinary prices! One seller put a piece of chewing gum which had been spat out by pop star Britney Spears up for sale on eBay. The seller said he found the gum on the pavement outside a London hotel when he saw Britney spit it out. The description that went with the gum on the Internet read: It is completely preserved as you can see, with Britney's teeth marks highly visible! This is the chance to own a piece of pop history – right from the mouth of the princess of pop herself!
There is no guarantee that the gum is authentic, but potential buyers can contact the seller direct and then use their own judgement to decide. It may not just be the gum which is fake; the bids may be fake too. During the bidding for Britney's gum, fake bids went up as high as $14,000 although the winning bid for the gum was reportedly closer to $100.
It is not only celebrity items that have been making news on eBay. Three boys in Texas, USA got a shock last Christmas after their father had given them constant warnings about their bad behaviour. He had bought them $700-worth of video console and games for Christmas but when there was no improvement in their behaviour, he decided to auction off their Christmas presents on eBay. The father sold the items for $1,700 and gave the profit to the local church.
So, it seems that almost anything can be bought and sold and that ridiculously high prices will be paid for sometimes completely useless items ...

Unit 7 Recording 5

1 One man bid £5,000 for a small antique chair.
2 Ten CDs for only £50 – that's a bargain!
3 I asked for a discount, but the shop assistant said no.
4 I'd like to buy a motorbike but I can't afford it.
5 This DVD player broke after only a week. I'd like a refund please.
6 I always try and haggle with market traders.
7 The rent on that tiny flat isn't worth it.
8 Don't forget to keep the receipt.

Unit 7 Recording 6

W=Woman R=Recorded message M=Mark

W: Hello. I'd like to speak ...
R: Hello. Welcome to FDS. In order to deal with your call efficiently, please listen to the following options. If you're phoning to arrange a delivery date, press 1. If you're phoning to change or cancel an existing appointment, press 2. If you're phoning about a faulty machine, press 3. If you're ...
W: Hello ...
R: Hello. For all hi-fi, television, DVD and video player faults, press 1. For all kitchen appliances faults, press 2. For all ...
M: Hello, Customer Services. Kitchen appliances. Repairs and replacements. Mark speaking. How may I help you?
W: Oh, hello. I'd like to speak to the manager please.
M: Well, this is Customer Services. Can I be of any assistance? What seems to be the problem?
W: Well, I bought a washing machine from you about three weeks ago and there have been problems with it ever since I first used it.
M: Oh, I'm very sorry about that, madam. Can I take your customer number please?
W: Oh, yes. It's 45002315.
M: ... Thank you ... OK. Alison Bentley, is it?
W: Yes. That's right.
M: So, you've had problems with your washing machine. What sort of problems?
W: Well, it often stops for no reason in the middle of a cycle and then starts again, but it keeps making strange noises. Now it's stopped completely and there's a load of washing stuck inside ... I phoned to make an appointment for one of your engineers to come and look at it yesterday, but your computers were down and I couldn't get through. Now it's really urgent ...
M: We did indeed have technical problems yesterday. I can only apologise for the difficulties you experienced in getting through. Would you like to make an appointment now?
W: Yes, please. I need an engineer urgently – today.
M: Just bear with me and I'll see if we've got any appointments available ... It looks like the earliest appointment we've got is Friday morning between 8 and 1. Shall I book that in for you?
W: Friday morning? That's three days time! What am I supposed to do about the clothes stuck inside the machine? They'll be ruined. Haven't you got anything sooner?

M: ... I'm afraid not. If you had the 3-star Service Plan, you could've got a priority appointment on the same day. But you've got the basic guarantee which says that we'll repair your appliance within a week if we can. And if not, we'll provide a replacement free of any extra charge. Shall I book an appointment for Friday for you?
W: Well ... I suppose I'll have to.
M: ... OK. That's fine. That's all booked for you. An engineer will be with you Friday between 8 and 1. Is there anything else I can help you with?

Recording 7.7

A feathers
B wings
C claws
D beak
E fur
F paws
G tail
H whiskers
I horns
J hooves
K fins

Unit 7 Recording 9

1 I'd forgotten to set the alarm clock that day so I overslept and woke up three hours later than I was supposed to ... Then, I'd seriously underestimated the time it would take me to get there. On the way, it started pouring with rain and I got completely soaked to the skin. In the end, it took me nearly two hours which meant that I was really, really late. When I did finally arrive – wet through – I walked into the interview room and who was sitting there, waiting to interview me, but my ex-boss from my previous job! I felt so awful because I know for a fact that he hates me and I'd made such a fool of myself.
2 A couple of years ago I decided to have a change of career. Having been a Spanish teacher for nearly 20 years, I decided to retrain as a translator and interpreter. It's a really difficult job and I found the training very hard work, but I'm really pleased with myself for having done it. I was brought up bilingual so the language itself wasn't difficult for me, but you have to learn completely different skills. I now work for a huge multinational holiday company specialising in organised trips around South America and I really love it! It's the best job I've ever had.
3 I can't believe the trouble I've had over this jacket I ordered off the Internet. It was unusual because I've ordered stuff from the same company before and never had one single problem. But this time, I ordered a waterproof rain jacket and when it came it was an extra-large even though I'd ordered medium. When I sent it back, the same thing happened. I sent it back about three or four times. So, eventually I phoned the customer services department but the man I spoke to was so rude I couldn't believe it. Throughout the whole conversation, he spoke to me in a sort of bored, monotonous voice and clearly wasn't interested in my problem at all. He didn't even apologise!

Unit 7 Recording 11

Dialogue 1
W=Waitress M=Man C=Woman customer
W: Good evening. Have you got a reservation?
M: Yes, we booked a table for two in the name of Morrison.
W: Madison ... I don't think we've got a booking from ...
M: Er ... no, it's Morrison ...
W: Sorry, Morrison ... ah, yes. If you'd like to follow me ...
M: Thank you ...
W: Can I get you some drinks?
M: Yes, please. A bottle of the house red and some mineral water please.
W: Sorry ... Did you say a bottle or a glass of red?
M: A bottle ... of the house red.
W: Certainly, Sir.
W: Are you ready to order?
M: Yes ... I think so.
W: Madam?
C: I'll have the steak please.
W: How would you like it?
C: Rare please.
W: Rare. Thank you. And for you, Sir?
M: I'll have the grilled tuna, please.
W: Sorry, the tuna's finished ...
M: Oh! Well, I'll have the swordfish then.
W: Mmm ... I'm very sorry but there's no swordfish either.
M: Oh!! Is there any fish on the menu today?
W: Yes, we have the grilled seabass.
M: I'll have that then please. And I'll have new potatoes with it, please.
W: I'm terribly sorry but we've run out of new potatoes but you can have it with rice.
M: Well, OK ... but I'm not very happy about all this ...

Dialogue 2
A=Assistant C=Customer
A: Can I help you?
C: Oh, yes ... I'd like to try these on, please.
A: Yes of course. What size are you?
C: Umm ... well, usually a 38 but sometimes a 39. Perhaps I could try both ...
A: Yes, that's fine. I'll bring both for you. I won't be a minute. Was it black you wanted?
C: Yes.
A: OK fine. Would you like to take a seat over there?
OK. I've got black in size 38, but not in 39. I've brought brown in size 39 for you to try.
C: Thanks. I'll try the 38 first.
A: Oh, they look really nice on you. How do they feel?
C: I really like them but they feel a bit tight actually. I think I'll try the 39s, though I don't like brown.
C: Ah, yes ... these are better ... mmm. The 39s fit much better, but I really don't like the colour. Are you sure you haven't got black in 39?
A: I'll just make sure if you like.
C: Yes, please. I really prefer black.
A: No, I'm sorry ... only brown in 39.
C: Oh! Can you phone your other branch and see if they've got them. I don't like brown ... they don't go with any of my clothes ...
A: Yes, of course ...

Dialogue 3
C=Customer R=Receptionist
C: Good morning. I'd like to book an appointment to have my hair done please.
R: Yes, of course. When would you like to come?
C: Have you got anything for tomorrow morning before 12.00?
R: Umm ... yes, there's 10.30, 11.15 or 11.45?
C: Oh, 10.30 please.
R: Fine, 10.30. That's with Tina. And what would you like to have done? Just a cut and blow-dry?
C: Well, a cut and blow-dry yes ... but I'd also like some highlights done. In fact, I was thinking of having multicoloured highlights this time. Would that be possible?
R: Oooh yes. That sounds fun. There's also a special offer on tomorrow. We're offering all customers an Indian head massage. I'm sure you'll like it. It's very relaxing.
C: Oh, yes please. That would be great.
R: Lovely. We'll see you tomorrow at 10.30.
C: Thank you. Bye.

Unit 8 Recording 2

B=Boss E=Employee
B: So, generally things are going fine. We've talked about your attitude to work, which is very good. Over the three years that you've worked here, you've shown a consistently professional approach to your work.
E: Thank you ... I must say that I've enjoyed it very much. Testing computer games is great fun ... and my colleagues are very helpful and supportive.
B: So, the next part of this appraisal is to think about the future. What do you see yourself doing next?
E: Well, as I say, I've really enjoyed the games testing work that I've been doing, but I feel that it's time I moved on now ... I mean I think I'd like to have a bit more responsibility.
B: Yes, I think we need to think about that. You've shown some good leadership skills and I wonder how you would feel about becoming a team leader. You know, then you'd be supervising a team of games testers and making sure everything gets done properly.
E: Oh, yes ... I'd like to very much ... though I'm not sure that I've got all the necessary skills to be honest. I mean, I'd like the responsibility, but err ... would there be any management training?
B: Yes, of course. We run some excellent in-house courses which I think would give you confidence. There's one coming up next week and then another in 2 months' time. And I think I'd rather you did the first one, so that we don't waste any more time. What do you think?
E: Well, yes. I'd be very interested. It would be great to get some training underway as soon as possible. I mean, I'd rather not wait for two months, if that's OK with you. I'd like to be as prepared as I can.
B: OK. Great. In that case, I'd better get your name on the list for the one next week immediately. I hope it's not full up already. I don't think it will be. Perhaps I'll just check with Jeannie now. Excuse me just one minute ... Oh, hello Jeannie. I just wanted to check if you've still got places on the Management

Skills course for next week ... ah, you have ... great ... Could I put Will Scott's name down please? ... Yes, S-C-O-double T ...

Unit 8 Recording 3

1 I feel that it's time I moved on now.
2 I think I'd rather you did the first course.
3 I'd rather not wait for two months.
4 I'd better get your name on the list immediately.

Unit 8 Recording 5

1 She isn't very strict and she hardly ever gets upset or worried.
2 He's the kind of person who has one aim and works hard to achieve it, doesn't he?
3 She's determined to do what she wants and won't listen to advice from anyone.
4 He uses words in a funny, intelligent and interesting way.
5 She really enjoys meeting and talking to people, doesn't she?
6 He's one of those people who is always honest and doesn't keep secrets from anyone.
7 He has very strong views about a lot of things in a way that annoys a lot of people.
8 She's the kind of person who cares only about herself rather than other people.
9 He's good at making things happen and change. He doesn't just react to events, does he?
10 She's one of those people who is good at secretly controlling or tricking people to get what she wants.

Unit 8 Recording 6

P=Presenter T=Tony Greenwood

P: Today on *Sports Alive* we are looking at success and achievement in sport. Who are the most successful sportspeople in the world and just how do they achieve their success? There is a huge sports psychology industry working with almost all athletes these days. But does it work? Is it all really necessary? We've got sports psychologist, Tony Greenwood here to help us answer these questions. Hello, Tony. Welcome to the programme.
T: Hello ...
P: So, first of all, Tony, let's think about that question. Is sports psychology really necessary? Some people would say that you've either got the determination to succeed or you haven't. What do you think?
T: Well, I suppose that's sometimes true. There are examples of sports people who are extremely successful and have never needed any help with their mental determination. Mohamed Ali was probably the most famous of all. He had complete self-belief that he was the best and absolutely unbeatable.
P: That's right. Nobody needed to remind him to focus on the goal!
T: No ... and there are other examples of sportspeople who seem to be totally committed to their own success: tennis player Bjorn Borg, racing driver Michael Schumacher and basketball player Michael Jordan to name a few. But these people are actually quite rare ... most sportspeople do a lot of work on mental preparation and get a lot of help with staying focussed on winning.
P: OK ... so what do the sports psychologists do? How do you help people to succeed?
T: Well, our basic job is to prepare the mind and we can do this in different ways depending on who we're working with. One of the most important things we do is to help people change negative thoughts into positive ones. I did some work with a footballer recently. He missed a really important goal and started thinking that he couldn't do it anymore. I told him he could do it by thinking about something different, not on missing the goal. After practising thinking about the way the ball was turning instead, his whole game improved dramatically.
P: Kelly Holmes is a good example of that too, isn't she?
T: Yes, that's right. For much of her career, she was constantly getting injured and then worrying that it would happen again. I remember that she admitted feeling totally out of control when she got injured all the time. But the fact is, athletes have to get over that and start to take control mentally. That's exactly what she did – and then of course won two gold medals at the Athens Olympics, which was a fantastic achievement!
P: Yes, she was really brilliant!
T: There are other things we can do to help with mental preparation too. Things like routines to get the players focussed and working as a team can really help.
P: Routines? What do you mean?
T: Well, the New Zealand All Blacks rugby team do their Haka war dance to focus themselves and to try and worry the other team. Then there are people who have their own personal lucky routines. Footballer Andy Cole said he always wanted to be the last player onto the pitch. It might seem a bit silly, but if it works ...

Unit 8 Recording 7

1 Kelly Holmes must be really ecstatic about her success.
Kelly Holmes must be absolutely ecstatic about her success.
2 The sports psychologist who worked with Kelly Holmes must be really ecstatic about her success.
The sports psychologist who worked with Kelly Holmes must be absolutely ecstatic about her success.
3 An extremely big sports centre near here has just opened.
A very big sports centre near where here has just opened.
4 If you want to get to the top in athletics, it's really vital to get yourself a professional trainer.
5 Whenever he plays football, he comes back with really filthy.
Whenever he plays football, he comes back absolutely filthy.
6 She was absolutely exhausted at the end of the race.
7 I love running. I'd be really devastated if I had to give it up.

Unit 8 Recording 8

1 I want to be the last player onto the pitch.
2 I won the race easily.
3 I'm not going to train today.
4 You can do it by thinking about something different.
5 Why are you feeling so negative?
6 Will you help me tomorrow?

Unit 8 Recording 10

Dialogue 1
H=Host J=Julie

H: ... and our next caller is Julie. So, what's on your mind, Julie?
J: ... Well ... guys basically, Chris ...
H: Ahh ... now where have I heard that before?
J: I know, I know ... but it feels like I've tried everything and I'm just not getting anywhere.
H: So ... what exactly do you mean when you say you've 'tried everything'?
J: Well ... I mean ... there was this guy I fancied a couple of months ago ... at work ... We used to have a bit of a laugh and a joke around the office ... and had lunch together a few times. It all seemed to be going pretty well. I'd text him now and then ... but then he seemed to just start avoiding me .
H: What ... like overnight?
J: Well ... I don't know about that ... but it was pretty strange.
H: And nothing had really changed?
J: No ... well ... like I said I had been texting him quite a bit..
H: What kind of things?
J: ... oh nothing much ... silly things ... telling him I thought he was really cute ... you know ...
H: Anything else?
J: Well ... I did send him the odd card ... and a big cake on his birthday ... to the office ...
H: To the office?
J: Yeah ... well ... maybe that was a bit over the top ...

Dialogue 2
H=Host M=Martina

H: So Martina ... apparently you're some kind of sportsperson ... is that right?
M: Yeah, well, I do a lot of long-distance running ... you know marathons and stuff.
H: Oh yeah ... so what exactly were you phoning about?
M: Well, just recently, I had this race ... you know, a really big one, televised and everything and ... well, how can I put it, I, you know, I just couldn't do it.
H: What do you mean ... 'couldn't do it'?
M: Well, it was really hot ... but about half-way, I was losing touch with the leaders and I just had to stop – which is really unusual for me ... and then I just couldn't get going again ... and I just gave up.
H: Wow ... I see ...
M: And since then, I've lost all my confidence ... I'm thinking I may have to give up running altogether ... But really, it's been my life until now.
H: That sounds really difficult. Have you talked to anyone about how you're feeling.
M: Yes, well, I work with a sports psychologist but she's just telling me to ...

Dialogue 3
H=Host T=Tim
H: So what's your issue today Tim?
T: ... my job I suppose ...
H: And what do you suppose about it?
T: Well ... I've been in my company for quite some time now ... and it's just ... well ... I seem to have got a bit stuck I think ...
H: Stuck?
T: Yeah well ... Other people who started around the same time have got promoted and moved up ... and I'm still doing exactly the same job as when I started ...
H: And you feel like you've been doing your current job ok?
T: Umm ... well ... I suppose there have been one or two problems. I mean I didn't really get on with one of my biggest clients ... but that wasn't all my fault as they were really annoying ... but, anyway, they didn't renew their contract with us so I got into a bit of trouble about that ... and then I have been told off a few times about being late ..
H: So, are you late for work often?
T: Yeah, well, I guess so ...
H: Just how often, Tim?
T: Well, maybe a couple of times a week ...
H: What ... every week?
T: Pretty much I suppose ... it's just that I sleep really well ... and I never hear my alarm clock ... I've tried different types but it doesn't seem to make any difference ...

Unit 9 Recording 2

M=Man W=Woman
M: Did I tell you about this really funny lawyer story that a friend of mine sent me on email the other day?
W: No, go on.
M: Well ... the way it goes is that ... there's this lawyer in the USA ... North Carolina or somewhere ... and he buys this box of really rare and very, very expensive cigars ...
W: Ok ...
M: And because they're so expensive he decides to insure them ... against fire amongst other things.
W: Fair enough.
M: Yes ... except that, within a month, having smoked his complete collection of these fantastic cigars and without having made even his first payment for the insurance policy, the lawyer made a claim against the insurance company.
W: What on earth for?
M: Well, in his claim, the lawyer stated that the cigars were lost in a series of small fires.
W: How ridiculous!
M: And unsurprisingly, the insurance company refused to pay for the obvious reason that the man had smoked the cigars in the normal way. But then, the lawyer sued the insurance company ... and won! When he gave his decision, the judge agreed with the insurance company that the claim appeared ridiculous BUT concluded that the lawyer had a policy from the company in which it guaranteed they could be insured against fire, without defining exactly what did or did not count as 'fire'. And so the company would have to pay the claim.
W: No! You're kidding.
M: But that's not all! You see, rather than going through a long and expensive appeal, the insurance company accepted the decision and paid $15,000 to the lawyer for his loss of the valuable cigars in the 'fires'. But now comes the best part!
W: Go on ... I can't wait ...
M: Then ... after cashing the cheque, the lawyer was arrested! The insurance company had him charged with 24 counts of arson! With his own insurance claim and evidence from the previous case being used against him, the lawyer was convicted of deliberately burning his insured property and so – can you believe it? – he was sentenced to 24 months in jail and a $24,000 fine.
W: No! Is that really true?
M: Cross my heart! My friend said he got it from a real newspaper.
W: How amazing.

Unit 9 Recording 3

W=Woman M=Man
W: Did you see these photos in the paper? It says they're of someone who was in the middle of stealing computer equipment from someone's house ...
M: Really? So, how did they manage to do that?
W: I'm not sure, I suppose they must have fixed up some kind of security camera.
M: What ... inside their own house?
W: Yeah. That would be pretty unusual. Do you think the thief realised he was being caught on camera?
M: He can't have done, can he? Otherwise, he'd have taken the camera too!

Unit 9 Recording 5

P=Presenter
P: ... and finally today, a house burglar was given an 11-month prison sentence today after admitting breaking into a local house and stealing thousands of pounds worth of computer equipment.
The householder, Duncan Grisby, who had been burgled on a previous occasion, set up a webcam which would start recording as soon as it detected movement in the room. But the particularly clever thing was that even though the burglar stole the computer and webcam, the images had already been sent via the Internet to a private email address.
The police officer in charge of the case, commented after the trial: After the break-in was discovered, Mr Grisby simply gave us the email address and we were able to watch several minutes of footage and identify the thief who is quite well known to us. When he initially denied breaking in to the property we were simply able to show him the footage. The webcam made our job really easy. It was a pleasure to show him the pictures and see his expression when we interviewed him.

Unit 9 Recording 6

I=Interviewer S.H.=Sherlock Holmes
I: Mr. Sherlock Holmes, I must ask you first ... How is it that you have the same name as Sherlock Holmes, the great detective from London?
S.H: Please, call me Holmes – that's what my friends and family call me – well, you see, my parents were great fans of the original Conan Doyle stories. Both parents, my father, especially, would spend hours reading the adventures to me – even as a child.
I: Really!?
S.H: Yes ... and when I was born, they discussed a number of first names. They wanted to give their son a name that was uncommon – but also that represented something special. They didn't take long to decide on Sherlock Holmes as he was their favourite literary figure – and they knew no one would forget me once they'd heard my name. And boy, were they right!
I: So, how do people in general react when you introduce yourself to them?
S.H: Well, I get all kinds of reactions really – everything from the usual 'Where's Dr Watson' type comments to people just thinking I'm being funny.
I: I can imagine ... And do you mind?
S.H: No, not at all. I never have done. I think, the best reaction was when I was in San Francisco one time. I went into an electronic store to buy a TV. The clerk behind the counter was a young lady about 18 or so. When she saw the name on my credit card she stared at it for about 10 full seconds. She slowly lifted her face to look at me and she said, in all sincerity, I didn't know you were real! Wait 'til I tell my friends I saw the real Sherlock Holmes!
I: No!
S.H: Yes! You could have knocked her over with a feather. The expression on her face was as if she'd seen a ghost. It was very amusing.
I: Given your name, do you feel that you have any special talent or ability to solve mysteries in everyday life?
S.H: Well, I will say that having such a name does mean that people often turn to me if anything unusual happens. For example, if I'm watching TV with a friend or family member and a magician comes on and does some kind of trick – all eyes turn to me to explain how it's done.
I: Really? How funny!
S.H: It's not as if I've even ever been interested in magic! Anyway, about two years ago, an old family friend suddenly disappeared from work with about $7,000. His mother hadn't heard from him for days. Even though we hadn't been in touch for years, she called me after the local police said they couldn't help. To keep her calm, I met her at her son's house, pulled out my torch and magnifying glass, and slowly went through the house looking for clues.
I: And did you actually find any?
S.H: Well, fortunately, he had left some of his email messages un-deleted in his computer system. It seemed to suggest that he'd deliberately taken the money to leave town and live in a warmer climate which was what I

told his mother. In the end, it turned out that he realized he couldn't really start a new life on only $7,000 and he returned to face the justice system. It was hard for him, but I was pleased to have worked out what happened!
I: Just like your namesake ...

Unit 9 Recording 7

P=Presenter

P: Nick Leeson's life started as a classic rags-to-riches story. He was born into a working class family and left school with almost no qualifications. Nonetheless, in the early 1980s, he got a series of clerical jobs with different banks, ending up with Barings, a well-known investment bank, where he did well and received rapid promotion.
Before long, he was making millions for Barings by betting on the future direction of the Japanese stock exchange. His bosses back in London were delighted with his large profits and put more and more trust in him. By the end of 1993, he had made more than £10m – about 10% of the total profit of the bank for that year. However, what the bank didn't know was that Leeson had a special account where he was hiding his losses.
By December '94 the losses hidden in that account totalled $512 million. As the losses grew, Leeson requested extra funds to continue trading, hoping to get himself out of the mess by more deals. In the end, Leeson managed to lose the bank $1.3 billion and effectively destroyed Barings
As the direct result of his actions, he had wiped out the 233 year old Barings investment Bank, who proudly counted the Queen as a client. Investors saw their savings wiped out, and some 1,200 of Leeson's fellow employees lost their jobs.
What became of Leeson? After going on the run, the world's most wanted man, on the cover of every newspaper, checked in on a flight to Europe using his own name and hiding beneath a baseball cap. The German authorities were alerted and the police were there to arrest Leeson as he touched down. In December 1995 a court in Singapore sentenced him to six and a half years. In jail, he is said to have spent a lot of time doing exercise and he also, apparently, found God.
He was released early, in the summer of 1999 and, after his return to the UK, found that he was effectively homeless and without a job. Leeson though, has managed to bounce back and make the most of his experiences. He has made an estimated £50,000 from his book, and the fee for selling his story to the newspapers is reported to be about three times that amount. The story has also been turned into a film called 'Rogue Trader', starring Ewan McGregor.

Unit 10 Recording 1

1 Once I had a premonition that something awful was going to happen to an old school friend of mine, Carola, who'd moved to Australia and I hadn't seen for ages. I somehow knew something was going to happen and then later that day, another friend of mine phoned to say that Carola had had an accident and was in hospital. A few other things like that have happened recently, so nowadays I take my premonitions a bit more seriously than I used to!

2 It was really weird the other day because I was at my brother's 30th birthday party and was talking to some people there ... And then in the middle of the conversation, I suddenly had a really strong feeling of déjà vu. I just felt that the whole thing ... you know, the place, the people, the exact conversation, had all happened before in exactly the same way. It made me feel quite strange for a couple of minutes.

3 More and more in my life, I think I've learned to trust my intuition ... It could be anything really, like deciding which job to apply for, or knowing which road to take if I get lost, or having a feeling that someone's lying to me. I find if I start analysing things and trying to work it out, I get confused. But if I go with my gut feeling, without thinking about things too much, it's funny but I find I'm usually right.

4 My cousins are twins and they have always been incredibly close. Now they are older, they still have an amazing sixth sense about each other. They always seem to know when something happens to the other one, even if they're miles apart. One of them knows if something important has happened to the other one, especially if they're in trouble or hurt in some way.

5 I've only been unconscious once in my life and that was when I was playing football with some friends. We used to play every Sunday and I really enjoyed it, but I often got injured! One day, I was knocked unconscious by someone ... I still don't really know how it happened ... I just remember waking up, lying on the grass looking up at a group of about twenty people all staring down at me, and I hadn't got a clue what was going on!

6 I think that I'm a very single-minded person – I mean, I really drive myself hard to succeed at everything I do ... The other day, I was wondering why I let myself work so hard and get so stressed about things, and I think it's maybe because I have a subconscious fear of failure. I think that deep down, without really being aware of it most of the time, I'm really scared of not succeeding in everything I do. Maybe it's to do with my parents. They always expected me to be the best at school.

Unit 10 Recording 2

Dialogue 1

I=Interviewer W=Woman M=Man

I: How do you feel about Paul McKenna?
W: Well, I reckon he's probably genuine myself. It sounds as if his clients go away satisfied. So even if we don't really understand how he does it, if you ask me, it doesn't really matter. He must be doing something right! Some people want to know how everything works, but I'm in favour of just accepting it if it works for you, and not analysing things too much!

Dialogue 2

I: What are your views on hypnosis? Do you have any strong feelings about it?
M: Yes, I do. I've always believed that people like Paul McKenna are just good showmen. To my mind, it's all rubbish – he's just good at being nice to people, so they're a bit happier at the time. But, I have my doubts about how much he can actually do for people in the long-term. I'm sceptical that hypnosis has any effect at all and I'm against people paying for a service and getting nothing real in return. I mean, I doubt hypnosis actually works for anyone.

Dialogue 3

I: What do you think of hypnosis?
M: From my point of view, I have to say that when I went for a session to a hypnotist, it was fantastic. It saved me my job. I mean, I was able to deal with the stress of my job much better after that and I'm convinced that it was the hypnosis that helped me. In fact, if I hadn't gone to the session, I suspect I would've left my job by now.

Unit 10 Recording 3

I=Interviewer E=Expert

I: Welcome to *Modern World*. On the programme today, we're talking to Jo Carlson about the power of persuasion. All around us, there are images on television, jingles on the radio, adverts in magazines, sound bites on the news, offers in the shops. They're all hard at work – trying to make us believe something or persuading us to buy something. Fear not, however, Jo Carlson is here to reveal their secrets and show us how to resist all this persuasion! Hello, Jo.
E: Hello.
I: First, persuading people is big business, isn't it? I mean, supermarkets and politicians, advertisers and salespeople, they all take it very seriously, don't they?
E: Yes. They spend a lot of money on working out the best psychological tricks to guarantee that even the most cautious among us are open to manipulation.
I: Let's take supermarkets then. How do they make us buy things we don't necessarily want? What are some of their tricks?
E: Well, firstly, they try to relax us by playing music and by pumping the smell of freshly-baked bread into the store. Studies have shown that the smell makes people buy more.
I: I know I've done that without even thinking about it ...

E: Exactly ... most of the time, we are completely unaware of what's happening. It's subconscious persuasion ...
I: And what about 'reward' cards?
E: Ah yes! Well, from the supermarket's point of view, reward cards are a huge success story. As customers, we think we're being rewarded for shopping at that particular supermarket. What's really happening, however, is that the store is basically not only tempting us to shop there again, but also getting vital information about what we're buying.
I: More information to help them work out how to persuade us to buy even more things ...
E: That's right!
E: So, what about the advertising industry? What secrets can you reveal about that? In what ways does it persuade us to buy particular products?
E: Well ... there's so much. And no matter how much we think we know about what the advertisers are doing ... they still tend to win! We still fall for the advert and end up buying the product.
I: Yes ...
E: Basically, there are two types of ads ... those that appeal to the thinking part of our brain and those that appeal to the emotional part.
I: So, for what type of products would they advertise by appealing to the thinking part of our brain?
E: Well, they are mostly used for things which have little emotional appeal, for example, cleaning products. They give us information about the product and try to influence us that way. However, adverts which go for our emotions are usually much more successful. In using emotion, adverts exploit psychoanalytical theories about the subconscious. I mean, they know that images can reach our emotions at a level that we are not aware of and so are much more powerful in persuading us to do things.
I: So, what kinds of emotions are used?
E: Well, adverts for different brands of clothes often want to make us feel that we belong, for example by showing us how to buy the right clothes to fit in with our friends. And adverts for insurance play on our need to feel safe. For example they might show a family happily spending their insurance money buying new things when their house has been burgled. Self-esteem is an important one too. Many ads for luxury products like expensive cars, work on making us feel good about ourselves and the lifestyles that we could have.
I: Celebrities are used a lot too, aren't they?
E: Yes, that's very popular. Celebrities are often used as a quick way of getting the message across. Their success and familiarity makes them feel safe, interesting, cool, ... whatever ... We see our favourite pop star drinking a particular fizzy drink and we're immediately persuaded to buy it!

Unit 10 Recording 5

1 They persuade us to buy things we may not want.
2 We carry on using reward cards at the same supermarket.
3 Adverts for clothes often want to make us feel that we belong.
4 I try to resist buying expensive designer clothes but it's difficult!
5 You could try leaving your credit card at home if you don't want to spend so much.

Unit 10 Recording 7

S=Student
S: I can't believe that spelling is so difficult in English. In Spanish, it's so easy! There are so many exceptions in English that every time I think I've learned a rule, I find a word that breaks it!
But I do think there are some quite nice words in English. I mean, they are hard to spell, but I like the fact that some of them are so strange ... like the g-h-t words, for example ... brought, caught, fight, ... you know ... why do they have g-h-t?
I think the best way to remember how to spell words, is just to repeat them ... I write them down lots of times and I also chant the spelling to myself ... You know, like, for example, brought ... I say ... B – R – O – U – – G – H – T. B – R – – O – U – – G – H – T.
B – R – – O – U – – G – H – T. It's a bit like brainwashing ... or mind control ... in the end, it works!

Mark Foley

UPPER INTERMEDIATE

Book 2

Total English

Workbook (with key)

PEARSON
Longman

Contents

6.1 Explore

Reading

1 **a** Read the newspaper article quickly and choose the best title.

1 Chinese Motorways
2 Speed Tourists
3 Europe's New Destination

(1) For years tourists (1) ______ to Europe to enjoy its many attractions. From the beaches of the Mediterranean to the castles of Scotland, Europe has something for every kind of holidaymaker to enjoy. Now travel agents (2) ______ a new and rather unexpected attraction to the list – the German motorway system. For the last three years travel companies (3) ______ Chinese tourists to Germany to experience the thrill of driving on its 'autobahns'. This year more than 120000 are expected to arrive.

(2) What is it about Germany's autobahns that tempts tourists to travel from halfway across the world? The answer is simple – speed. More than 8000 kilometres of German motorways have no speed limit – something which is virtually unique in the modern world. Few Europeans realise that Germany's superb roads have an almost mythical reputation in Asia, where highways are often overcrowded, poorly maintained and full of potholes.

(3) Tour operators (4) ______ that offering a Mercedes, Audi or BMW capable of 240 kilometres per hour to holidaymakers is the best way of bringing in much-needed foreign exchange.

For the last few years the Chinese economy (5) ______ rapidly and as a result there are plenty of Chinese travellers wealthy enough to afford the €3000 charged for a six-day 'autobahn tour'. The prices they are charging may seem high, but the 'speed tourists' claim that the thrill of driving at speeds which would almost certainly lead to prison sentences back at home far outweighs the expense involved.

(4) But this new form of tourism (6) ______ so popular with the locals. German road safety groups (7) ______ negatively to the arrival of the Chinese speed tourists. Figures published by the World Health Organisation show that more than 600 people die on China's roads every day. Even taking into consideration the huge population of China, this is still a horrifying statistic. But the Chinese drivers are undeterred, pointing out that since they first started coming three years ago there (8) ______ no major accidents involving speed tourists.

b Read the text again. Write the questions for these answers.

1 three years
______
2 120000
______
3 speed
______
4 8000
______
5 Mercedes, Audi or BMW
______
6 240
______
7 €3000
______
8 600
______

c Find these words or phrases in the text.

1 two more nouns that mean *tourists*
______ ______
2 three more nouns that mean *roads*
______ ______ ______
3 another expression that means *travel companies*
______
4 an adverb that means *almost*
______
5 an adjective that means *like something from a story or legend*
______
6 an *-ed* adjective that means the opposite of *put off/discouraged*
______

Grammar | Present Perfect Simple and Continuous

2 Complete the newspaper article in Ex. 1 using Present Perfect Simple or Continuous forms of the verbs in the box. You may need to use negative or passive forms.

add be bring discover expand flock prove react

3 Write responses using the prompts and appropriate forms of the Present Perfect Simple or Continuous. Add any other words that are necessary.

Why are you so red?

I/lie/sun/all morning

I've been lying in the sun all morning.

1 Can we go back to the car now?
no/I/not pay/shopping/yet
______

2 Why are the children soaking wet?
they/swim/the lake
______

3 Have you tried that new French restaurant yet?
no/never/go/there
______

4 Michael looks tanned.
yes/he/just/come back/Miami Beach
______

5 Why aren't you having any pudding?
I/follow/strict diet/for/last two months
______

6 Shall I feed the cats?
no/I/already/do/it
______

7 Is Maria still working on that report?
yes/she/type/lunchtime
______

8 You're a good teacher and you seem very experienced.
yes/teach/karate/more than/ten years
______

9 You look exhausted.
I/wash/the floors/all afternoon
______

10 Do you still go to the tennis club?
no/I/not be/member/2004
______

Vocabulary | adjectives with *-ed*/*-ing* endings

4 Complete the summaries using suitable *-ed* or *-ing* adjectives from the list on page 87 of the Students' Book.

1 **Miranda:** Daniel's behaviour made me very angry.
Miranda feels ______.
Daniel's behaviour was ______.

2 **David:** After listening to her speech, I decided to become a doctor.
Her speech was ______.
David felt ______ by the speech.

3 **Mary:** I thought the exhibition was incredibly interesting.
The exhibition was ______.
Mary was ______ by the exhibition.

4 **José:** That was the scariest film I've ever seen. I've never been so scared!
José was ______ by the film.
The film was ______.

5 **Eloise:** I know the job is quite difficult, but that hasn't put me off doing it.
Eloise doesn't think the job is ______.
She isn't ______ by the job.

Writing

5 You are about to finish a three-month holiday in Kenya. As part of the holiday you have been helping a charity project which teaches English to young children. Complete this email to your friend Sara. Follow this paragraph plan and look at page 162 of the Students' Book to help you.

Paragraph 1
where you are/why you are there/how you feel about it

Paragraph 2
what you do in the morning/in the afternoon/in your free time

Paragraph 3
how you feel about the experience/how feel about finishing and coming home

Hi Sara
I'm having an amazing experience here! I'm

Reading

1 **a** Read the web page quickly and match the headings A–G with the paragraphs 1–5. Two headings are not needed.

A Facilities ☐
B Reservations ☐
C Location ☐
D Lapland ☐
E History ☐
F The Ice Hotel ☐
G Construction ☐

b Read the web page again and decide if the statements are true (T) or false (F).

1 The Ice Hotel isn't the sort of building people expect to find in a northern country. ☐
2 People in Jukkasjärvi don't speak Swedish. ☐
3 It takes two days to build the hotel. ☐
4 The hotel is mainly built of ice. ☐
5 A French artist built the first Ice Hotel. ☐
6 Guests sometimes worry about the cold temperatures. ☐
7 Guests can watch films. ☐
8 Visitors can hunt reindeer in the daytime. ☐

c We often use particular adverb and adjective combinations, e.g. *heavily insulated* (paragraph 1). Find five more examples of this type of collocation in the text.

File Edit View History Bookmark help

Unusual Destinations – number 22

(1) People often choose to have holidays in strange and unusual places. But there can be few places stranger than the Ice Hotel in Sweden, which is visited by almost 37000 people each winter. Built entirely of snow and ice, the hotel is the very opposite of the heavily insulated, centrally heated buildings we normally associate with northern countries. Rather than insulate itself from the cold subzero environment all around it, the hotel embraces the wintry surroundings and makes them into part of its attraction.

(2) The Ice Hotel is situated in the small village of Jukkasjärvi, next to the river Tornealven. Jukkasjärvi lies 200 kilometres north of the Arctic Circle in Saamiland (formerly known as Lapland), the most northerly part of Sweden. Before the arrival of the Ice Hotel there were almost no tourists in this sparsely populated region, where the local people speak Saami, not Swedish, and there is no industry or pollution.

(3) The Ice Hotel is not a permanent building but is rebuilt each winter. Construction of the 5000 square metre building starts in late October when special snow cannons shoot tons of snow onto steel sections. After two days the steel sections are removed leaving solid snow arches five or six metres wide. Over the following weeks the sections are reused to make more arches. Huge ice blocks are carved from the frozen river to make walls and pillars. About 30000 tons of snow and 4000 tons of ice are used to build the hotel.

(4) The story of the Ice Hotel began in the winter of 1989–90. There was an exhibition of ice art in the local village and a cylinder-shaped igloo made of ice was built for an exhibition by French artist Jannot Derid. Some of the visitors decided to sleep on reindeer skins in the igloo and found it a surprisingly relaxing and stimulating environment. Yngve Bergqvist, the owner of the small local inn, realised that others might want to share this unique experience and the concept of the Ice Hotel was born.

(5) Visitors to the Ice Hotel are sometimes nervous about staying in a place where the outside temperature in winter is often minus forty degrees Centigrade. But of course local people have been living in this environment for thousands of years, and conditions inside the Ice Hotel are reasonably comfortable. The temperature is usually around minus four degrees, and guests are provided with specially made sleeping bags and their beds are lined with reindeer skins. To keep visitors amused in the evenings the hotel includes an 'ice cinema' and a well stocked 'ice bar'. During the day the hotel company organises sports activities such as white water rafting, dogsledding and fishing, and there are tours of local villages and 'safaris' to observe reindeer in their natural habitat.

Vocabulary | weather

2 Use the clues to complete the crossword.

Across

1 very hot
5 light rain
6 no clouds
9 rain from time to time
11 not warm or very cold

Down

2 grey sky
3 never the same
4 a light wind
7 adjective from clue 4
8 quite cold
10 move liquid

Grammar | questions

3 Match the questions and answers. Then complete the questions with one word.

1 Have you ______ a holiday this year?
2 Where ______ you go?
3 When ______ you go?
4 ______ did you get there?
5 ______ you go on your own?
6 ______ went with you?
7 How ______ did you go for?
8 What ______ it like?
9 ______ it expensive?
10 ______ you going to go again?

a We flew via Dubai.
b Fantastic!
c Three weeks.
d Yes, probably.
e To Thailand.
f Yes, it was.
g No, I didn't.
h Yes, I have.
i My boyfriend.
j Last January.

4 Put the words in the correct order to make questions.

get when a refund me can you tell I'll
Can you tell me when I'll get a refund?

1 to was who talking she
______________________________?
2 if my do know you this seat is
______________________________?
3 much costs it can tell you me how
______________________________?
4 they car where the did take
______________________________?
5 ask to the open could I you window
______________________________?
6 the how you computer do turn off
______________________________?
7 correct are the answers these
______________________________?
8 been how you here long have working
______________________________?

5 Rewrite the direct questions as indirect questions. Start with the words given.

Where are you from?
Can you *tell me where you are from?*

1 What's your email address?
Can you ______________________________
______________________________?
2 Does Graham Randall live here?
Could I ______________________________
______________________________?
3 Is this the correct platform for the train to Brighton?
Do you ______________________________
______________________________?
4 Which seats in the plane have the most legroom?
I'd like to ______________________________
______________________________.
5 Is the doctor available now?
Can I ______________________________
______________________________?
6 Where exactly does she live?
Can you explain ______________________________
______________________________?
7 How much do the tickets cost?
Do you ______________________________
______________________________?
8 Who is in charge?
Would you tell ______________________________
______________________________?

Listening

1 **a** 6.1 Cover the tapescript. Listen to five people talking to a researcher. Match them to the statements A–E.

A used to live abroad ☐
B has seen TV programmes about emigrants ☐
C definitely isn't interested in living abroad ☐
D is planning to live abroad at some point ☐
E would like to live abroad but hasn't got any definite plans ☐

b Listen again and match these descriptions to the people.

1 is a university student ☐
2 had problems with travel documents ☐
3 is in a hurry ☐
4 is worried about being identified ☐
5 has family responsibilities ☐

c Now read the tapescript. Find words and phrases that mean:

1 thought about *(n)* ____________
2 make someone leave their home *(v)* ____________
3 interested in/fascinated by *(-ed adj + prep)* ____________
4 depressing *(adj)* ____________
5 giving you a feeling you want to do something *(-ing adj)* ____________
6 this is my true feeling/opinion *(phrase)* ____________
7 clearly *(adv)* ____________
8 chances *(n)* ____________

TAPESCRIPT

1

R: Excuse me. Can I ask you some questions about living abroad?
W: Sure.
R: Have you ever considered moving to a foreign country?
W: Not really. I'm quite happy with my life as it is! And I've got four kids, so it would be a bit difficult to uproot them from their schools and things, wouldn't it?

2

R: Hello. I'm doing some research on emigration. Can I talk to you for a minute?
M: OK. If it's quick. I'm a bit late for an appointment.
R: Thanks. Er. Have you ever thought about moving abroad?
M: Yes. I'm quite intrigued by the idea of living somewhere else.
R: Any particular reason?
M: The weather, I suppose. It's so grim here in the winter, isn't it?
R: So you'd prefer somewhere hotter?
M: Probably. But I'm not really sure where ...

3

R: Excuse me. Can I ask you some questions about living in a foreign country?
M: Alright. You don't need my name or anything, do you?
R: No, nothing like that. I'd just like to ask you how you feel about the idea of moving abroad.
M: Oh, yes. I've seen those TV programmes about people moving to Australia. It always looks tempting.
R: Have you ever considered doing it yourself?
M: Myself? I've not really thought about it to be honest.

4

R: Excuse me. Hello. Could I just take a few minutes of your time? I'm doing some research on people emigrating for my college course.
W: Really? I lived in Canada for a year when I was younger.
R: Oh. But obviously you came back ...
W: Well, I had this Canadian boyfriend. But it didn't really work out. And it was really difficult getting the right visas and things ...

5

R: Hi. Would you mind answering a few questions? It'll only take a minute or two.
M: Of course. No problem.
R: Have you ever considered emigrating?
M: I certainly have. I'd love to do it.
R: Why?
M: Well, the job opportunities, really. I'm in the middle of an engineering degree and when I finish I'm going to apply for jobs in the Middle East. There are loads of well-paid engineering posts over there ...

Vocabulary | verb phrases about moving/travelling

2 Match the sentence halves.

1 I've always dreamed about ☐
2 See you later. I'm ☐
3 Make sure you've got your passport and tickets before ☐
4 We hate the cold weather here so we're going ☐
5 Now that I'm eighteen I think it's time ☐
6 She went to Greece and ☐
7 His girlfriend didn't even bother to go to the station ☐
8 We don't have enough bedrooms so we need ☐

a to emigrate.
b to move house.
c off to work.
d to see him off.
e roamed around the beaches.
f setting off.
g living abroad.
h to leave home.

Grammar | comparative & superlative adjectives and adverbs

3 Complete the newspaper article using appropriate comparative or superlative forms of the words in brackets. Add any words that are necessary.

The Ultimate Thrill

With the latest technological developments, new rollercoaster rides

are much (1) ______ (exciting) ever before. But thrill seekers looking for the ultimate rollercoaster ride are now torn between two monster rides on opposite sides of the world. (2) ______ (big) is Steel Dragon 2000 in Nagashima Spaland, a theme park in Japan, about 200 miles west of Tokyo. The ride is over one and a half miles long, lasts four minutes and includes a 68 degree drop. At times riders reach speeds (3) ______ (great) 95 miles per hour. Costing $55 million, the ride is also (4) ______ (expensive) ever built.

Steel Dragon 2000's arch rival is the brand new Kingda Ka ride at Six Flags Great Adventure Park, near Philadelphia, USA. It (5) ______ (not long) as its Japanese competitor, but what it lacks in size it makes up for in speed and height. With riders travelling at up to 128 miles per hour (206 kilometres per hour) it is by far (6) ______ (fast) rollercoaster ride on earth. It is also (7) ______ (tall), with a maximum height of 456 feet (139 metres). But at less than one minute, the ride is much (8) ______ (short) the four-minute experience of Steel Dragon 2000.

4 There is one mistake in each sentence. Find the mistakes and correct them.

1 I think Jeremy's got the most heavy bag.
2 This exercise is bit more difficult than the last one.
3 He was bad hurt in the accident.
4 I'm sorry I arrived so lately; I missed the bus.
5 The Mayback is most expensive car BMW has ever made.
6 They say Seville is always hoter than Madrid.
7 This novel isn't as interesting than his previous one.
8 Mobile phones are quite lot cheaper than they used to be.
9 Antonio lives more far from the school than I do.
10 I'm not as taller as my sister.
11 She speaks Italian very good.
12 That was the most bad DVD I've ever watched.

Pronunciation

5 **a** 6.2 Are the underlined sounds in each sentence the same (S) or different (D)? Listen and check.

1 Life at university is harder than at home, but it isn't as hard as at school. ☐
2 He's isn't as fat as his father. ☐

b 6.3 Mark the underlined sounds in the sentences the same (S) or different (D). Then listen and check.

1 This hat isn't as expensive as that plate. ☐
2 I worked harder than my brother. ☐
3 They're not as certain as they need to be. ☐
4 The fridge was more expensive than the cooker. ☐
5 Is it as expensive as the morning class? ☐

Vocabulary

1 There is one mistake in each sentence. Find the mistakes and correct them.

1 I didn't go with a group; I went as an independence traveller.
2 Experiencing culture shocked can be one of the most difficult parts of living in a foreign country.
3 Do you make itchy feet or are you happy to stay in your home town?
4 My sister has always loved travelling – she was bitten by the journey bug as a teenager.
5 I love the unknown; I adore going through uncharted territory.
6 We never go on organised tours, we prefer to wonder around on our own.

Present Perfect Simple and Continuous

2 Complete the text about Bono using Past Simple, Present Perfect or Present Perfect Continuous forms of the verbs in brackets.

BONO (1) _____ (be) a rock star for the last 25 years. But recently he (2) _____ (become) famous for something completely different – his work for charity. Since 2004 Bono (3) _____ (lead) the fight against poverty in Africa, trying to get more people to understand that continent's terrible problems of famine and disease. For several years now he (4) _____ (appear) regularly on TV shows and at international events, attempting to get the world's media to pay attention to this issue. He (5) _____ (have) meetings with many world leaders and in 2005 he (6) _____ (help) organise the Live8 concerts in London and around the world. Bono lives in Dublin but spends much of his time travelling with his group, U2. Bono believes his position as an international celebrity (7) _____ (give) him a unique opportunity to influence young people. He (8) _____ (visit) Africa several times and these experiences (9) _____ (clearly influence) his political views. In 2003 Bono (10) _____ (meet) Nelson Mandela in Cape Town and in July 2005 he (11) _____ (speak) to world leaders at the G8 Conference in Scotland, helping to influence their decisions on reducing Africa's debt. Critics sometimes say that Bono (12) _____ (only do) this for the last few years to compensate for his group's declining popularity. But with their latest CD high in the charts, this can hardly be the case.

Vocabulary

3 Use the clues to complete the crossword.

Across

3 It's a ___ story, full of twists and turns that keep you hooked.
4 I can't stand cabbage soup, I think it's ___.
7 Babies are often ___ by brightly coloured objects.
8 That new horror film was absolutely ___.
9 It's very ___ when people push in front of you at the supermarket check-out.
10 A lot of people would feel ___ by running a marathon but I take it in my stride.

Down

1 I'm a bit ___ about Miriam. Is there something wrong with her?
2 She found the task ___ but she managed to achieve it in the end.
5 You shouldn't have told the children that scary story, they were ___.
6 Picasso was ___ by African tribal art.

4 Match the words 1–8 with their opposites a–h.

1 humid	a grey
2 clear	b settled
3 bright	c warm
4 drizzle	d calm
5 cool	e dry
6 chilly	f pour
7 breezy	g scorching
8 changeable	h overcast

Questions

5 There are eight incorrect questions in this dialogue. Find the mistakes and correct them.

Woman: I'm doing some market research. Could I ask you some questions?
Man: Sure.
Woman: Where went you for your holidays?
Man: We went to Florida.
Woman: Who did go on holiday with you?
Man: My girlfriend.
Woman: Can I ask what is her name?
Man: Of course. Her name's Lucy.
Woman: Could you tell me what does she for a living?
Man: Yes. She's a hotel receptionist.
Woman: Do you know how old she is?
Man: She's twenty-one.
Woman: Can you tell me is she British?
Man: No. She's Australian.
Woman: How long she has lived here?
Man: About six months.
Woman: I'd like to know where did you meet her.
Man: We met at a party.
Woman: Why did you go to Florida?
Man: Well, we wanted to see Miami and Key West.
Woman: Would you tell me how long did you stay in Florida?
Man: We stayed there for three weeks.

Vocabulary

6 Choose the correct alternative.

1 The neighbours were very noisy so I had to *move/change* house.
2 When I left for university my parents came to the station to see me *out/off*.
3 Their daughter lives *abroad/outside* so they don't see her very often.
4 Over a million Scots *migrated/emigrated* to the USA in the 19th century.
5 The police found a small child roaming *round/around* in the streets.
6 You must be very excited about your trip. When do you *go/set* off?
7 When I was sixteen I left *home/house* to join the army.
8 I can't talk now; I'm *off/out* to meet my brother from the bus station.
9 Are you going *over/away* for the bank holiday or are you staying here?
10 She *walked/set* out after they had a terrible argument.

Comparative & superlative adjectives and adverbs

7 Tick (✓) the phrases which can be used to fill the gaps and put a cross (✗) by those that cannot. Sometimes more than one is possible.

1 I don't think Barcelona is ___ Malaga.
A as sunny as ☐ B sunnyer than ☐
C sunnier than ☐
2 My new mobile is ___ my old one.
A more good than ☐ B a lot better than ☐
C many better than ☐
3 Bill Gates is ___ in America.
A the richest man ☐
B the man richest ☐
C the most rich man ☐
4 This model is ___ in the shop.
A the less expensive ☐
B the most less expensive ☐
C the least expensive ☐
5 Los Angeles is usually ___ San Francisco.
A not as hot as ☐ B hoter than ☐
C hotter than ☐
6 Ella arrived ___ the others.
A a bit later than ☐ B much later than ☐
C just as late as ☐
7 Did you drive ___ we did?
A more far than ☐ B as far as ☐
C further than ☐
8 He takes life ___ most people his age.
A more serious than ☐
B more seriously than ☐
C just as serious as ☐

Vocabulary

8 Complete the sentences with expressions with *go*.

1 Which car did you decide to go ______ in the end?
2 I'd love to ______ a go at ice-skating; I've never tried it before.
3 Do you think Johan will be able to ______ a go of the new business?
4 Of course we'll pay – that goes ______ saying.
5 Trust me; I never go ______ on a promise.
6 I hope you like this CD. I went to great ______ to find it for you.
7 What's going ______ in the Big Brother house?
8 Kieran's always on ______ go – she never seems to stand still!

7.1 Excess

Listening

1 **a** 7.1 Cover the tapescript. Listen to the conversation and answer the questions.

1 How many speakers are there?
2 What are they trying to decide?
3 What do they decide to do in the end?

b Listen again and tick (✓) the correct column.

	Tom	Ben	Alice
1 fancies eating a burger	☐	☐	☐
2 likes fried chicken	☐	☐	☐
3 suggests going to a pizza place	☐	☐	☐
4 loves pizza	☐	☐	☐
5 is supposed to be on a diet	☐	☐	☐
6 thinks burgers aren't as fattening as pizzas	☐	☐	☐
7 doesn't like vegetarian burgers	☐	☐	☐
8 loves king prawns	☐	☐	☐

c Now look at the tapescript. Find the following adjectives and phrases and write them in the correct column.

greasy to be sick of something starving
delicious not too keen on disgusting
yummy tasteless ravenous
I could eat a horse scrumptious

Feeling very hungry	Positive opinion	Negative opinion

TAPESCRIPT

Tom: I haven't eaten since lunch time and I'm starving. Do either of you feel like popping out for a take-away?
Ben: Great idea, Tom. I'm ravenous.
Alice: Me too. I could eat a horse! Could you get something for me as well?
Tom: What do you fancy?
Alice: Um. I'm not sure. A burger, I suppose.
Tom: OK. What about you, Ben?
Ben: I'm not too keen on burgers, really. How about fried chicken or something?
Alice: Oh, that's disgusting, so greasy.
Tom: Actually, I was thinking of pizza for myself. There's that new pizza place near the station. It's called Pizza Delight, or something like that. Does that appeal to either of you?
Alice: Yummy. I love pizza.
Ben: Yuk. I'm sick of pizzas. I've had them twice this week already.
Tom: I thought you were on a diet, Ben.
Alice: Yeah. He's on the pizza diet!
Ben: Very funny, Alice. And I suppose burgers are super healthy, are they?
Alice: Well I'm sure they're not as fattening as pizzas. Anyway, I was going to have a vegetarian burger.
Ben: A vegetarian burger? They're completely tasteless. Like eating cardboard!
Tom: Look. There's no point arguing. We need to agree on something.
Ben: What about kebabs?
Tom: Oh no. I had one of those a couple of days ago and it gave me a bit of a stomach-ache.
Alice: I know. What about Chinese?
Ben: Good idea. There's a Chinese take-away in Arnold Street. It's just around the corner from the supermarket. They do that delicious Peking Duck ...
Tom: Yes. And they've got those scrumptious king prawns. Great. Chinese it is!

Grammar | countable and uncountable nouns

2 Choose the correct words to complete the text.

Riverside Technical College
Student Facilities

Here are just (1) ___ the facilities we provide for our students. We hope you'll agree we have something to offer everyone!

Computer and Internet Centre
You're always connected at Riverside! We have (2) ___ computers available, all with free access to the Internet. There are (3) ___ printers too – so you can print out your essays with ease. And if you need (4) ___ advice, we have two full-time computer technicians available.

Student Café and Bar
(5) ___ students enjoy taking their lunch here. We have a range of delicious snacks, including healthy salads and sandwiches. We're open until midnight, so why not invite (6) ___ friends and spend the evening with us? Or just pop in for (7) ___ coffee and a slice of our homemade cake.

College Sports Centre
Why not improve your health with (8) ___ exercise? Riverside has an extensive range of sports facilities. We have state of the art exercise machines in our gym and a fabulous heated swimming pool. In fact, some of our students spend (9) ___ their free time here. There are (10) ___ colleges in the country which can rival our sports provision, and it's all free for students!

1 A few B some C a few of
2 A much B many C any
3 A lots of B any C much
4 A an B many C some
5 A Few B A lot of C Much
6 A a few B a little C few
7 A a B a piece of C little
8 A many B little C a little
9 A a great deal of B many C a lot
10 A a few B little C few

3 Decide if the sentences in each pair are correct (✓) or incorrect (✗). Sometimes both sentences are correct.

1 A I eat two eggs every morning. ☐
  B She got egg all down the front of her dress. ☐
2 A He bought me some chocolates for my birthday. ☐
  B She's diabetic so she can't eat chocolate. ☐
3 A I need some legal advice. ☐
  B The doctor gave her three advices. ☐
4 A My new car has excellent equipments. ☐
  B Will you bring the camping equipment? ☐
5 A Pedro's knowledge of computers is impressive. ☐
  B Knowledge are very important in the modern world. ☐
6 A I often feel nostalgic for the old times. ☐
  B There never seems to be enough time. ☐

Vocabulary | food and cooking

4 **a** Combine words from box A with words from box B to make ten expressions.

A	B
an electric grilled grated a wooden a talented a complicated scrambled a china sour a frying	milk eggs cook cheese recipe pan cooker sausages plate spoon

b Complete the sentences using expressions from Ex. 4a.

1 I love putting ______ on top of pasta.
2 We don't have gas in our area so we had to buy ______ for the kitchen.
3 We're having a barbeque with ______ and burgers.
4 Would you prefer toast or ______ for breakfast tomorrow?
5 Edwina's husband is ______.
6 The smell of ______ is revolting.

Reading

1 **a** Read the text quickly and choose the best title.

1 Impressionist Paintings at Sotheby's
2 The Story of Sotheby's
3 Britain's Greatest Auction House

b Read the text again and match the information 1–8 with the information a–h.

1 Sotheby's ☐
2 Samuel Baker ☐
3 James Christie ☐
4 the auction of Talleyrand's library ☐
5 Peter Wilson ☐
6 the first public auction of impressionist masterpieces ☐
7 Parke-Bernet ☐
8 Alfred Taubman ☐

a John Sotheby's rival
b 1958
c chairman of Sotheby's
d the most famous auction house
e an American businessman
f John Sotheby's uncle
g 1793
h a New York auction house

c Find words or phrases in the text that mean:

1 worth a lot of money (*adj*) ______
2 state an opinion that others might disagree with (*v*) ______
3 competitor (*n*) ______
4 copy someone's example (*phrase*) ______
5 effect/impression/influence (*n*) ______
6 best/highest quality examples of works of art (*n*) ______
7 time when the economy is bad (*n*) ______
8 completely (*adj*) ______

(1) There is little doubt that Sotheby's is the oldest and most famous auction house in the world. It has been going for more than two and a half centuries and has sold many of the most famous and valuable treasures and works of art ever created. Its rivals might disagree but many would argue that the international art market as it exists today (1) ______ (create) by Sotheby's. The idea of enormously valuable works of art being sold at public auction is something we take for granted, but in fact it is a relatively new phenomenon. So how did it all come about?

(2) It all began back in 1744 when a book dealer called Samuel Baker opened a small book store in the Strand in London. After his death in 1778 the business (2) ______ (take over) by his nephew, John Sotheby. Sotheby had a great rival, James Christie, who (3) ______ (start) the Christie's auction house in 1776. Buying and selling things at auction was made fashionable by James Christie but John Sotheby was quick to follow his lead. In 1793 he

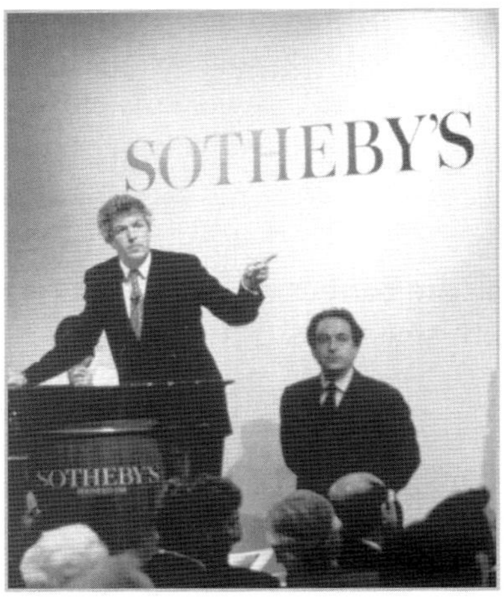

auctioned Talleyrand's library and in 1823 he (4) ______ (score) a public relations triumph by auctioning Napoleon's collection of books from St Helena.

(3) Sotheby's business grew throughout the 19th century but it was only in the middle of the 20th century that Sotheby's began to make a huge impact internationally. In 1958 its charismatic chairman, Peter Wilson, (5) ______ (organise) the first ever public auction of impressionist masterpieces by Cezanne, Renoir and Van Gogh. Before that time extremely valuable works such as these (6) ______ (sell) privately or through dealers. Wilson turned the whole auction into a fashionable event. He sent invitations to film stars and politicians and held the auction in the evening. Journalists from the leading papers (7) ______ (invite) and everyone was asked to wear black tie or evening dress. Not surprisingly, the auction got a huge amount of publicity and the prices set new records.

(4) With its growing reputation in London Sotheby's decided to expand into the American market and bought the New York auction house Parke-Bernet. But things began to go wrong during the oil crisis and the recession of the 1970s and the company started to get into financial difficulties. In 1971 they even tried to raise money by launching a Sotheby's brand of cigarette. Eventually, in 1983 Sotheby's (8) ______ (buy) by American businessman, Alfred Taubman. Based in Detroit, Taubman transformed Sotheby's into a wholly American company. It was certainly a long way from the little bookshop in the Strand.

Vocabulary | verb phrases about money

2 One word in each sentence is incorrect. Find the word and correct it.

1 It's a good idea to keep the refund when you buy expensive things.
2 If we buy ten of these, can we get a bargain of 10%?
3 Auctions are fun but I do get nervous when people start haggling for something I want.
4 I want to buy a new computer but I can't worth it yet.
5 I love buying things in street markets – it's great fun bidding with the market traders.
6 They're moving house next year so they're not sure if it's afford buying a new sofa.

Grammar | passives

3 Complete the text in Ex. 1 using appropriate active or passive forms of the verbs in brackets.

4 Rewrite the sentences in *italics* in the text using only passive forms.

Money Factsheet 8

(1) ***How does the Mint make coins?***

Long sheets of metal arrive at the mint.
(2) *Somebody feeds the metal strips into a cutting machine.*
(3) *The cutting machine cuts the metal into round shapes called 'blanks'.*
(4) *After the machine has cut them out somebody heats the blanks in a furnace.*
(5) *Somebody washes the blanks while somebody is heating them.*
The hot blanks go into a pressing machine and (6) *the machine stamps each coin with a pattern on both sides.*
(7) *Somebody cools the coins and a special machine counts them.*
(8) *Somebody distributes the coins to the banks.*

1 *How are coins made?*
2 ______
3 ______
4 ______
5 ______
6 ______
7 ______
8 ______

5 Rewrite each sentence beginning with the words given.

Peter published the report last year.
The report *was published last year.*

1 The doctor has given Alison a new prescription.
Alison ______.
2 You mustn't open the present until your birthday.
The present ______.
3 The police are investigating the crime.
The crime ______.
4 They are going to open the hotel in November.
The hotel ______.
5 We will drive the children to the party.
The children ______.
6 You can see my house from the top of the hill.
My house ______.
7 Somebody was watching them.
They ______.
8 They haven't released that DVD yet.
That DVD ______.
9 Somebody might have seen the burglar.
The burglar ______.
10 They didn't take anything.
Nothing ______.

Writing / How to ... | write a letter of complaint

6 Rewrite this informal letter as a formal letter of complaint. Look at page 163 of the Students' Book to help you.

Dear James O'Brien

I'm writing to tell you about a mobile phone I bought in your shop the other day.

When I got home it didn't work. I was really shocked because it cost €250!

Please send me another phone or give me a refund immediately.

I'd love to get a reply soon.

Love from
Mandy Smith

Listening

1 a 7.2 Cover the tapescript. Listen to five people talking about animals. Match each person with an animal from the box. Three animals are not needed.

snake cats spider tropical fish
mouse horse goldfish dog

1 ______ 3 ______ 5 ______
2 ______ 4 ______

b Listen again and match the statements with the animals 1–5 in Ex. 1a.

1 is always hungry ______
2 lives in a big field ______
3 need a lot of care and attention ______
4 loves going for walks ______
5 doesn't jump any more ______
6 provide companionship ______
7 moves very slowly ______
8 costs a lot of money to maintain ______

c Now look at the tapescript. Find the words in the box and put them in the correct columns. There are three words in each column.

dart crawl tank sinuous gentle
kennel trot playful stable

Ways animals move (verbs)	Places animals live (nouns)	Animal characteristics (adjectives)

TAPESCRIPT

1
Well, I'm not sure you'd call them pets, really. I mean you don't have to take them to the vet, or for walks, obviously. But they do require quite a lot of care and attention. I seem to spend ages cleaning out the pond and repairing the water filters. It's a nightmare in autumn with all the fallen leaves. And in winter you have to make sure the surface doesn't get covered in ice. But they do give me a lot of pleasure, watching them darting around.

2
We've had him for about four years now. He's got a kennel in the back garden. His name's Wolfie. David bought him for the children, really. Everyone knows retrievers are great with kids – so gentle and playful. He's got beautiful blond fur and he loves being cuddled. Of course, he adores being taken for walks – which is a great excuse for us to get some exercise as well! The only downside is the amount of food he eats. And whatever we give him, he always seems to be starving.

3
Some people think keeping a reptile is a bit weird, but you'd be surprised at how popular it is. I know loads of people that do it. I got Sarah from a friend and I wasn't too sure about it at first. It's a bit of a fuss because you have to have a big tank and keep it at a certain temperature. And when she sheds her skin it's a bit disgusting. But I think she's beautiful – the way she moves is so slow and sinuous. I love letting her crawl up my arms and around my neck.

4
When I was younger I used to take her out jumping and things, but I hurt my back a few years ago so now we just go for walks. Or a bit of a gentle trot if I'm feeling energetic! We've got a big field behind the house so she's got plenty of room, and there's a small stable for the winter months. Big animals are always quite expensive to look after, but I think it's worth it. I mean I get plenty of exercise, and I feel we have a really strong bond. I certainly wouldn't let anyone else ride her.

5
I never had any children, but I think in some ways they're better than children. A lot less trouble! I've got two at the moment, Tiddles and Spark. Tiddles is just a kitten, really. Now that I'm retired I don't really get out much so they're ideal for me, and they're much easier to look after than dogs. They're pretty independent but they give me a lot of companionship. I talk to them all the time, which is a bit stupid I know, but at least I don't get lonely.

Grammar | *have/get something done*

2 Complete the picture labels using forms of *have/get something done*. Use verbs from box A and words/phrases from box B.

A	B
check paint do test service wash	car blood pressure house boiler hair eyes

1 Mrs Alderson ____________ every month.
2 Daniel ____________ once a week.
3 The Smiths ____________ every five years.
4 Liz ____________ once every six months.
5 Mr Grant ____________ when he goes to the clinic.
6 We ____________ before the beginning of winter.

3 Rewrite the sentences using the words in brackets.

He needs to finish that project soon. (done)

He needs to get that project done soon.

1 Somebody left the bag behind. (got)

____

2 The maid washes Linda's clothes. (has)

____

3 They forward my post to me. (I)

____

4 Will somebody cut your hair this week? (get)

____

5 How often do they clean your windows? (you)

____

6 I should finish my homework by six o'clock. (done)

____

Vocabulary | animals

4 Use the clues to complete the crossword with animal words.

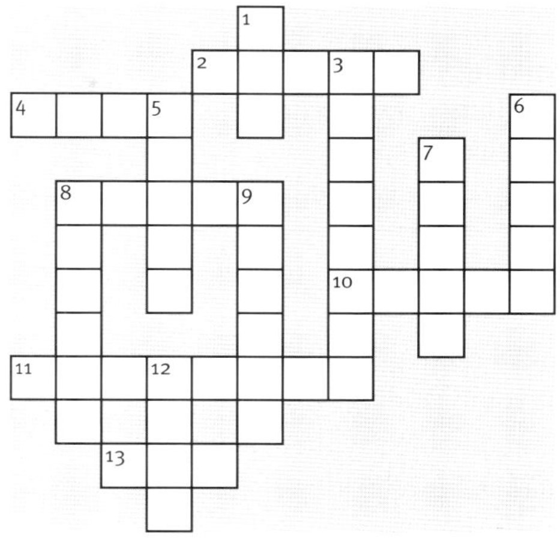

Across

2 they can be very sharp
4 it lives in the sea
8 to take the bull by the ___
10 symbol of the USA
11 they keep birds warm
13 if you see this above the water it could be a shark

Down

1 planes and birds do this
3 cats have very long ones
5 straight from the ___'s mouth
6 the biggest animal
7 birds couldn't fly without them
8 toenails for a horse
9 lots of people are afraid of this insect
12 it's at the back of a horse or dog

Pronunciation

5 7.3 Look at the underlined sounds in each group of words. Circle the odd one out. Then listen and check.

1 horns claws cow
2 feathers beak bear
3 wings fins tiger
4 eagle whale tail
5 horse fur paw

Vocabulary

1 Complete the sentences using words from the box. Two words are not needed.

spending	excessive
extra-large	far-fetched
overpriced	spoilt
luxury	extravagant

1 My car isn't a ______; it's a necessity.
2 You're renting a five-star hotel for your wedding? How ______!
3 Some people say there is life on Mars but the idea seems ______ to me.
4 After we moved we went on a ______ spree and bought lots of new furniture.
5 Don't buy anything from that shop – all their goods are very ______.
6 I think it's greedy to order ______ portions in restaurants.

Countable and uncountable nouns

2 Eight of the sentences contain mistakes. Find the mistakes and correct them.

1 Our shop stocks luggages from all over the world.
2 There are few places as beautiful as Kashmir.
3 There isn't many traffic around here on Sundays.
4 May I have little sugar in my coffee, please?
5 I'd like to have a lots of money.
6 They're not very busy, they only have a few work this week.
7 They don't have much money but they're happy.
8 Would you like a spaghetti, or do you prefer rice?
9 You can invite few of your friends to the party if you like.
10 The college offers much courses on foreign languages.

Vocabulary

3 Use the clues to complete the crossword.

Across

4 Heat the milk in a small ___.
5 You have to ___ the mixture quickly until it becomes stiff.
7 I don't eat meat. I'm a ___.
8 Don't cook my steak for very long, I like it ___.
12 The soup isn't ___ enough, add a little more.
13 This vegetable contains a lot of vitamins.
14 It's a fruit which we often serve with cream.
15 I don't put sugar in tea or coffee – I hate ___ drinks.

Down

1 They say ___ are very good for you.
2 You haven't cooked this, it's completely ___.
3 Coffee without sugar has this taste.
6 Do you prefer to ___ eggs or fry them?
9 This tastes delicious. Could you give me the ___?
10 I like to ___ a little parmesan cheese on top of my pasta.
11 Would you like a ___ of cake?

4 Complete the sentences using words from the box.

afford	bargain	bidding	discount
haggling	worth	receipt	refund

1 I only paid €10 for this DVD – I got a ______!
2 I'd love to get a new car but I'm not sure I can ______ it.
3 We love visiting the local markets and ______ for things.
4 I'm afraid you cannot return the goods if you do not have a ______.
5 Don't interrupt him; he's ______ for something on an Internet auction site.
6 We are offering a 20% ______ to any customers who buy more than five CDs.
7 It's a really expensive trip but we think it's ______ it.
8 Due to the cancellation of tonight's performance we are offering a full ______ to all ticket holders.

Passives

5 You have just booked a holiday on the Internet. Read the web page and complete the sentences below. Use appropriate passive forms.

> ***Thank you*** **for making a booking with** GoAway Travel
>
> Your booking reference is HJ980L
>
> We have debited €450 from your credit card. For your security we use 128 KB protection software for all credit card payments.
> We are sending your itinerary by email. We will send your flight tickets by first class post.
> Please note the following:
>
> - You must bring your passport to check-in one hour before departure.
> - You cannot change the date and time of your flights.
> - You can pre-book seats on the website.
> - GoAway Travel does not allow smoking on any of its flights.
> - You may purchase meals on the plane.
> - The price includes transfers from the airport.
>
> Please see our FAQs if you have any further queries.

1 €450 ______________________________.

2 128 KB protection software ______________________________.

3 Your itinerary ______________________________.

4 Your tickets ______________________________.

5 Your passport ______________________________.

6 The date and time of your flights ______________________________.

7 Seats ______________________________.

8 Smoking ______________________________.

9 Meals ______________________________.

10 Transfers from the airport ______________________________.

have/get something done

6 Complete each sentence with one word.

1 I ______ the central heating checked last month so it should be fine now.
2 She never received her new credit card – it must have ______ lost in the post.
3 I'm sorry about spilling wine on your jacket. I'll have it ______ for you.
4 Tell the boss that Jamie will ______ the report finished by four o'clock.
5 Have you got the broken chair ______?
6 He ______ arrested by the local police.
7 Do you ______ your photocopying done locally?
8 I like to have my hair ______ by Silvia. She's the best stylist in the salon.
9 I'm going to get my photo ______; I need it for the job application.
10 It blocks the light so we are ______ that big tree removed.

Vocabulary

7 **a** Circle the incorrect word in each group.

1 A bull has: horns hooves fin tail
2 A cat has: whiskers beak paws claws
3 An eagle has: wings paws feathers beak
4 A bear has: fur paws hooves claws

b Complete the sentences.

1 She was in such a bad mood she was like a ______ with a ______ head.
2 Don't ask grandma to read the instructions; she's as ______ as a ______.

8 Choose the correct alternative.

1 It doesn't take long to prepare, just *rewarm/reheat* it in the microwave.
2 He's got a fantastic job with a huge *multinational/manynational* company.
3 Can I have the *ex-large/extra-large* burger, please?
4 We thought the seats on the plane were very *uncomfortable/incomfortable*.
5 Sue's *bilanguaged/bilingual*; she speaks English and German equally well.
6 The children get very badly behaved when they're *extra-tired/overtired*.
7 Have you seen your *ex-boyfriend/exboyfriend* recently?
8 The film was *monotonous/monologue* and quite boring.
9 That chicken was *less-cooked/undercooked* – it was pink in the middle.
10 I've just bought a *multipurpose/monopurpose* printer. It can print, scan and photocopy.

8.1 Success

Reading

1 **a** Read the text quickly and choose the best heading for each paragraph. Two headings are not needed.

A The Fight for Freedom
B Independence
C Studying in London
D Introduction
E Gandhi's Legacy
F Gandhi's Early Life
G Life in Prison
H Philosophy

b Read the text again and decide if these statements are true (T) or false (F).

1 Gandhi was president of India. ☐
2 Gandhi worked in South Africa. ☐
3 South Africa used to be part of the British empire. ☐
4 Local people were sometimes treaded badly in the colonies. ☐
5 The British were never able to put Gandhi in prison. ☐
6 Some elements of Satyagraha come from Hinduism. ☐
7 Gandhi wanted India to be mainly Hindu. ☐
8 A religious extremist killed Gandhi. ☐

c Write brief notes to complete this time-line of Gandhi's life.

1869	*born in Porbandar,*
1893	
1915	
1947	
1948	

Leading by Example

① ______
Gandhi is one of history's great leaders. But unlike other leaders he never led an army, he was never a president or prime minister and he never used force or violence to impose his leadership on people. His principle of leadership was simple – he led by example. He believed that the best way to influence events was through peaceful protest rather than by violent revolution or bloodshed.

② ______
Mohandas Karamchand Gandhi was born on 2nd October 1869 in Porbandar in western India. He was sent to England to study law and was offered a job in South Africa after he qualified in 1893. At that time both India and South Africa were colonies of Britain. Working as a lawyer, Gandhi soon began to experience the prejudice that local people suffered under the colonial regime.

③ ______
Gandhi returned to India in 1915, determined to fight against colonialism and injustice. He realised that Indians would never be able to build a fair society until they had independence from the British empire. He joined the Indian nationalist movement and began to fight for Indian independence. The British regarded Gandhi as a troublemaker and he was arrested many times. Rather than resist, Gandhi was quite prepared to be sent to prison for his beliefs. Altogether he spent more than seven years behind bars.

④ ______
Most independence movements in history have depended on violence and revolution to achieve their aims. Gandhi was sure that the same effect could be achieved through non-violent protest and a policy of civil disobedience. He developed a philosophy known as 'Satyagraha' which was partly based on the teachings of Hinduism. According to Satyagraha the best way to change society was through peaceful means. Through his own behaviour Gandhi provided an example of this philosophy in action.

⑤ ______
After more than thirty years of struggle India eventually achieved independence in 1947. Gandhi's policy of peaceful protests, strikes, trade boycotts and civil disobedience had worked. Gandhi wanted India to be a single country which included all races and religions but his wish was not granted. The Indian sub-continent was split into two states – the mainly Hindu India and the largely Muslim Pakistan.

⑥ ______
Gandhi's belief in religious freedom was to cost him his life. On 30th January 1948 he was assassinated by a young Hindu fanatic, Nathuram Godse. But his legacy was to last long after his death. Gandhi's philosophy of peaceful protest and civil disobedience has been an inspiration to numerous people around the world. By his own actions he showed that the best leaders are those who lead by example rather than by force.

Grammar | *It's time/I'd rather/I'd better*

2 Tick (✓) the sentence which has the same meaning as the sentence in *italics*.

1 *It's time you went to bed.*
 A You should be in bed by now. ☐
 B You are already in bed. ☐
2 *I'd rather take the bus.*
 A There is no other way to get there. ☐
 B I prefer buses to trains. ☐
3 *We'd better take the earlier flight.*
 A We prefer early flights. ☐
 B The later flight might not arrive in time. ☐
4 *Would you rather I replied by email?*
 A I prefer to send emails. ☐
 B Do you want me to send an email? ☐
5 *It's high time you looked for a job.*
 A You've been looking but you haven't found the perfect job yet. ☐
 B You are unemployed. ☐
6 *I'd rather she didn't come.*
 A I don't want her to come. ☐
 B She doesn't want to come. ☐
7 *You'd better take the car.*
 A There's a bus strike today. ☐
 B You prefer driving. ☐
8 *It's about time we left.*
 A It's quite late. ☐
 B We left on time. ☐

3 Rewrite the sentences using the words in brackets.

1 I really think you should move to a bigger flat. (high)
____
2 You should take an umbrella. (better)
____
3 I prefer going the cinema. (rather)
____
4 John needs to get a better computer. (about)
____
5 Do you want me to bring my camera? (would)
____
6 I would prefer her not to smoke. (didn't)
____
7 I don't like working at the weekend. (rather)
____
8 I think it's safer if you have the salad. (you'd)
____

Vocabulary | describing personality

4 Use the clues to complete the crossword with words to describe personality.

Across

1 Carol's really high ___; she needs expensive presents all the time!
5 I've got strong ideas about everything; I suppose I'm pretty ___.
6 He doesn't have any secrets. He's very ___ and honest.
10 Actors love an audience because they like to be the centre of ___.
11 Dorinda's ___; she likes meeting new people and she talks to everybody.
12 We always laugh when Jake tells a story because he's so ___.
13 My boss is very single-___; he never gets distracted.

Down

1 My girlfriend tricks people into doing what she wants; she's very ___.
2 Lizzie never makes a fuss or complains; she's very ___-going.
3 ___ people always do what they want and refuse to listen to advice.
4 To succeed in business you need to be ___-to-earth and realistic.
7 I wish I could be more ___ but I tend to let other people take the lead.
8 Juanita goes out to clubs every night, she's a real ___ animal.
9 You shouldn't be a ___; try to be more assertive and independent.

8.2

Listening

1 **a** 8.1 Cover the tapescript. Listen to Amanda and Steven and answer the questions.

1 Where are they?
2 What is Amanda's job?
3 What are Steven's aims?

b Listen again and complete each statement with one word.

1 Steven has been training for ______ weeks.
2 He hasn't done any real exercise for ______ years.
3 Steven thinks three months is an ______ long time.
4 He is ______ eating desserts.
5 He ______ hungry all the time.
6 Amanda asks Steven about his ______ levels.
7 Steven used to feel ______ in the afternoons.
8 Amanda hasn't prepared the ______ sheet for Steven yet.

c Now read the tapescript. Match the phrases in *italics* with the reporting verbs in the box.

ask	admit	complain	promise	remind	explain	suggest

TAPESCRIPT

Amanda: Come on Steven, keep going.
Steven: This is exhausting ...
Amanda: One more repetition. You can do it ... Great. Well done. Let's take a short break now.
Steven: Phew! Good idea!
Amanda: You're doing really well, you know.
Steven: (1) *I'm still finding it quite difficult.*
Amanda: Well, you can't expect to get completely fit in just a month.
Steven: (2) *Actually, it's been six weeks.*
Amanda: Six weeks then. You know it usually takes about three months to get fit. After all, you haven't done any real exercise for more than five years, so you've got some catching up to do.
Steven: Mm. It seems an awfully long time.
Amanda: Be positive. We're almost half way there.
Steven: (3) *How long before I start to lose weight?*
Amanda: That depends. Have you cut out all those sweet snacks?
Steven: Er, sort of. But I'm afraid I'm still eating desserts. I just feel so hungry all the time.
Amanda: (4) *How about trying fruit instead of a dessert?*
Steven: OK. (5) *I'll give it a try.*
Amanda: (6) *If you cut down the amount of sugar you eat, you're bound to lose weight.* Now, how about your energy levels? Are you still feeling lethargic in the afternoons?
Steven: No, that's definitely improved. I haven't really felt as tired as I used to.
Amanda: That's great.
Steven: Oh, have you prepared that nutrition sheet for me?
Amanda: Sorry. (7) *I'm afraid I forgot.* I'll do it next week. So, are you ready to move on to the next machine?
Steven: Gosh. You trainers are such slave drivers!

Vocabulary | adjectives and intensifiers

2 Complete the sentences using intensifiers. Use *absolutely* with non-gradable adjectives and *really* with gradable adjectives.

1 Saturday's game is ______ vital for our hopes of promotion.
2 I always feel ______ hungry after swimming.
3 I often feel ______ tired at the end of the day.
4 Terry was ______ devastated when the factory closed down.
5 Suzanne was ______ exhausted after the race.
6 Poor Joe! He's ______ upset about his exam results.
7 What's there to eat? I'm ______ starving!
8 Take your time to decide. This is a ______ important decision for you.

Pronunciation

3 **a** 8.2 Underline the two words that have the main stress in these sentences. Then listen and check.

1 When the children got back from the park they were absolutely filthy.
2 Clare was really devastated when she heard the news.

b 8.3 Look at the completed sentences Ex. 2 above. Underline the two words with the main stress in each sentence. Then listen and check.

Grammar | reported speech

4 8.4 Cover the tapescript. Listen to six examples of direct speech from the conversation in Ex. 1. Write them in reported speech, using reporting verbs from the box.

admit ask promise suggest ~~warn~~ explain

1 Amanda ______________________________
____

2 Amanda *warned Steven (that) he couldn't expect to get completely fit in just a month.*

3 Steven ______________________________
____

4 Amanda ______________________________
____

5 Steven ______________________________
____

6 Amanda ______________________________
____

5 Choose the correct words to complete the sentences.

1 When we were young our parents ___ not to talk to strangers.
A told B told to us C told us

2 James asked me what ___ for my birthday.
A I wanted B did I want C wanted me

3 My girlfriend asked me ___ go to the party with her.
A will I B if I would C that I would

4 He said ___ already bought the tickets.
A me he had B he had C to me he had

5 The sales assistant suggested ___ a new MP3 player.
A buying B to buy C me buying

6 Davina asked me ___ been the day before.
A where I had B where had I C where was I

7 The police officer warned me ___ so fast in future.
A not driving B not to driving C not to drive

8 Michael asked us ___ the film last Wednesday.
A did we enjoy B if we had enjoyed
C if we enjoy

9 She asked me whether ___ a school uniform when I was at infant school.
A I must wear B I had to wear
C did I have to wear

10 The criminal promised ___ out of trouble.
A to stay B staying C he will stay

6 Report these examples of direct speech using suitable reporting verbs from the box. Use each verb once.

admit decide explain promise ~~remind~~ suggest warn

David Don't forget to lock the back door.

David reminded me to lock the back door.

1 **My brother** Why don't we go out for a meal?
____
____

2 **John** I can't come because I have to work that evening.
____
____

3 **The children** We'll never do it again.
____
____

4 **The lifeguard** Swimming there can be very dangerous.
____
____

5 **Maria** I haven't done my homework.
____
____

6 **Customer** I'll take the smaller model.
____
____

Reading

1 **a** Read the newspaper article and match the sentence halves.

1 Piers Sharma ☐
2 Mike Ryde ☐
3 Arran Fernandez ☐
4 Francesca ☐
5 Frederick ☐

a took Maths GCSE at the age of five.
b is a college principal.
c is taking a GCSE next year.
d is six years old.
e is waiting for his exam results.

b Read the text again and correct the factual mistakes in these statements.

1 Exam results are coming out later this month.
2 Piers Sharma got an A* in the exam.
3 There are five students in Piers' class at school.
4 The college has a maths course for babies.
5 Mike Ryde's son is top of the class at school.
6 The parents decide when children are ready to take an exam.
7 Mike says the older children love working with computers.
8 Mike thinks few children could take a GCSE at the age of eleven.

c Match the following words and phrases from the text with the meanings a–j.

1 trepidation ☐
2 momentarily ☐
3 extraordinarily ☐
4 embarked ☐
5 coincidence ☐
6 knock-on effect ☐
7 gravitate ☐
8 horrified ☐
9 dumb down ☐
10 lowest common denominator ☐

a when two things are the same for no reason
b surprisingly
c lower the standard
d causes other things to happen
e slight nervousness or fear
f shocked, frightened
g least difficult thing that everyone understands
h for a very short period of time
i are attracted towards
j began

Who's a clever boy then?

Is it wise for children aged six and seven to be taking GCSE exams, asks Zoe Brennan

Like many youngsters across the country, Piers Sharma will be waiting for the postman with trepidation next month, when exam results come out. Being seven years old, he is not the average GCSE student, however.

'It was a bit hard, and a bit easy,' he says of the exam in computer skills. 'The hard bit was the video conferencing, the applications bit was easy.'

Does he expect to pass? Sharma sounds momentarily stressed. 'I did really well in the practical, I got an A*,' he says. 'In the exam, I might have got a C+ or a B+.'

Most students do their GCSEs at the age of fifteen or sixteen, but Sharma is one of a growing number of pupils sitting exams extraordinarily early. This year, he is one of an entire class of nine children — four seven-year-olds and five six-year-olds — who in May took a GCSE in information and communication technology (ICT) at the private Ryde College in Hertfordshire.

The course takes a year to complete. Mike Ryde, principal of the college, confirmed that three of the children were five years old when they embarked on their GCSE studies, having 'graduated' from the college's baby and toddler computer course, where learning starts at eighteen months. At the age of three or four the infants attend 'primer' lessons. Then Ryde judges when they are ready to sit the exam.

'The most we've ever had before has been one or two children of this age doing a GCSE,' says Ryde. 'The very fact that we've got nine students this year shows that a lot of six and seven-year-olds would be capable of doing this. It is no coincidence that they all started in classes so early.'

The youngest ever to have taken a GCSE at Ryde was Arran Fernandez, who was five when he took Maths in 2001. Ryde's own daughter Francesca, seven, will take the ICT GCSE next year and his son Frederick, six, is on the primer course. 'The wonderful thing is that studying at a level designed for a fifteen-year-old has a knock-on effect,' he says. 'Francesca is topping the class at school.'

'We also have children doing English and Maths really early, but the younger children seem to gravitate towards ICT,' he says. 'They love working with computers.'

Many educationists and parents would be horrified, arguing that six is too young to burden a child with exams. Ryde, however, believes that early GCSEs should be introduced widely, claiming that such a system would reduce the stress on youngsters later on.

'At present, you see children taking upwards of ten GCSES at once at the age of sixteen,' he says. 'That's a tremendous pressure. Why not give them the opportunity to take one or two a year? It seems to me that most children are ready to do a GCSE by the age of eleven. We should not dumb down the system to the lowest common denominator – education is all about opportunity.'

Grammar | *hard* and *hardly*

2 Complete the sentences using the expressions in the box.

hard (x2) hardly (x2) hardly ever (x2) hardly anyone (x2) hardly anything hardly anywhere

1 You've ______ touched your food!
2 This is a treat; we ______ go to restaurants these days.
3 Although Sam studied ______, he wasn't able to pass the test.
4 By ten o'clock there was ______ left in the club.
5 Our teacher ______ gives us homework.
6 Monica pushed ______ but she couldn't open the door.
7 There's ______ to park in central London.
8 I didn't spend much; I bought ______.
9 I've ______ seen Isabel since she got married.
10 ______ in my street owns a car.

How to … | give your opinion

4 Read the dialogue and choose the correct alternative.

Sue: Did you see that item about students on the news? It said that nowadays more than half of them take a year off between school and university. They call it a 'gap year'.

Jake: What do they do?

Sue: They usually go travelling. I (1) *am thinking/think* it's a really good idea.

Jake: I disagree. As far as I'm (2) *concerned/concerning* it's a waste of time.

Sue: Well, I (3) *trust/believe* it can be a very useful experience.

Jake: Why do you think that?

Sue: Well, (4) *for/of* several reasons. (5) *Firstly/First one*, it gets them away from their parents and makes them more independent.

Jake: Getting a job and earning your own money is what makes people independent, (6) *of/in* my opinion.

Sue: That's true. But students on gap years often get jobs while they are travelling (7) *for/because* they need money to live on.

Jake: I thought their parents usually paid for everything.

Sue: Perhaps some of them do, but I don't think that's a very good idea. I mean, if the parents pay for everything, (8) *so/then* their children are never going to become independent.

3 Complete the picture labels using appropriate forms of *hard*, *hardly*, etc. Add any other words that are necessary.

1

It was very disappointing. ______ came to my barbecue.

2

Dennis tries really ______ but I don't think he'll ever succeed.

3

I can't help you. I've got ______ any money myself.

4

I'm not surprised Jane's work is so bad, she ______ comes to the class.

5

I'm afraid there's ______ left to eat in the fridge.

6

We looked ______ but we couldn't see where our friend was.

Review and consolidation unit 8

Vocabulary

1 Match the sentence halves.

1 If this product doesn't sell, the company will definitely ☐
2 Deborah's delighted – the book she wrote has become a ☐
3 People don't watch cowboy films any more; I think they've ☐
4 I think you'll have to pull it down and start again; this work really isn't ☐
5 People say that in this life you need a lot of luck in order to ☐
6 We've never done this before but we're willing to ☐
7 After failing the driving test four times, Jim has decided to ☐
8 Nobody bought their new CD; it was a complete ☐

a up to scratch.
b flop.
c succeed.
d best-seller.
e give up.
f go under.
g have a go.
h had their day.

It's time/I'd rather/I'd better

2 Complete each sentence with one word only.

1 It's getting late; I think it's ______ we left.
2 Would you ______ take the bus or the train?
3 Your bedroom's filthy; it's ______ time you tidied up.
4 Look at those dark clouds, you'd ______ take an umbrella.
5 I'm a bit tired; I ______ rather not go out this evening.
6 Don't you think it's about time you ______ your mother – you can use my mobile.
7 She's looking very ill; you ______ better call a doctor.
8 ______ you rather pay me now or wait until next week?
9 You'd better ______ interrupt him right now, he's with a client.
10 I'd rather ______ poor and happy than rich and unhappy.

Vocabulary

3 Choose the correct alternative.

1 My cousin doesn't have unrealistic ideas; he's very down to *ground/earth*.
2 I'm pretty *headstrong/proactive* – I don't take any notice of what other people think.
3 Isabel loves parties; she's very *outgoing/easy-going*.
4 My boss can be very *opinionated/manipulative* so I don't really trust him.
5 You must invite Carol to the party; she's very *high maintenance/witty* and she'll make us all laugh.
6 Everyone takes advantage of David, but then he's a complete *doormat/doorway*.
7 We're looking for a new marketing manager who will be *proactive/open* in developing the business.
8 Like all actors he loves to be the *heart/centre* of attention.
9 Don't be so *selfish/single-minded*; leave some of the chocolate for us.
10 She never listens to reasonable arguments; she's very *opinionated/single-minded*.

4 In seven sentences the adjective in *italics* is incorrect. Tick (✓) the correct sentences then replace the adjectives in the others.

1 Alex was very *devastated* when he heard the news.
2 The children were really *exhausted* after their skiing lesson.
3 Miranda loves cleaning, her kitchen is very *spotless*.
4 My flat is in a great location but it's absolutely *small*.
5 Without the air conditioning our office would get extremely *boiling*.
6 I'm really *hungry*. What's in the fridge?
7 The guided tour of the castle was absolutely *interesting*.
8 It's absolutely *vital* that you take out the correct insurance.
9 Robert was very *ecstatic* about his pay rise.
10 New York can be absolutely *cold* in January.

Reported speech

5 Match the examples of direct speech A–J with the reported speech sentences 1–10. Then complete the sentences.

A Don't touch these plates, they're very hot. ☐

B Where's your passport? ☐

C I'm afraid the doctor's sick today so he can't see you. ☐

D Don't forget to be at the airport two hours before your departure. ☐

E Do all the exercises on page 65 of the Workbook. ☐

F I'll pay back the loan within six months. ☐

G Are you feeling alright, darling? ☐

H Why don't we go to the cinema on Friday evening? ☐

I I stole the money. ☐

J I think I'll have the spaghetti Bolognese. ☐

1 The receptionist explained ________________ ________________.

2 Our teacher told us ________________ ________________.

3 My best friend suggested ________________ ________________.

4 The waitress warned us ________________ ________________.

5 The criminal admitted ________________ ________________.

6 The immigration officer asked me ________________ ________________.

7 My mother asked me ________________ ________________.

8 The customer decided ________________ ________________.

9 The travel agent reminded us ________________ ________________.

10 Elizabeth promised the bank manager ________________ ________________.

hard and *hardly*

6 Choose the correct word or phrase to complete the sentences.

1 Since he got married we ___ our son.
A hardly never see B hardly ever see
C hardly are seeing

2 Running the marathon was ___ work.
A really hard B hard of C really hardly

3 If you ___ you can just see the north star above the horizon.
A hardly look B look hard C hard look

4 I can't go out this week, I've got ___ left in my bank account.
A hardly no money B hardly money
C hardly any money

5 Hardly ___ came to the show.
A nobody B none C anyone

6 She ___ but she couldn't reach the top shelf.
A tried hard B hardly tried C hard tried

7 John made one last effort and hit the hammer as ___ as he could.
A hardly B hard C very hardly

8 After the accident I ___ my arm.
A could hardly move B could move hardly
C couldn't hardly move

9 I thought last night's homework was ___.
A so hardly B a lot hard C very hard

10 ___ in this shop is in our price range.
A Hardly nothing B Hardly anything
C Anything hardly

Vocabulary

7 Complete each gap with a word from the box to make expressions with phrasal verbs.

catch come cut for get look looking made on put to (x2) with (x4)

1 He's my hero. I really ______ up ______ him.

2 If you want to lose weight, you'll have to ______ down _____ all those sweets and cakes!

3 I hear you've got a new car; I'm ______ forward ______ seeing it.

4 Joe's snoring is very irritating – I don't know how you ______ up ______ it.

5 Carol has ______ up ______ a great new idea to make money.

6 They've caught the bank robbers; I'm glad they didn't ______ away ______ it.

7 The runner was slow at first but she ______ up ______ it in the last few metres and won.

8 He's just gone to the shops. You can _____ up ______ him if you run.

9.1 Crime

Vocabulary | law and insurance

1 **a** Each sentence contains one word which should be in a different sentence. Find the words and put them in the correct sentences.

1. The judge convicted the man to three years in prison.
2. There was a fire at the factory last week; the police think it is fraud.
3. I fell down the steps at work so I sentenced the company and got compensation.
4. You shouldn't use someone else's credit card, that's premium.
5. I'm glad to say I've never been sued of any driving offences.
6. The criminal decided to guarantee against his sentence.
7. The arson on our house insurance seems to get higher every year.
8. We appeal all our new cars for three years.

b Complete the sentences.

1. I was shocked when my next-door neighbour was convicted ______ fraud.
2. The injured pedestrian sued the driver ______ €10000.
3. The convicted man was sentenced ______ five years in prison.
4. Each new car is guaranteed ______ three years.

Reading

2 **a** Read the website on page 69 quickly and match the headings with the stories. Three headings are not needed.

A **Fatal Coffee**

B **The Unlucky Car Thief**

C **Imprisoned in a Garage**

D **Nightclub Accident**

E **Don't Ask the Jury**

F **Cruise Control**

b Read the text again and write questions for the following answers.

1. It maintains the vehicle's speed.
______
______
2. To make himself a cup of coffee.
______
______
3. A broken arm and leg and cuts to the head.
______
______
4. To avoid paying the entrance charge.
______
______
5. $12000.
______
______
6. For ten years.
______
______
7. Because the owners were on vacation.
______
______
8. A supply of dog food and some cans of Pepsi.
______
______

c Find the following words and phrases in the text and write them in the correct column. There are five words in each column.

accelerator awarded broke compensation court cruise control expenses fell jury knocked out mph owner's manual speed starvation suffered

Vehicles	Injuries/Harm	Legal

Compensation Culture or Legal Legends?

1 ________ [A]

In December 2002 Joseph Grazinski bought a brand-new motor home. He was thrilled because it had cruise control – a switch on the steering wheel which controls the accelerator and maintains the vehicle's speed at a constant rate. A few days after buying the motor home he decided to take it on a trip to Yellowstone National Park. Having joined the motorway, he set the cruise control at 65 mph and decided to step into the back of the motor home to make himself a cup of coffee. Within seconds the motor home had veered off the road, slid down a hillside and turned upside down. Mr Grazinski broke an arm and a leg and suffered cuts to his head.

Mr Grazinski sued the manufacturers because it did not say in the owner's manual that it was dangerous to leave the steering wheel while driving, even if the cruise control was switched on. The court awarded him $175000 and a brand-new motor home.

2 ________ [B]

In April 1998 Kara Walton of Claymont, Delaware wanted to get into the Black Cat nightclub but she didn't want to pay the $3.50 entrance charge. So she decided to sneak into the club by climbing through the window of the ladies toilet. Unfortunately, while struggling to get through the window she fell to the floor and knocked out her two front teeth. Ms Walton sued the owner of the Black Cat nightclub and was awarded $12000 compensation plus dental expenses.

3 ________ [C]

For ten years Terrence Dickson of Bristol, Pennsylvania, had had a successful career as a burglar who specialised in robbing people's houses while they were on holiday. In October 2004 he was about to leave a house he had just robbed when he got stuck in the garage. After entering the garage from the house he realised the door could not be opened from the inside. Because the owners were on vacation he was trapped in the garage for another eight days. During this time he lived on the supply of dog food and some cans of Pepsi which the owners kept at the back of the garage.

Mr Dickson sued the homeowner's insurance company, claiming that he had been the victim of kidnapping, starvation and mental torture. The jury awarded him $500000 compensation.

Grammar | sequencing devices

3 Underline three examples of sentences containing sequencing devices in the text in Ex. 2.

4 Read the sentences and decide which action happened (or started) first, A or B.

1 Having taken two aspirin, I began to feel a little sick.
A taking two aspirin B began to feel sick

2 Before going to bed, I have a glass of milk.
A going to bed B have a glass of milk

3 After leaving home, he got a job in a circus.
A leaving home B got a job in a circus

4 On hearing the news, I rushed out to tell my girlfriend.
A hearing the news B rushed out

5 Having crashed his car, Gerry had to come by taxi.
A coming by taxi B crashed his car

6 While waiting for the train, I noticed a small child crying on the platform.
A waiting for the train B noticed a child

5 Rewrite the sentences using the words in brackets.

Karl took the test then he went out to celebrate. (taken)

Having taken the test, Karl went out to celebrate.

1 Dave told his best friend before he announced the news to his colleagues. (having)
____

2 He got up and went into the village to get some food. (after)
____

3 They went to bed after they had watched the midnight movie. (going)
____

4 Surinda was watching TV when she heard a strange sound. (while)
____

5 Before we went to the computer shop we read lots of consumer reports. (reading)
____

6 Jackie had to get a taxi because she missed the bus. (having)
____

7 My uncle went to America and started a new business. (gone)
____

8 The kids usually do their homework and then watch TV for an hour. (doing)
____

Grammar | *must/might/can't have*

1 Match the questions 1–10 with the answers a–h.

1 Why didn't she pass the test? ☐
2 Why did she marry him? ☐
3 Why did she get an A+ in the test? ☐
4 Why did she divorce him? ☐
5 Why didn't she come to work? ☐
6 Why did she do that job? ☐
7 Why didn't she say hello to me? ☐
8 Why was she waving? ☐

a She must have fallen in love.
b She might have been sick.
c She can't have loved him any more.
d She can't have seen you.
e She might have needed the money.
f She can't have done enough revision.
g She must have seen you.
h She must have done lots of work.

2 Rewrite the sentences in *italics* using *must*, *might* or *can't have*.

1 The plants look very healthy. *Somebody definitely watered them.*
____

2 Emma isn't here. *Perhaps she didn't receive the invitation.*
____

3 *I'm sure he didn't go out.* I saw the light on in his bedroom.
____

4 Their flat is empty. *I'm certain they have left already.*
____

5 *I'm sure they haven't left the country.* They don't have passports.
____

6 Peter isn't answering his mobile. *Maybe he forgot to take it with him.*
____

7 *Maria's probably passed the exam.* She studied very hard.
____

8 Where's your umbrella? *I'm absolutely sure you forgot to bring it.*
____

3 Complete the text with *must/might/can't have*.

The Mystery of Tutankhamen's Tomb

The discovery of Tutankhamen's tomb is all thanks to one man, Howard Carter. If it hadn't been for Carter's endless curiosity and persistence, the incredible tomb (1) ______ been lost forever. Carter was working in the Valley of the Kings in Egypt when he noticed a pile of ancient rubbish near the entrance of the tomb of Rameses VI. Carter realised that the rubbish (2) ______ been there for a reason and he asked his men to dig into it. Three metres below the original surface they found a stone step carved into the side of the valley. From its depth and position he knew that this step (3) ______ been at least three thousand years old. It turned out to be the first of many steps that led down to the fabulous tomb of Tutankhamen.

It took Carter many months to fully excavate the tomb. But then the archaeologist was left with just as many questions as answers. Who exactly was Tutankhamen and how had he died? From the size of the body he knew that Tutankhamen was only a boy, he (4) ______ been more than eighteen or nineteen when he died. But what killed him? He (5) ______ been murdered by a jealous relative or he (6) ______ died from disease. From the inscriptions in the tomb Carter knew that Tutankhamen (7) ______ come to the throne at the age of about eight or nine. As he died young, he (8) ______ been on the throne for more than about ten years. Yet his tomb was filled with fabulous treasures, worthy of a great king.

Vocabulary | compound adjectives

4 Complete the sentences using compound adjectives. Add any other necessary words.

Damien uses his left hand for writing.
Damien *is left-handed.*

1 Mr Lockwood is fifty years old.
Mr Lockwood ______________________________.

2 She made the chocolate cake herself.
The chocolate cake ______________________________.

3 My sister only works for two hours a day.
My sister ______________________________.

4 It took me weeks and weeks to complete the project.
The project ______________________________.

5 Elizabeth finds it easy to concentrate and get things done.
Elizabeth ______________________________.

6 I want a ticket to Hong Kong; I'm not coming back.
I want a ______________________________.

7 I had a change of mind just before I was due to leave.
I ______________________________.

8 There's a really modern hospital here; it's just opened.
There's ______________________________.

Listening

5 **a** 9.1 Cover the tapescript. Listen to a radio programme and choose the best answers.

1 The radio programme is probably designed for
A lawyers. B sixteen- to eighteen-year-olds. C young children.

2 How many guests will there be on the programme?
A none B one C more than one

3 Emily says the majority of lawyers work
A in court. B for criminals. C in offices.

4 Divorce is part of
A civil law. B criminal law. C court.

5 Emily thinks the most important quality of a barrister is
A self-confidence. B communication. C a good memory.

b Listen again and complete the sentences.

1 There's a factsheet that you can ______ from the website.
2 Emily will help listeners ______ the mysteries of the legal profession.
3 Barristers present a case for the prosecution or ______ the accused.
4 Only a small ______ of lawyers work in court in England.
5 What ______ qualities do you think a good barrister needs?
6 You've got to ______ you know what you're doing.

c Complete the sentences with words and phrases from Ex. 5b.

1 I am writing this letter ______ the board of directors.
2 You're very tanned. You ______ you've been somewhere sunny.
3 I'm going to ______ some MP3 songs from the Internet.
4 This isn't the ______ behaviour I expect from someone like you.
5 Can you help me ______ these cables, they are all jumbled up.
6 You should try to have a large ______ of vegetables in your diet.

TAPESCRIPT

Voice: It's three o'clock and time for this week's edition of *Job Spotlight* with Zack Desmond.

Zack: Hello everyone and welcome once again to *Job Spotlight*. In today's programme we'll be looking at job opportunities in the legal profession. From your letters and emails I know this is a career that a lot of you are considering, so we've also put together a factsheet which you can download from our website. Now, as usual we have several guests here to help us unravel some of the mysteries of this particular profession. My first guest in the studio today is top lawyer Emily Waterstone.

Emily: Hello.

Zack: Welcome to the programme, Emily. Now, you're a barrister, aren't you?

Emily: Yes, a criminal barrister.

Zack: Can you tell us exactly what a barrister does?

Emily: I'll do my best. Actually, I think most people are familiar with barristers from TV and films. We're the people who stand up in court and present the case for the prosecution or on behalf of the accused, that's the person accused of a crime.

Zack: Don't all lawyers do that?

Emily: Not really. In England only a small proportion of lawyers work in court. Most lawyers work in offices – helping people buy houses, make their wills, get divorces – that kind of thing.

Zack: You said you were a criminal barrister. Does that mean you work for criminals?

Emily: No, not exactly. It means I work in criminal law rather than civil law.

Zack: So, what's the difference?

Emily: Well, criminal law is to do with actual crimes – murder, arson, robbery and so on. Civil law isn't about crimes at all; it's the law that governs things like contracts, inheritance, business, things like that.

Zack: So, you wouldn't be able to help me if I wanted to get a divorce.

Emily: I'm afraid not. Well, not unless divorce suddenly became a crime!

Zack: Right. Now for our listeners who are thinking about becoming barristers, what sort of qualities do you think a good barrister needs?

Emily: The main one is self-confidence I think. You've got to look like you know what you're doing. And communication is very important, especially in court.

Zack: I suppose a good understanding of human nature comes in useful.

Emily: Yes, and a good memory helps, too.

Zack: OK. Let's talk about the training you need to do ...

Reading

1 a Read the text quickly. Which statement is correct?

1 It summarises the complete plot and characters of *The Hound of the Baskervilles*.
2 It describes Conan Doyle's career using *The Hound of the Baskervilles* as an example.
3 It gives the background to *The Hound of the Baskervilles* and introduces the story.

b Read the text again and decide if the statements are true (T) or false (F).

1 *The Hound of the Baskervilles* was originally a series of magazine stories. ☐
2 People believe that a hound has killed Sir Charles Baskerville. ☐
3 Sir Charles was Henry Baskerville's uncle. ☐
4 Henry Baskerville comes to see Sherlock Holmes. ☐
5 Dr Mortimer is a friend of Sherlock Holmes. ☐
6 Dr Mortimer has some shocking new evidence about the mystery. ☐
7 Sherlock Holmes believes in scientific explanations. ☐
8 Holmes and Watson immediately solve the mystery. ☐

c Find the following words in the text. Decide if they are verbs, nouns or adjectives and match them with the definitions a–h.

1 cliff-hanger ☐
2 curse ☐
3 beast ☐
4 estate ☐
5 heir ☐
6 consult ☐
7 inquest ☐
8 rational ☐

a (*n*) an animal (especially a wild or dangerous animal)
b (*n*) a court case which examines the causes of a person's death
c (*v*) ask for advice from an expert
d (*n*) a promise or legend that something terrible will happen
e (*n*) a large area of land with a house belonging to one person or family
f (*adj*) scientific and logical
g (*n*) an exciting development in a plot that makes the reader want to know more
h (*n*) somebody who inherits land or money when a relative dies

Sherlock Holmes and *The Hound of the Baskervilles*

(1) *The Hound of the Baskervilles* is one of the most famous and admired detective stories ever written. Published in 1901 and 1902, it originally appeared in nine monthly instalments in *The Strand* magazine. Like Dickens's serialised novels of the same era, each instalment ended with a suspenseful 'cliff-hanger' that kept author Arthur Conan Doyle's audience clamouring for more.

(2) In the story, the old and noble Baskerville family is threatened by a curse: 'A great, black beast, shaped like an enormous wild dog or hound, yet larger than any hound that has ever been seen' terrorises and kills any family member who comes to live at the Baskerville estate. As the story opens, the hound seems to have claimed its latest victim, Sir Charles Baskerville. Sir Charles's nephew, Henry, the new heir to the estate, is about to take up residence the next day. A friend of the family, Dr Mortimer, comes to consult the famous Sherlock Holmes in his rooms at 221b Baker Street, though he admits he doesn't know if the case is more suitable 'for a detective or a priest'. The first instalment of the novel originally ended as Dr Mortimer explains:

(3) *'... One false statement was made by Barrymore at the inquest. He said that there were no traces upon the ground round the body. He did not observe any. But I did – a short distance away, but fresh and clear.'*

'Footprints?'

'Yes, footprints.'

'A man's or a woman's?'

Dr Mortimer looked strangely at us for an instant, and his voice sank almost to a whisper as he answered: 'Mr Holmes, they were the footprints of a gigantic hound!'

(4) Into this atmosphere of ancient secrets, deadly curses and supernatural beasts comes the supremely rational Sherlock Holmes – a man described by his friend Watson as 'the most perfect reasoning and observing machine the world has ever seen'. Piece by piece Holmes and Watson solve the mystery and find the culprit. In the end, they reassure the characters in the novel (as well as Conan Doyle's Victorian readers), that behind the threat of a supernatural 'hound of hell' is a perfectly scientific explanation.

Grammar | relative clauses

2 Match the statements 1 and 2 with the explanations A and B.

1
- 1 We stayed in the only hotel in the town which had a sea view. ☐
- 2 We stayed in the only hotel in the town, which had a sea view. ☐
- A There were several hotels but only one had a view of the sea.
- B There was only one hotel in the town.

2
- 1 My sister, who lives in Paris, has just had a baby. ☐
- 2 My sister who lives in Paris has just had a baby. ☐
- A I have several sisters and one of them lives in Paris.
- B I only have one sister.

3
- 1 All the students, who can speak French, were invited to the party. ☐
- 2 All the students who can speak French were invited to the party. ☐
- A All of the students were invited to the party.
- B Some of the students were invited to the party.

4
- 1 The cinema, which is opposite the station, is going to become a nightclub. ☐
- 2 The cinema which is opposite the station is going to become a nightclub. ☐
- A There is only one cinema in our town.
- B There is more than one cinema in our town.

3 Complete the sentences with relative clauses using the information in the box. Add commas and relative pronouns if necessary.

> We met the girl on holiday. The hospital is very old. It was elected last year. Her boyfriend lives in Athens. ~~She is Spanish~~. We stayed in the hotel last summer. He was Scottish. I'm living in that house. I saw that film yesterday.

John's sister-in-law, *who is Spanish*, is training to be an opera singer.

1 Miranda's boyfriend ____________ is a doctor.
2 The house ____________ is over a hundred years old.
3 Arthur Conan Doyle ____________ was born in 1859.
4 The government ____________ has introduced a new tax.
5 Our local hospital ____________ is about to be closed down.
6 The girl ____________ is coming to stay next weekend.
7 Spielberg's new film ____________ was fantastic.
8 The hotel ____________ had a heated swimming pool.

Pronunciation

4 **a** 9.2 The symbol () in these sentences represents the place where we usually pause in normal speech. Are the symbols in the correct place? Listen and check.

1 I bumped into Jane (), who used to be married to Steven (), last night.
2 I bumped into the girl () who used to be married to Steve.
3 My old friend Steve (), who used to be married (), was at our school party.

b 9.3 Mark the pauses in these sentences. In some sentences there may be no pauses. Listen and check.

1 We found our car, which had been towed away two hours earlier, at the police car pound.
2 It was my car that was towed away.
3 The police took the car, which had been blocking someone's gate, to the car pound in Lennard Street.
4 This is the gate that our car was blocking when it was towed away.

Writing

5 Write a short article based on the story in this cartoon strip. Use the guidelines in Ex. 13 on page 126 of the Students' Book to help you.

Vocabulary

1 Use the clues to complete the crossword.

Across

1 The criminal had to pay a ___ of $500.
2 We filed an insurance ___ after our suitcase was stolen.
5 In English courts the ___ wears a wig.
8 £2 million was stolen in the bank ___.
10 The murderer was given a ___ of thirty years in prison.
13 The police found him because he left his ___ on the weapon.
14 My car insurance ___ went up by 20% this year.

Down

1 He's going to ___ a claim with his insurance company.
3 Although she has been convicted, her lawyer is going to make an ___ to a higher court.
4 After the car crash we had to ___ the other driver for compensation.
6 The DVD player comes with a 12-month ___ from the manufacturers.
7 The pictures from the shop's cameras helped to ___ the shoplifter.
9 The ___ stole my handbag while I was dancing.
11 That wasn't an accidental fire, it was ___.
12 Credit card ___ is one of the fastest-growing crimes.

Sequencing devices

2 Choose the correct alternative.

1 Before *leaving/left* the meeting, she handed me her business card.
2 Having *seeing/seen* the film myself, I wouldn't recommend it.
3 *At/On* arriving at the airport the tourist group were met by the travel agent.
4 *After/Before* taking the tablets I felt a lot better – they were very effective.
5 Having opened the door, she *runs/ran* into the garden.
6 Before *booking/booked* the holiday, we did a lot of research.
7 While *lived/living* in New York, Kirsten made many new friends.
8 *To have/Having* taken the express train, Derek arrived in plenty of time.
9 On *the finish/finishing* his speech, the politician got a round of applause.
10 Having *learned/being learned* Spanish at school, the children were able to communicate during their holiday.

must/might/can't have

3 Read the situation and complete the sentences using appropriate forms of *must/might/can't have*.

Last night £50,000 was stolen from the safe of Western United Bank. None of the doors or locks was broken so the police think somebody working in the bank stole the money. There were no fingerprints on the safe door, but the police found a cigarette end on the floor near the safe. Nobody is allowed to smoke in the bank. Only three members of staff have keys to the safe: Mr Briggs the manager, Jennifer the assistant manager and Darren, the chief cashier. Mr Briggs was at home with his wife all last night. His wife confirms this. Jennifer says she was at home, but she lives alone. Darren says he was at home. He lives with his parents. His mother says he was at home all night, except when he went outside to take the dog for a walk at midnight.

1 The money ______ been stolen by a member of staff because none of the doors or locks was broken.
2 It ______ been either Mr Briggs, Jennifer or Darren because they are the only ones with keys to the safe.
3 The thief ______ been a smoker because there was a cigarette end on the floor.
4 It ______ been Mr Briggs because he was at home with his wife all night.
5 Jennifer ______ stolen the money because she can't prove she was at home last night.
6 Darren ______ stolen the money when he went out for a walk at midnight.

Vocabulary

4 Complete the sentences with compound adjectives. The first letter of each adjective is given.

1 This cake is delicious, is it h______?
2 I never buy second-hand things, I like everything to be b______.
3 Yes, sir. A first class ticket to Glasgow – o______ or return?
4 I'm afraid we only have p______ jobs available at the moment.
5 You can tell from her writing that she's l______.
6 It was a l______ decision to come here because we didn't know our holiday dates until last week.
7 I find filling in my tax form incredibly t______.
8 She's really determined and s______ about getting what she wants.
9 Car insurance is much cheaper for m______ people than for youngsters.
10 I really wouldn't trust that s______ friend of yours; she's quite dishonest.

Relative clauses

5 Six sentences contain mistakes with grammar and punctuation. Rewrite the incorrect sentences. Add relative pronouns and commas where necessary.

1 My brother that works in Cardiff is an opera singer.
2 Jenny of who I told you about last week is getting married.
3 The house we saw last weekend is worth over £1 million.
4 The children didn't pass the test had to take it again.
5 Our car which, we bought last year has been stolen, from our garage.
6 The film was on TV last night was absolutely fascinating.
7 Pilar, who guided us around the town, is a real expert on Spanish history.
8 My colleague, which showed us how to use the computer has been promoted, to the Los Angeles office.

6 Use defining and non-defining relative clauses to make each numbered pair of sentences into one sentence. The first one has been done as an example.

1 The house has been sold. It is the house where I used to play as a child.
2 It belonged to an old lady. The old lady died.
3 When I was young the old lady allowed me to play in her garden. The old lady used to be a schoolteacher.
4 The garden had lots of lemon trees. The garden was huge.
5 I used to pick the lemons from the trees. The trees grew there.
6 The old lady used the lemons to make lemonade. I had picked the lemons.

1 *The house where I used to play as a child has been sold.*
2 ______________________________
3 ______________________________
4 ______________________________
5 ______________________________
6 ______________________________

Vocabulary

7 Read the newspaper headlines and decide if the statements are true (T) or false (F).

Manchester United bids for top Portuguese player

BBC to axe top comedy show

Ministers clash over immigration

French Actress quits Hollywood

Prime Minister backs strikers

CHILDREN RESCUED FROM HOTEL BLAZE

Oscar-winning director in divorce drama

Government aid for homeless rises 25%

1 Manchester United has bought a Portuguese football player. ☐
2 The BBC will cancel a popular comedy show. ☐
3 Government ministers disagree about immigration. ☐
4 A French actress has left Hollywood. ☐
5 The Prime Minister wants the strikers to go back to work. ☐
6 Firefighters have rescued some children from a hotel fire. ☐
7 An award-winning director is making a film about a divorce. ☐
8 The Government says a quarter of homeless people have a disease. ☐

10.1 Memories

Listening

1 **a** 10.1 Cover the tapescript. Listen to the extract from a radio programme and choose the best summary.

1 The extract is a book review.
2 The extract is an interview with a writer.
3 The extract is about a famous French hypnotist.

b Listen again and use the information to complete the notes on Franz Mesmer's life. Write one word or number in each gap.

1734	• born in (1) ______
1766	• (2) as a doctor from (3) ______ university • started using (4) ______ on sick patients
1777	• moved to (5) ______. • became famous treating French (6) ______, he even treated the (7) ______ . • he cured people but he also (8) ______ them.
1785	• he was (9) ______ to go back to Germany.
(10) ______	• he died

c Match the words and phrases 1–8 with the things they refer to A–D. Then listen again or read the tapescript to check your answers.

1 quite unique ☐
2 a kind of magic ☐
3 a great showman ☐
4 a recently discovered phenomenon ☐
5 were treated by Mesmer ☐
6 surprisingly effective ☐
7 like theatrical displays ☐
8 gullible ☐

A Franz Anton Mesmer
B Mesmer's treatments of patients
C French aristocrats
D magnetism

TAPESCRIPT

I: This week's biography choice is *Mesmer – The Original Hypnotist*. It is the story of Franz Anton Mesmer, the 18th-century scientist who is often regarded as the founder of hypnotism. With me in the studio is its author, Alexander Bond. Alexander, can I start by asking you what attracted you to this character?

B: Yes. Well, I've always been interested in hypnotists and I wanted to find out how hypnotism first started, so obviously that led me to Franz Mesmer.

I: Now, Mesmer is quite unique, isn't he?

B: Yes. He's one of the very few people whose name has become an English verb.

I: As in 'to be mesmerised by something' ...

B: Exactly. And that shows just how influential and important he was.

I: He was French, wasn't he?

B: Actually he was born in Germany, in 1734. And he studied medicine in Austria – at the university of Vienna, in fact.

I: So how did he first became famous?

B: Well, after he qualified as a doctor in 1766 he started doing experiments with magnets. Magnetism was a recently discovered phenomenon but it wasn't properly understood. People saw metal objects flying towards each other and it seemed to be a kind of magic. Anyway, Mesmer started applying magnets to his sick patients ...

I: To sick people?

B: Yes. In fact, it was surprisingly effective. Lots of his patients got better and Mesmer soon became the best-known doctor in Vienna. But the other doctors resented his success and forced him to move to Paris in 1777.

I: And that's where he became really famous?

B: Yes. Paris was pretty much the centre of European culture at the time, and the French were fascinated by Mesmer and his magnetic cures. Many members of the French aristocracy were treated by him. Even King Louis XVI became one of his patients. But then Mesmer was a great showman, his treatments were more like theatrical displays, so as well as curing people he entertained them.

I: But how did it work?

B: Well, we think that what he was really doing was hypnotising people. From detailed descriptions written at the time it seems he probably used the power of hypnotism to convince his patients they were feeling better.

I: He must have made a lot of money from those gullible French aristocrats!

B: Yes, he made a fortune. But his success didn't last for long. He failed to cure some influential members of French society and in 1785 he was forced to go back to Germany.

I: Did he carry on his medical work there?

B: Not really. But he had a happy and contented retirement. And he lived until 1815.

Vocabulary | belief and opinion

2 There is one unnecessary or incorrect word in each sentence. Correct the mistakes.

1 Are you in favour that the law against smoking in restaurants?
2 I'm quite sceptic that anyone can read another person's mind.
3 My friend is reckons that there are ghosts in his house.
4 He's convenienced that the government is lying to us.
5 The police suspect of the murderer knew the victim.
6 I'm against give money to beggars.

Grammar | reflexive pronouns

3 Complete the sentences with the correct words.

1 They've got an oven that cleans ___.
A himself B itself C them
2 Our teacher told ___ to do exercise 3.
A ourselves B we C us
3 Successful team work depends on people helping ___.
A each other B ourself
C each others
4 When he went on holiday David took his computer with ___.
A itself B himself C him
5 I hurt ___ when I was lifting a heavy suitcase.
A myself B me C my
6 Emma sat down and relaxed ___ twenty minutes.
A her for B herself for C for
7 The children really enjoyed ___ on the rollercoaster.
A themselves B itself C each other
8 We couldn't afford builders so we decided to build the house ___.
A myself B each other C ourselves
9 It's very important to concentrate ___ you are driving.
A while B yourself while
C yourselves
10 At the end of the presentations I want you to give ___ marks out of ten.
A themselves B each other C you

4 Rewrite the sentences using reflexive pronouns or *each other.*

Janna looked at her reflection in the mirror.
Janna looked at herself in the mirror.

1 Darren cut his hand while he was gardening.
______
2 I made the cake without anyone's help.
______
3 We've made all the arrangements; nobody helped us.
______
4 Mandy sent a text message to Sylvia and Sylvia sent one to Mandy.
______
5 My central heating turns on automatically if the temperature drops.
______
6 The Bensons often send packages to their home address when they are abroad.
______
7 Did you paint this picture on your own?
______
8 Isabel doesn't work for anybody else; she's self-employed.
______

How to ... | ask about other people's views

5 Put the words in the correct order to make questions. Then answer the questions with your own opinions.

1 about do you strong feelings have pollution any ?
______?
2 poverty feel how about do you
______?
3 the for are death penalty you or against
______?
4 on what fast food are views your
______?
5 think divorce of what do you
______?

Reading

1 a Read the newspaper article quickly and choose the best summary.

1 Artificial smells haven't lived up to expectations.
2 Artificial smells have huge potential for business.
3 Banks hope artificial smells will increase their profits.

b Read the text again and decide if the following statements are true (T) or false (F).

1 Dale Air has produced an artificial 'smell of money' for Barclays Bank. ☐
2 The bank is having problems with its air conditioning systems. ☐
3 It is difficult to isolate the real smell of money. ☐
4 Shoppers are aware of the effect smells have on their spending. ☐
5 The smell of coconuts seems to encourage people to buy holidays. ☐
6 Cafés often put coffee machines near the entrance. ☐
7 The human sense of smell is highly developed. ☐
8 Most of the scientific problems of producing artificial smells have now been solved. ☐

c Find the following words and phrases in the text.

1 a compound adjective to describe bread which has just been made ______
2 an adjective meaning the opposite of *pessimistic* ______
3 a phrasal verb which means *to collect or attract something* ______
4 a compound noun that describes a machine used to store money in a shop ______
5 an adverb we use when something is done in a clever and almost invisible way ______
6 a scientific phrase which describes the parts of the body we smell things with ______
7 an adjective made from the verb *to evoke* ______
8 a verb which means *to control something and use it for your own benefit* ______

The Smell of Money

(1)
For many years large supermarkets have been encouraging us to spend money by pumping the smell of freshly-baked bread into their stores. Now Dale Air, a leading firm of aroma consultants, has been approached by Barclay's Bank to develop suitable artificial smells for their banks. Researchers have suggested that surrounding customers with the 'smell of money' will encourage them to feel relaxed and optimistic and give them added confidence in the bank's security and professionalism.

(2)
But before a smell can be manufactured and introduced into banks' air conditioning systems it must be identified and chemically analysed, and this has proved to be difficult. The problem is that banknotes and coins tend to pick up the smell of their surroundings. So cash that has been sitting in a cash register at a fishmonger's will smell of fish, and banknotes used to pay for meals in restaurants will tend to smell of food.

(3)
It may be a challenge, but aroma experts have little doubt that the use of artificial smells can be an effective form of subconscious advertising. Lunn Poly, a British travel company, introduced the smell of coconuts into its travel agencies and saw a big increase in spending by holiday makers. Many cafés now have electric dispensers that release the smell of freshly roasted coffee near their entrances, subtly encouraging customers to come in and have a drink or snack. Even prestige car maker Rolls-Royce has been spraying the inside of its cars to enhance the smell of the leather seats.

(4)
'The sense of smell is probably the most basic and primitive of all human senses,' explains researcher Jim O'Riordan. 'There is a direct pathway from the olfactory organs in the nose to the brain.' It is certainly true that most people find certain smells incredibly evocative, stirring memories and feelings in a way that few other stimulants can rival. It is a phenomenon marketing consultants have long recognised, but until recently have been unable to harness. 'We've made great progress but the technology of odour production is still in its infancy,' says O'Riordan. 'Who knows where it will take us.'

Vocabulary | advertising

2 Label the texts/words 1–4 using the following words (not all the words are needed):

publicity makes advertisement
classified ad marketing target market
slogan

'You deserve the best'

1 ________________

Siemens
Sony
Boeing
Rolls-Royce

2 ________________

For Sale
2003 Toyota Corrolla
40,000 miles
Excellent condition.
£3,000
Tel 03303778899

3 ________________

Married women living in the United States between the ages of 30 and 45 with annual incomes in excess of $25,000.

4 ________________

Pronunciation

3 10.2 How many syllables do these words have? Put the words into the correct column and mark the main stress on each word. Then listen and check.

advertisement commercial customers
information magazines persuasion
politicians supermarket

Three syllables	Four syllables

Grammar | gerunds and infinitives

4 Choose the correct alternative.

1 Did your colleagues *refuse/suggest* working at the weekends?
2 The boss suggested *join/joining* her for lunch.
3 Let me know when you've finished *writing/to write* the report.
4 He encouraged *her to get/to get her* a new job.
5 Could you *promise/imagine* living without a mobile phone?
6 Sheila should practise *speaking/to speak* Spanish before she goes to Madrid.
7 Will you *miss/agree* playing football on Saturdays?
8 Did you persuade her *coming/to come*?

5 Match the sentence halves.

1
1 I stopped watching TV ☐
2 I stopped to watch TV ☐
A and answered the phone.
B because there was a fascinating documentary on.

2
1 I regret to say ☐
2 I regret saying ☐
A you were lazy, it was very rude of me.
B that you have not been selected for the team.

3
1 I remember locking the door before ☐
2 Remember to lock the door before ☐
A you go home.
B I left.

4
1 Hilary tried closing the door but ☐
2 Hilary tried to close the door but ☐
A there was still a cold draught in the room.
B it was jammed and she couldn't do it.

Writing

6 Look at your answers in Ex. 5 on page 77. Write an essay, using one of these titles.

- Pollution is the most serious threat facing the modern world.
- The death penalty should be used for all convicted murderers.
- Fast food is dangerous to people's health and should be banned completely.

Look at the guidelines in Ex. 11 on page 137 of the Students' Book to help you.

10.3

Reading

1 **a** Read the text quickly and choose the best heading for each paragraph. Two of the headings are not needed.

A Subconscious Suggestion
B The Future
C Advertising
D Fiction or Reality?
E Pavlov
F New Drugs
G Conditioning and Indoctrination

b Read the text again and write questions for the answers.

1 ______________________________?
Memories of a failed romance.
2 ______________________________?
Changes in brain chemistry.
3 ______________________________?
More than forty.
4 ______________________________?
Through subtle suggestion and manipulation
5 ______________________________?
By endlessly repeating tasks and sequences.
6 ______________________________?
Which parts of the brain control individual movements.

c Find words or phrases in the text that mean:

1 something invented/not true (*n*, para 1) ______
2 people who study the brain (*n*, para 2) ______
3 chemicals made from several different ingredients (*n*, para 2) ______
4 take away/remove (*v*, para 2) ______
5 surprised/impressed (*-ed adj*, para 3) ______
6 getting people to do what you want by secretly tricking them (*n*, para 3) ______
7 instructions given to you by a superior (*n*, para 4) ______
8 do a task (*phrasal v*, para 4) ______
9 distorted information given to people by a government or organisation to influence them (*n*, para 4) ______
10 sudden desire or wish (*n*, para 5) ______

Mind Control – is it real?

(1)
With the release of *Eternal Sunshine of the Spotless Mind* the subject of mind control is once again in the news. In the film Joel has bad memories of a failed romance removed from his mind by the sinister Lacuna organisation. Of course, the film is only fiction. But could such a thing happen in real life?

(2)
Scientists point to the recent development of several drugs which appear to influence the brain. Known as memory-management drugs, these new compounds can cause changes in brain chemistry, and seem to directly influence the part of the brain that stores and processes past experiences. Neuroscientists hope to make products which can improve memory skills and even erase negative thoughts. The American Food and Drug Administration (FDA) is testing more than forty such products.

(3)
Drugs are not the only way the mind can be controlled. Viewers of Channel 4's series on mind control featuring Derren Brown have been amazed at how he can put ideas into people's minds through subtle suggestion and manipulation. Similar effects are achieved by hypnotists, although they always claim they are only harnessing the mind's own hidden desires and wishes. Some even claim that advertisements include invisible triggers that stimulate the subconscious to make us want particular products.

(4)
More traditional forms of mind control are well-known. For centuries armies have been training soldiers to obey orders without thinking using a method now known as Pavlovian conditioning, named after Russian psychologist Ivan Pavlov. By endlessly repeating tasks and sequences and by employing simple tactics of punishment and reward, people can be persuaded to carry out instructions without question. On a larger scale the technique of indoctrination can be employed. Through the use of education and propaganda, dictators and governments throughout history have convinced people of things which are obviously untrue.

(5)
The future holds even more worrying possibilities. Research has shown us exactly which parts of the brain control individual movements. Once we have learned how to stimulate these areas we will be able to make people move in whichever way we want. The concept of a human robot, its mind and body obedient to another person's every whim, has become a distinct possibility.

Vocabulary | speaking

2 Complete the crossword using the clues below.

Across

1 Please ___; I don't want anyone else to hear us.
4 You should speak more clearly – don't ___.
5 I'm afraid I ___ whenever I see a spider.
7 The news was so shocking I was ___ for words.
8 She's never afraid to speak her ___.

Down

2 Please don't ___ me when I'm in the middle of telling a joke.
3 I can't keep a secret; I ___ things out at the worse times!
6 Excuse me. Can I have a ___ with you about this invoice?

Grammar | *If* structures (2)

3 **a** Match the sentence halves to make correct conditional sentences.

If clause

1 If we hadn't missed the plane, ☐
2 If you don't like Coldplay, ☐
3 Provided you pay for the tickets, ☐
4 If I had plenty of money, ☐
5 If we'd gone to the concert, ☐
6 As long as I work overtime, ☐
7 Unless you pay for it, ☐
8 If we hadn't managed to get tickets, ☐

Main clause

a I'd take a six-month holiday.
b we wouldn't have seen Coldplay.
c we would be on holiday now.
d I'll go to the concert with you.
e I can have an extra week's holiday.
f you shouldn't have bought tickets for their show.
g we would have seen the band.
h I won't go to the concert with you.

b Answer these questions about the completed sentences in Ex. 3a.

1 Is sentence 1 3rd Conditional or Mixed Conditional?
2 Is sentence 6 Zero Conditional or 1st Conditional?
3 Is sentence 5 3rd Conditional or Mixed Conditional?
4 Which type of conditional is sentence 4?
5 Which type of conditional is sentence 2?

4 Complete the second sentence so that it means the same as the first.

You can put on the life jacket, but only if there is an emergency.

Don't put on the life jacket *unless there is an emergency.*

1 We went to the sales and bought an incredibly cheap sofa.
If we hadn't gone ______________________
______________________.

2 Charles forgot to turn on his alarm clock so he overslept.
Charles wouldn't have overslept ______________________
______________________.

3 Plants grow when you give them water.
If you ______________________
______________________.

4 One day I might get a pay rise and then I'll be able to buy a nice house.
If I got a pay rise ______________________
______________________.

5 Only use the generator if there is a power failure.
Don't use the generator ______________________
______________________.

6 We will give you a guarantee if you pay by credit card.
Provided ______________________
______________________.

7 If the neighbours complain, you can't have a party.
You can have a party ______________________
______________________.

8 If you show us a receipt, we can give you a refund.
As long as ______________________
______________________.

Vocabulary

1 Choose the correct alternative.

1 Harold was knocked *subconscious/unconscious* by the falling tree.
2 Although I had never been there before I had a strong feeling of *sixth sense/déjà vu*.
3 I always *trust/believe* my intuition about new people I meet.
4 Before we left for the airport I had an awful *premonition/intuition* that something bad was about to happen.
5 It isn't really difficult to learn new skills; it's just a question of *brain/mind* over matter.
6 You need a lot of *premonition/willpower* to give up smoking.
7 My brother gets very stressed about his work; I think he has a *subconscious/unconscious* fear of failure.
8 Hypnotists are experts at using the power of *persuasion/intuition*.

Reflexive pronouns

2 Six of the sentences contain mistakes with pronouns. Find the mistakes and correct them.

1 Emma cut her while doing the washing up.
2 Mike takes his laptop with himself when he goes on business trips.
3 Juanita and Mario phone each others every day.
4 I'm going to teach myself to play the violin.
5 To save money we painted our house ourself.
6 Mr and Mrs Wright decided to take their grandchildren with themselves when they went on holiday.
7 I have no objections to the product itself; it's the advertisement that annoys me.
8 I repaired me the broken chair.

Vocabulary

3 Rewrite the sentences using suitable forms of the phrases in the box. Use each phrase once only.

to have always believed that	to be against	to be sceptical about	to be convinced	~~to have your doubts about~~	reckon	to be in favour of

Janet isn't really sure about this new job.
Janet has her doubts about this new job.

1 I am absolutely certain that Jimmy is guilty of the crime.
______
2 Emily supports the idea of longer prison sentences for criminals.
______
3 I think she could be our new manager.
______
4 All my life I have had the opinion that people are basically honest.
______
5 Some politicians don't support the new tax.
______
6 I really don't completely trust or believe in hypnosis.
______

4 Use the clues to complete the crossword.

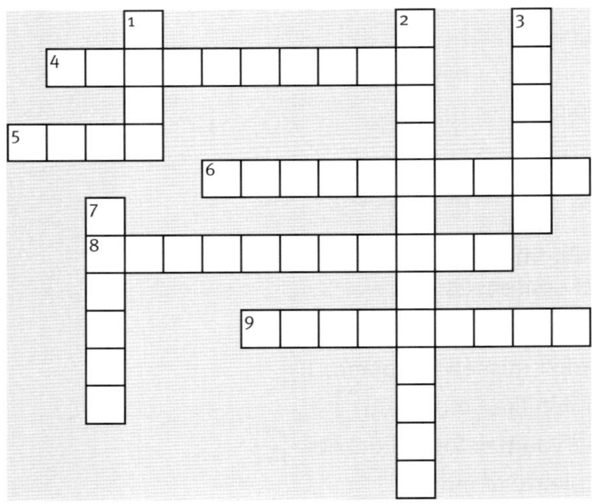

Across
4 A small advertisement in a newspaper is a ___ ad.
5 Publicity that makes something seem important.
6 A ___ break is a series of advertisements between TV programmes.
8 A noun made from the verb *to advertise*.
9 Deciding where and how to sell products, how much to charge, etc.

Down
1 What ___ is it? Sony or Philips?
2 Pictures/Words/Short film that tries to sell you a product.
3 A short clever phrase used by advertisers or politicians.
7 For this product our target ___ is teenagers.

Gerunds and infinitives

5 Complete the sentences using appropriate forms of the words in brackets.

1 Jane's father agreed ____________ from the nightclub. (collect/us)
2 Did you remember ____________ before you left? (turn on/the burglar alarm)
3 Have you considered ____________ in other countries? (apply/to universities)
4 We regret ____________ that your job application has been unsuccessful. (inform/you)
5 My grandfather carried on ____________ until he was 80. (work/as a doctor)
6 It was an expensive city but we enjoyed ____________. (live/there)
7 I would avoid ____________ – they taste disgusting. (eat/the prawns)
8 It was a very long drive so at one o'clock I stopped ____________. (have/lunch)
9 Her new job involves ____________ and publicity materials. (design/websites)
10 My teacher persuaded ____________ the first certificate exam next summer. (me/take)

Vocabulary

6 Match the descriptions 1–6 with the phrases a–h. Two of the phrases are not needed.

1 When you speak quietly because you only want one person to hear you. ☐
2 When you can't think what to say. ☐
3 When you tell people exactly what you think about something, even if it is shocking. ☐
4 When you say something quickly without thinking about it. ☐
5 When you speak quietly and not very clearly. ☐
6 When you say something while another person is still speaking. ☐

a to be lost for words
b to shriek
c to interrupt
d to whisper
e to have a word with
f to mumble
g to blurt out
h to speak your mind

If structures (2)

7 Complete the sentences with the correct words.

1 I'll go to the party ___ you agree to come with me.
A unless B as long as C if not
2 If we ___ stuck in this traffic jam, we would be there by now.
A didn't get B don't get C hadn't got
3 If the film hadn't ended so late, we ___ the last bus home.
A would miss B wouldn't have missed C don't miss
4 We'll give you a refund ___ back the receipt.
A provided you bring B provided you brought
C unless you bring
5 If she isn't at home, ___ the invitation through the letter box.
A you would put B put C you have put
6 If I ___ to a part-time job, I'd have a lot more time with the children.
A changed B will change C had changed
7 If you've lived there all your life, you ___ how beautiful it is.
A will already know B had already known
C already knew
8 If we'd arrived earlier, we ___ the film stars arriving.
A might see B saw C might have seen
9 You mustn't use that expensive mobile phone ___ it's a real emergency.
A if B provided C unless
10 Darren ___ in the winning team if he hadn't broken his leg.
A wasn't B could have been C can be

Vocabulary

8 Match the letters in the box with the gaps in the words. Each gap may be two or three letters long.

cc ea ei el ell il iou ou ss syc

1 int___igence
2 p___hologist
3 subconsc___s
4 th___r
5 responsib___ity
6 definit___y
7 chang___ble
8 nece___ary
9 gener___s
10 o___asionally

Unit 6 Explore

Lesson 6.1

Reading

1a 2

b (suggested answers) **1** How long have Chinese 'speed tourists' been coming to Germany? **2** How many tourists are expected to arrive this year. **3** What is it that tempts the Chinese tourists to drive on the autobahns? **4** How many kilometres of German motorways have no speed limit? **5** What makes/types of car do the tour operators offer to the tourists? **6** What speed are these cars capable of?/How fast can these cars go? **7** How much does a six-day autobahn tour cost? **8** How many people die on China's roads each day?

c **1** holidaymakers, travellers **2** autobahns, motorways, highways **3** tour operators **4** virtually **5** mythical **6** undeterred

Grammar: Present Perfect Simple and Continuous

2 **1** have been flocking **2** have added **3** have been bringing **4** have discovered **5** has been expanding **6** has not proved **7** have reacted **8** have been

3 **1** No, I haven't paid for the shopping yet. **2** They've been swimming in the lake. **3** No, I've never been/gone there. **4** Yes, he's just come back from Miami Beach. **5** I've been following a strict diet for the last two months. **6** No, I've already done it. **7** Yes, she's been typing it since lunchtime. **8** Yes, I've been teaching karate for more than ten years. **9** I've been washing the floors all afternoon. **10** No, I haven't been a member since 2004.

Vocabulary: adjectives with *-ed*/*-ing* endings

4 **1** annoyed, annoying **2** inspiring, inspired **3** fascinating, fascinated **4** petrified, petrifying **5** daunting, daunted

Lesson 6.2

Reading

1a **1** F **2** C **3** G **4** E **5** A

b **1** T **2** T **3** F **4** F **5** F **6** T **7** T **8** F

c Built entirely centrally heated formerly known sparsely populated surprisingly relaxing reasonably comfortable well stocked

Vocabulary: weather

2

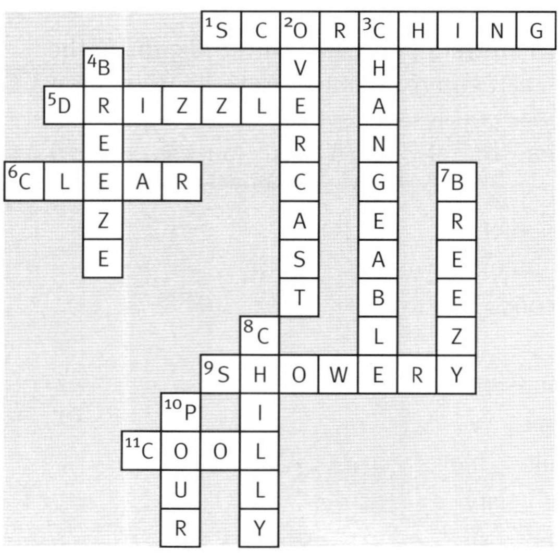

Grammar: questions

3 **1** (had) h **2** (did) e **3** (did) j **4** (How) a **5** (Did) g **6** (Who) i **7** (long) c **8** (was) b **9** (Was) f **10** (Are) d

4 **1** Who was she talking to? **2** Do you know if this is my seat? **3** Can you tell me how much it costs? **4** Where did they take the car? **5** Could I ask you to open the window? **6** How do you turn off the computer? **7** Are these the correct answers? **8** How long have you been working here?

5 **1** Can you tell me what your email address is? **2** Could I ask you if/whether Graham Randall lives here? **3** Do you know if this is the correct platform for the train to Brighton? **4** I'd like to know which seats in the plane have got the most legroom. **5** Can I ask you if/whether the doctor is available now? **6** Can you explain exactly where she lives? **7** Do you know how much the tickets cost? **8** Would you tell me who is in charge?

Lesson 6.3

Listening

1a **A** 4 **B** 3 **C** 1 **D** 5 **E** 2

b **1** 5 **2** 4 **3** 2 **4** 3 **5** 1

c **1** considered **2** uproot **3** intrigued by **4** grim **5** tempting **6** to be honest **7** obviously **8** opportunities

Vocabulary: verb phrases about moving/travelling

2 **1** g **2** c **3** f **4** a **5** h **6** e **7** d **8** b

Grammar: comparative & superlative adjectives and adverbs

3 **1** more exciting than **2** The biggest **3** greater than **4** the most expensive **5** isn't as long **6** the fastest **7** the tallest **8** shorter than

4 **1** ~~most heavy~~ heaviest **2** ~~is bit~~ is a bit **3** ~~bad hurt~~ badly hurt **4** ~~lately~~ late **5** ~~is most~~ is the most **6** ~~hoter~~ hotter **7** ~~than~~ as **8** ~~quite lot~~ quite a lot **9** ~~more far~~ farther/further **10** ~~taller~~ tall **11** ~~good~~ well **12** ~~most bad~~ worst

Pronunciation

5a **1** All the underlined sounds are the same (/ə/ schwa) **2** All the underlined sounds are different /ə/, /æ/, /ə/, /ɑː/.

b **1** D **2** S **3** S **4** S **5** D

Review and consolidation unit 6

Vocabulary

1 **1** ~~independence~~ independent **2** ~~shocked~~ shock **3** ~~make~~ have **4** ~~journey~~ travel **5** ~~through~~ into **6** ~~wonder~~ wander

Present Perfect Simple and Continuous

2 **1** has been **2** has become **3** has been leading/has led **4** has been appearing **5** has had **6** helped **7** has given **8** has visited **9** have clearly influenced **10** met **11** spoke **12** has only been doing

Vocabulary

3

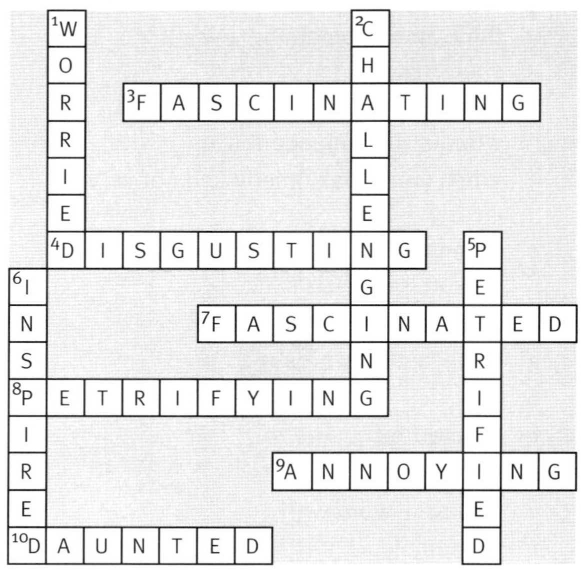

4 **1** e **2** h **3** a **4** f **5** c **6** g **7** d **8** b

Questions

5

(line 4) Where ~~went you~~ for your holidays? → Where did you go ...

(line 6) Who ~~did go~~ on holiday with you? → Who went on holiday ...

(line 8) Can I ask what ~~is her name~~? → Can I ask what her name is?

(line 10) Could you tell me what ~~does she~~ for a living? → what she does for a living ...

(line 15) Can you tell me ~~is she British~~? → ... if/whether she is British.

(line 17) How long ~~she has~~ lived here? → ... has she lived here?

(line 19) I'd like to know where ~~did you meet her~~. → ... where you met her.

(line 25) Would you tell me how long ~~did you stay~~ in Florida? → ... how long you stayed ...

Vocabulary

6 1 move 2 off 3 abroad 4 emigrated 5 around 6 set 7 home 8 off 9 away 10 walked

Comparative & superlative adjectives and adverbs

7 1 A✓ B✗ C✓ 2 A✗ B✓ C✗ 3 A✓ B✗ C✗ 4 A✗ B✗ C✓ 5 A✓ B✗ C✓ 6 A✓ B✓ C✓ 7 A✗ B✓ C✓ 8 A✗ B✓ C✗

8 1 for 2 have 3 make 4 without 5 back 6 lengths 7 on 8 the

Unit 7 Excess

Lesson 7.1
Listening

1a 1 Three. 2 Which take-away restaurant to go to. 3 To go to the Chinese take-away.

b 1 Alice 2 Ben 3 Tom 4 Alice 5 Ben 6 Alice 7 Ben 8 Tom

c **Feeling very hungry:** starving, ravenous, I could eat a horse
Positive opinion: yummy, delicious, scrumptious
Negative opinion: not too keen on, disgusting, greasy, to be sick of something, tasteless

Grammar: countable and uncountable nouns

2 1 C 2 B 3 A 4 C 5 B 6 A 7 A 8 C 9 A 10 C

3 1 A✓ B✓ 2 A✓ B✓ 3 A✓ B✗ 4 A✗ B✓ 5 A✓ B✗ 6 A✓ B✓

Vocabulary: food and cooking

4a an electric cooker grilled sausages grated cheese a wooden spoon a talented cook a complicated recipe scrambled eggs a china plate sour milk a frying pan

b 1 grated cheese 2 an electric cooker 3 grilled sausages 4 scrambled egg 5 a talented cook 6 sour milk

Lesson 7.2
Reading

1a 2

b 1 d 2 f 3 a 4 g 5 c 6 b 7 h 8 e

c 1 valuable 2 argue 3 rival 4 follow his lead 5 impact 6 masterpieces 7 recession 8 wholly

Vocabulary: verb phrases about money

2 1 ~~refund~~ receipt 2 ~~bargain~~ discount 3 ~~haggling~~ bidding 4 ~~worth~~ afford 5 ~~bidding~~ haggling 6 ~~afford~~ worth

Grammar: passives

3 1 was created 2 was taken over 3 had started 4 scored 5 organised 6 had been sold 7 were invited 8 was bought

4 2 The metal strips are fed into a cutting machine. 3 The metal is cut into round shapes called 'blanks'. 4 After they have been cut out the blanks are heated in a furnace. 5 The blanks are washed while they are being heated./While they are being heated the blanks are washed. 6 each coin is stamped with a pattern on both sides. 7 The coins are cooled and counted. 8 The coins are distributed to the banks.

5 1 Alison has been given a prescription. 2 The present mustn't be opened until your birthday. 3 The crime is being investigated. 4 The hotel is going to be opened in November. 5 The children will be driven to the party. 6 My house can be seen from the top of the hill. 7 They were being watched. 8 That DVD hasn't been released yet. 9 The burglar might have been seen. 10 Nothing was taken.

Writing/How to: a letter of complaint

6 (suggested answer)

Dear Sir/Madam,

I am writing to complain about a mobile phone I bought in your shop on 6th January.

When I got home I was shocked to find that it did not work, especially as it cost €250.

I would be grateful if you could send me another phone. If this is not possible, I would like a full refund of my money as soon as possible.

I look forward to hearing from you.

Yours faithfully,

Mandy Smith

Lesson 7.3
Listening

1a 1 goldfish 2 dog 3 snake 4 horse 5 cats

b 1 dog 2 horse 3 fish 4 dog 5 horse 6 cats 7 snake 8 horse

c **Ways animals move:** trot, dart, crawl
Places animals live: tank, stable, kennel
Animal characteristics: sinuous, playful, gentle

Grammar: *have/get something done*

2 1 has her hair done 2 has his car washed 3 have their house painted 4 has here eyes tested 5 has his blood pressure checked 6 have our boiler serviced

3 1 The bag got left behind. 2 Linda has her clothes washed (by the maid). 3 I have my post forwarded (to me). 4 Will you get your hair cut this week? 5 How often do you have your windows cleaned? 6 I should have my homework done by six o'clock.

Vocabulary: animals and animal expressions

4

					[1]F						
				[2]C	L	A	[3]W	S			
[4]F	I	S	[5]H		Y		H				[6]W
			O				I		[7]W		H
	[8]H	O	R	N	[9]S		S		I		A
	O		S		P		K		N		L
	O		E		I		[10]E	A	G	L	E
	V				D		R		S		
[11]F	E	A	[12]T	H	E	R	S				
	S		A		R						
		[13]F	I	N							
			L								

Pronunciation

5 1 cow 2 beak 3 tiger 4 eagle 5 fur

Review and consolidation unit 7

Vocabulary

1 1 luxury 2 extravagant 3 far-fetched 4 spending 5 overpriced 6 extra-large

Countable and uncountable nouns

2 1 ~~luggages~~ luggage 2 ✓ 3 ~~many~~ much 4 ~~little~~ a little 5 ~~a lots~~ a lot OR a lots 6 ~~a few~~ a little 7 ✓ 8 ~~a~~ spaghetti OR (some) spaghetti 9 ~~few~~ a few 10 ~~much~~ many

Vocabulary

3

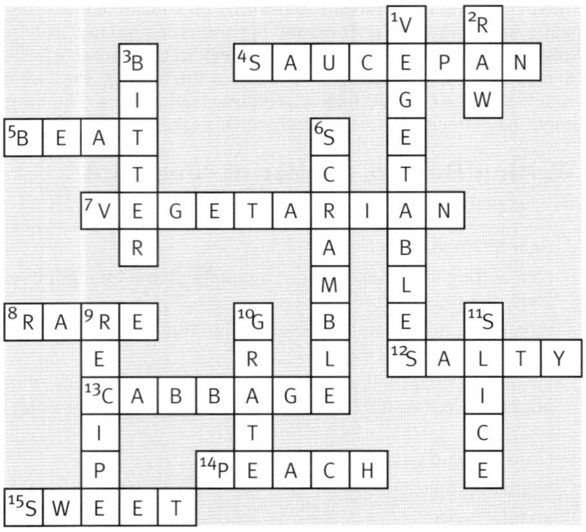

4 1 bargain 2 afford 3 haggling 4 receipt 5 bidding 6 discount 7 worth 8 refund

Passives

5 1 €450 has been debited from your credit card. 2 128 KB protection software is used for your security. 3 Your itinerary is being sent by email. 4 Your tickets will be sent by first class post. 5 Your passport must be brought to check-in one hour before departure. 6 The date and time of your flights cannot be changed. 7 Seats can be pre-booked on the website. 8 Smoking is not allowed on any GoAway Travel flights. 9 Meals may be purchased on the plane. 10 Transfers from the airport are included in the price.

have/get something done

6 1 had 2 got/been 3 (dry-)cleaned 4 have/get 5 repaired/fixed/mended 6 got/was 7 get/have 8 done 9 taken/printed/copied 10 having/getting

Vocabulary

7a 1 fin 2 beak 3 paws 4 hooves

b 1 bear, sore 2 blind, bat

8 1 reheat 2 multinational 3 extra-large 4 uncomfortable 5 bilingual 6 overtired 7 ex-boyfriend 8 monotonous 9 undercooked 10 multipurpose

Unit 8 Success

Lesson 8.1

Reading

1a 1 D 2 F 3 A 4 H 5 B 6 E

b 1 F 2 T 3 T 4 T 5 F 6 T 7 F 8 T

c

1869	*born in Porbandar, western India*
1893	*qualified as a lawyer*
1915	*returned to India, determined to fight against colonialism*
1947	*India gained independence*
1948	*assassinated by a Hindu fanatic*

Grammar: *It's time/I'd rather/I'd better*

2 1 A 2 B 3 B 4 B 5 B 6 A 7 A 8 A

3 1 It's high time you moved to a bigger flat. 2 You'd better take an umbrella. 3 I'd rather go to the cinema. 4 It's about time John got a better computer. 5 Would you like me to bring my camera/ Would you rather I brought my camera? 6 I'd rather she didn't smoke. 7 I'd rather not work at the weekend. 8 You'd better have the salad.

Vocabulary: describing personality

4

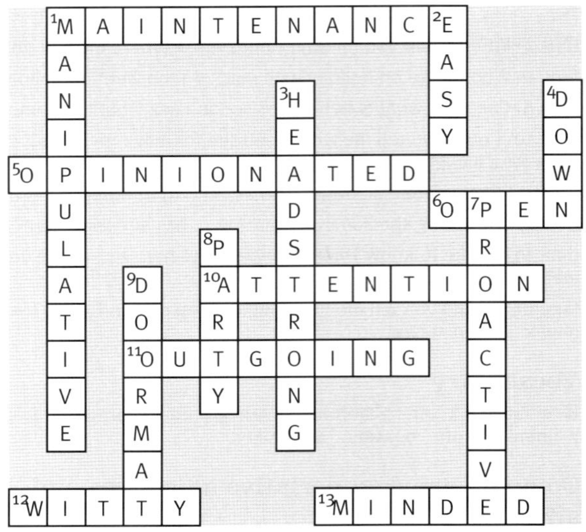

Lesson 8.2

Listening

1a 1 They are in a gym. 2 She is a trainer/fitness instructor. 3 To get fit, lose weight and improve his energy levels.

b 1 six 2 five 3 awfully 4 still 5 feels 6 energy 7 lethargic/tired 8 nutrition

c 1 complain 2 remind 3 ask 4 suggest 5 promise 6 explain 7 admit

Vocabulary: adjectives and intensifiers

2 See answers to Ex. 3b below.

Pronunciation

3a 1 When the children got back from the park they were absolutely filthy. 2 Clare was really devastated when she heard the news.

b 1 Saturday's game is absolutely vital for our hopes of promotion. 2 I always feel really hungry after swimming. 3 I often feel really tired at the end of the day. 4 Terry was absolutely devastated when the factory closed down. 5 Suzanne was absolutely exhausted after the race. 6 Poor Jo! He's really upset about his exam results. 7 What's there to eat? I'm absolutely starving! 8 Take your time to decide. This is a really important decision for you.

Grammar: reported speech

4 1 Amanda suggested taking a short break then. 3 Amanda explained (that) it usually takes/took about three months to get fit. 4 Steven admitted (that) he was still eating desserts. 5 Steven asked (Amanda) if/whether she had prepared that nutrition sheet for him. 6 Amanda promised to do it the following week.

5 1 C 2 A 3 B 4 B 5 A 6 A 7 C 8 B 9 B 10 A

6 1 My brother suggested going out for a meal. 2 John explained that he couldn't come because he had to work that evening. 3 The children promised (that) they would never do it/that again. 4 The lifeguard warned (us) that swimming there could be very dangerous. 5 Maria admitted that she hadn't done her homework. 6 The customer decided to take the smaller model.

Lesson 8.3

Reading

1a 1 e 2 b 3 a 4 c 5 d

b 1 ~~this month~~ next month 2 ~~exam~~ practical 3 ~~five~~ nine 4 ~~maths~~ computer 5 ~~son~~ daughter 6 ~~The parents~~ Ryde 7 ~~older~~ younger 8 ~~few~~ most

c 1 e 2 h 3 b 4 j 5 a 6 d 7 i 8 f 9 c 10 g

Grammar: *hard* and *hardly*

2 1 hardly 2 hardly ever 3 hard 4 hardly anyone 5 hardly ever 6 hard 7 hardly anywhere 8 hardly anything 9 hardly 10 hardly anyone

3 1 hardly anyone 2 hard 3 hardly 4 hardly ever 5 hardly anything 6 hard

How to: give your opinion

4 1 think 2 concerned 3 believe 4 for 5 Firstly 6 in 7 because 8 then

Review and consolidation unit 8

Vocabulary

1 1 f 2 d 3 h 4 a 5 c 6 g 7 e 8 b

It's time/I'd rather/I'd better

2 1 time 2 rather 3 high/about 4 better 5 would/'d 6 phoned/called/spoke to/rang 7 had/'d 8 Would 9 not 10 be

Vocabulary

3 1 earth 2 headstrong 3 outgoing 4 manipulative 5 witty 6 doormat 7 proactive 8 centre 9 selfish 10 opinionated

4 1 upset 2 ✓ 3 clean 4 tiny 5 hot 6 ✓ 7 fascinating 8 ✓ 9 happy 10 freezing

Reported speech

5 1 [C] (that) the doctor was sick that day so he couldn't see me. 2 [E] to do all the exercises on page 65 of the Workbook. 3 [H] going to the cinema on Friday evening.
4 [A] not to touch those plates because they were very hot.
5 [I] stealing the money/(that) he had stolen the money.
6 [B] where my passport was. 7 [G] if/whether I was feeling alright. 8 [J] to have the spaghetti Bolognese. 9 [D] to be at the airport two hours before our departure. 10 [F] (that) she would pay back the loan within six months.

hard and *hardly*

6 1 B 2 A 3 B 4 C 5 C 6 A 7 B 8 A 9 C 10 B

Vocabulary

7 1 look, to 2 cut, on 3 looking, to 4 put, with 5 come, with 6 get, with 7 made, for 8 catch, with

Unit 9 Crime

Lesson 9.1

Vocabulary: law and insurance

1a 1 ~~convicted~~ sentenced 2 ~~fraud~~ arson 3 ~~sentenced~~ sued 4 ~~premium~~ fraud 5 ~~sued~~ convicted 6 ~~guarantee~~ appeal 7 ~~arson~~ premium 8 ~~appeal~~ guarantee

b 1 of 2 for 3 to 4 for

Reading

2a 1 F 2 D 3 C

b 1 What does cruise control do? 2 Why did the Mr Grazinski step into the back of the motor home? 3 What injuries did he suffer from? 4 Why did Kara Walton climb through the window of the ladies toilet? 5 How much compensation was she awarded? 6 How long had Terrence Dickson's career as a burglar lasted? 7 Why was he trapped in the garage for eight days? 8 What did he live on while he was trapped in the garage?

c **Vehicles:** cruise control, accelerator, speed, mph, owner's manual
Injuries/Harm: suffered, fell, broke, knocked out, starvation
Legal: court, awarded, compensation, expenses, jury

Grammar: sequencing devices

3 1 Having joined the motorway, he set the cruise control at 65 mph and decided to step into the back of the motor home to make himself a cup of coffee. 2 ... while struggling to get through the window she fell to the floor and knocked out her two front teeth. 3 After entering the garage from the house he realised the door could not be opened from the inside.

4 1 A 2 B 3 A 4 A 5 B 6 A

5 1 Having told his best friend, Dave announced the news to his colleagues. 2 After getting up, he went into the village to get some food. 3 They watched the midnight movie before going to bed./Before going to bed, they watched the midnight movie.
4 While (she was) watching TV Surinda heard a strange sound./Surinda heard a strange sound while she was watching TV.
5 We went to the computer shop after reading lots of consumer reports./After reading lots of consumer reports, we went to the computer shop. 6 Having missed the bus, Jackie had to get a taxi.
7 My uncle started a new business after he had gone to America./Having gone to America, my uncle started a new business.
8 The kids usually watch TV for an hour after doing their homework./After doing their homework, the kids usually watch TV for an hour.

Lesson 9.2

Grammar: *must/might/can't have*

1 1 f 2 a 3 h 4 c 5 b 6 e 7 d 8 g

2 1 Somebody must have watered them. 2 She might not have received the invitation. 3 He can't have gone out. 4 They must have left already. 5 They can't have left the country. 6 He might have forgotten to take it with him. 7 Maria must have passed the exam. 8 You must have forgotten to bring it.

3 1 might have 2 must have 3 must have 4 can't have 5 might have 6 might have 7 must have 8 can't have

Vocabulary: compound adjectives

4 1 Mr Lockwood is middle-aged. 2 The chocolate cake is home-made. 3 My sister works part-time. 4 The project was time-consuming. 5 Elizabeth is single-minded. 6 I want a one-way ticket to Hong Kong. 7 I had a last-minute change of mind. 8 There's a brand-new hospital here.

Listening

5a 1 B 2 C 3 C 4 A 5 A

b 1 download 2 unravel 3 on behalf of 4 proportion 5 sort of 6 look like

c 1 on behalf of 2 look like 3 download 4 sort of 5 unravel 6 proportion

Lesson 9.3

Reading

1a 3

b 1 T 2 T 3 T 4 F 5 F 6 T 7 T 8 F

c 1 g 2 d 3 a 4 e 5 h 6 c 7 b 8 f

Grammar: relative clauses

2 1 1A 2B 2 1B 2A 3 1A 2B 4 1A 2B

3 1 Miranda's boyfriend, who lives in Athens, is a doctor.
2 The house I'm living in is over a hundred years old. 3 Arthur Conan Doyle, who was Scottish, was born in 1859. 4 The government, which was elected last year, has introduced a new tax. 5 Our local hospital, which is very old, is about to be closed down. 6 The girl we met on holiday is coming to stay next weekend.
7 Spielberg's new film, which I saw yesterday, was fantastic.
8 The hotel we stayed in last summer had a heated swimming pool.

Pronunciation

4a **Sentences 1 and 3:** pause marks are correct because we pause at the beginning and end of non-defining relative clauses.

Sentence 2: the pause mark is not correct because we don't pause at the beginning of defining relative clauses.

b 1 We found our car ( ), which had been towed away two hours earlier ( ), at the police car pound. 2 It was our car that had been towed away. 3 The police took the car ( ), which had been blocking someone's gate ( ), to the car pound in Lennard Street. 4 This is the gate that our car was blocking when it was towed away.

Review and consolidation unit 9

Vocabulary

1

					[1]F	I	N	E					
					I				[2]C	L	[3]A	I	M
		[4]S			L						P		
	[5]J	U	D	[6]G	E			[7]C			P		
		E		U			[8]R	O	B	B	E	R	Y
				A		[9]T		N			A		
				R		H		V			L		
				A		I		I					
		[10]S	E	N	T	E	N	C	E				
				T		F		T			[11]A		
				E			[12]F				R		
[13]F	I	N	G	E	R	P	R	I	N	T	S		
							A				O		
		[14]P	R	E	M	I	U	M			N		
							D						

Sequencing devices

2 1 leaving 2 seen 3 On 4 After 5 ran 6 booking 7 living 8 Having 9 finishing 10 learned

must/might/can't have

3 1 must have 2 must have 3 must have 4 can't have 5 might have 6 might have

Vocabulary

4 1 home-made 2 brand-new 3 one-way 4 part-time 5 left-handed 6 last-minute 7 time-consuming 8 single-minded 9 middle-aged 10 so-called

Relative clauses

5 1 My brother, who works in Cardiff, is an opera singer. 2 Jenny, who/whom I told you about last week, is getting married. 3 ✓ 4 The children that/who didn't pass the test had to take it again. 5 Our car, which we bought last year, has been stolen from our garage. 6 The film that was on TV last night was absolutely fascinating. 7 ✓ 8 My colleague, who showed us how to use the computer, has been promoted to the Los Angeles office.

6 2 It belonged to an old lady who died. 3 When I was young the old lady, who used to be a schoolteacher, allowed me to play in her garden. 4 The garden, which was huge, had lots of lemon trees. 5 I used to pick the lemons from the trees that grew there. 6 The old lady used the lemons (that) I had picked to make lemonade.

Vocabulary

7 1 F 2 T 3 T 4 T 5 F 6 T 7 F 8 F

Unit 10 Memories

Lesson 10.1

Listening

1a 2

b 1 Germany 2 qualified 3 Vienna 4 magnetism 5 Paris 6 aristocrats 7 king 8 entertained 9 forced 10 1815

c 1 A 2 D 3 A 4 D 5 C 6 B 7 B 8 C

Vocabulary: belief and opinion

2 1 ~~that~~ of 2 ~~sceptic~~ sceptical 3 ~~is~~ 4 ~~convenienced~~ convinced 5 ~~of~~ that 6 ~~give~~ giving

Grammar: reflexive pronouns

3 1 B 2 C 3 A 4 C 5 A 6 C 7 A 8 C 9 A 10 B

4 1 Darren cut himself while he was gardening. 2 I made the cake myself. 3 We've made all the arrangements ourselves. 4 Mandy and Sylvia sent text messages to each other. 5 My central heating turns itself on automatically if the temperature drops. 6 The Bensons often send packages to themselves when they are abroad. 7 Did you paint this picture yourself? 8 Isabel works for herself.

How to: ask about other people's views

5 1 Do you have any strong feelings about pollution? 2 How do you feel about poverty? 3 Are you for or against the death penalty? 4 What are your views on fast food? 5 What do you think of divorce?

Lesson 10.2

Reading

1a 2

b 1 F 2 F 3 T 4 F 5 T 6 F 7 F 8 F

c 1 freshly baked 2 optimistic 3 pick up 4 cash register 5 subtly 6 olfactory organs 7 evocative 8 harness

Vocabulary: advertising

2 1 slogan 2 makes 3 classified ad 4 target market

Pronunciation

3 (main stress underlined)
Three syllables: commercial, customers, magazines, persuasion
Four syllables: advertisement, information, politicians, supermarket

Grammar: gerunds and infinitives

4 1 suggest 2 joining 3 writing 4 her to get 5 imagine 6 speaking 7 miss 8 to come

5 1 1A 2B 2 1B 2A 3 1B 2A 4 1A 2B

Lesson 10.3

Reading

1a 1 D 2 F 3 A 4 G 5 B (not needed: C, E)

b 1 What is removed from Joel's mind in the film? 2 What do memory management drugs cause? 3 How many of these drugs is the FDA currently testing? 4 How does Derren Brown put ideas into people's minds? 5 How can people be persuaded to carry out instructions without question? 6 What has research shown us?

c 1 fiction 2 neuroscientists 3 compounds 4 erase 5 amazed 6 manipulation 7 orders 8 carry out 9 propaganda 10 whim

Vocabulary: speaking

2

			[1]W	H	[2]I	S	P	E	R
	[3]B				N				
	L				T				
[4]M	U	M	B	L	E				
	R				R				
	T		[5]S	H	R	I	E	K	
					U				
			[6]W		P				
		[7]L	O	S	T				
			R						
[8]M	I	N	D						

Grammar: *If* structures (2)

3a 1 c 2 f 3 d 4 a 5 g 6 e 7 h 8 b

b 1 mixed 2 zero 3 third 4 second 5 mixed

4 1 If we hadn't gone to the sales, we wouldn't have bought an incredibly cheap sofa. 2 Charles wouldn't have overslept if he hadn't forgotten to turn on his alarm clock. 3 If you give plants water, they grow. 4 If I got a pay rise, I would be able to buy a nice house. 5 Don't use the generator unless there is a power failure. 6 Provided you pay by credit card, we will give you a guarantee. 7 You can have a party unless the neighbours complain. 8 As long as you show us a receipt, we can give you a refund.

Review and consolidation unit 10

Vocabulary

1 **1** unconscious **2** déjà vu **3** trust **4** premonition **5** mind **6** willpower **7** subconscious **8** persuasion

Reflexive pronouns

2 **1** ~~her~~ herself **2** ~~himself~~ him **3** ~~others~~ other
4 ✓ **5** ~~ourself~~ ourselves **6** ~~themselves~~ them
7 ✓ **8** repaired ~~me~~ repaired the broken chair myself

Vocabulary

3 **1** I am convinced that Jimmy is guilty of the crime. **2** Emily is in favour of longer prison sentences for criminals. **3** I reckon she could be our new manager. **4** I've always believed that people are basically honest. **5** Some politicians are against the new tax. **6** I'm sceptical about hypnosis.

4

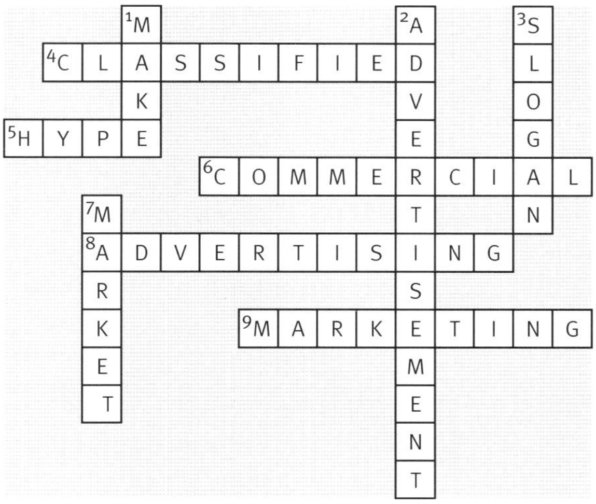

Gerunds and infinitives

5 **1** to collect us **2** to turn on the burglar alarm **3** applying to universities **4** to inform you **5** working as a doctor **6** living there **7** eating the prawns **8** to have lunch **9** designing websites **10** me to take

Vocabulary

6 **1** d **2** a **3** h **4** g **5** f **6** c (not needed: b, e)

If structures (2)

7 **1** B **2** C **3** B **4** A **5** B **6** A **7** A **8** C **9** C **10** B

Vocabulary

8 **1** intelligence **2** psychologist **3** subconscious **4** their **5** responsibility **6** definitely **7** changeable **8** necessary **9** generous **10** occasionally notes

notes